LANGUAGE AND STYLE
SERIES

General Editor
STEPHEN ULLMANN

II

VICTOR E. GRAHAM

THE
IMAGERY OF PROUST

BASIL BLACKWELL
OXFORD
1966

First printed 1966

PRINTED IN GREAT BRITAIN
BY A. T. BROOME AND SON, 18 ST. CLEMENT'S, OXFORD
AND BOUND BY THE KEMP HALL BINDERY, OXFORD

CONTENTS

PREFACE

This analysis of Proust's imagery was originally completed in 1953 at Columbia University under the direction of Professor Justin O'Brien to whom I should like to acknowledge my enduring gratitude. A summary of it appeared in *Dissertation Abstracts XIV* (1954), pp. 1409–10. I myself used some of the most significant material in a later article on water imagery in Proust,[1] and a number of other scholars interested in various aspects of the imagery in *A la recherche du temps perdu* at different times have drawn on other information contained in the thesis. Even so, it probably would have remained in manuscript form except for the kind encouragement of Professor Stephen Ullmann who invited me to publish the work in the Blackwell series on language and style. I have therefore revised it and brought it up to date although the basic plan remains the same.

It would have been useful, perhaps, to change the myriad references to *A la recherche du temps perdu* to correspond with the text of the Pléiade edition in three volumes but this would have been a Herculean task. Similarly, a comparison of the images in *Jean Santeuil* with those in *A la recherche du temps perdu* would no doubt have thrown new light on Proust's methods of composition but this, too, would have involved a long period of additional research.

As any of his admirers knows, the study of Proust is the work of a life-time. An exhaustive examination of all his imagery in itself would require almost as many volumes as there are in the whole of *A la recherche du temps perdu*, and the net result might not appear to be much more than a tissue of quotations from Proust. This essay therefore cannot pretend to be definitive, but it attempts to examine objectively features of Proust's methods which have never before been adequately treated. There has not been room to include all the data, but the generalizations which can be made from them offer startling and overwhelming proof of the existence in Proust of what T. S. Eliot calls 'the pattern below the level of plot and character'.[2]

The old dispute about whether or not Proust's novel has a plan has long since been settled in the writer's favour, but if any additional evidence were needed, it could readily be adduced from

---

[1] 'Water Imagery and Symbolism in Proust,' *Romanic Review* L (1959), pp. 118–28.

[2] Quoted by René Wellek and Austin Warren, *Theory of Literature*, New York (1949), p. 216.

our examination of imagery related to themes. Proust constantly
and consciously associates images from particular sources with
certain themes. The consistent pattern of the orchestration of each
of the individual *leit-motifs* which run through Proust's work gives
them a unity which is harmonious from the interior. At the same
time, the utilization of the same ultimate source of images in connection with various different themes adds to the unity of the work
by linking many themes by means of a stylistic device.

Proust is deeply concerned about the unity of his novel, and its
vast cycle is more tightly pulled together by many subsidiary cycles,
by the 'links' he so often talks about, by the 'threads' which join
together memories and phenomena long considered completely
unrelated. No small part of this process is achieved through
imagery.

Any study of imagery has to be, to a degree, a repertory of the
images a writer employs. In Proust's case, it would be undesirable
from many points of view to try to include references to every
single image he uses. For this reason, examples from the text have
been chosen critically and they have been listed in order of interest
or importance rather than chronologically.

It should be strongly emphasized that all references in this study
are references to images, and that treatment of themes has been
proscribed by the same consideration. What is said on Proust's
conception of love, for instance, is drawn entirely from the images
he uses in that connection. A complete treatment of a given theme
would require a consideration of many other factors.

It should also be noted that images have been considered only
from a literary point of view. Charles Briand has attempted a
psychoanalysis of Proust which is based partly on a consideration of
his images.[1] Such a treatment is alien to the purpose of our analysis.
Even so, it has been impossible not to arrive at some conclusions
regarding Proust's tastes and his prejudices. We may be accused of
falling into the 'intentional fallacy',[2] of attributing to Proust purposes
which were not in his mind at all, but the evidence could not be
denied.

VICTOR E. GRAHAM.

University of Toronto.

---

[1] Charles Briand, *Le Secret de Marcel Proust*, Paris (1950).
[2] See W. K. Wimsatt, Jr. and M. C. Beardsley, 'The Intentional Fallacy,' reprinted
in *Essays in Modern Literary Criticism*, New York (1952), pp. 174–89.

NOTE

All references to *A la recherche du temps perdu* are to the Gallimard edition of the *Nouvelle Revue Française* in 15 volumes. References to the *Pastiches et Mélanges* and *Les Plaisirs et les jours* are to the editions in the same series.

The following abbreviations have been used:

I

PRELIMINARY CONSIDERATIONS

Ce qui était caché derrière les clochers de Martinville devait être quelque chose d'analogue à une jolie phrase, puisque c'était sous la forme de mots qui me faisaient plaisir que cela m'était apparu.
— A LA RECHERCHE DU TEMPS PERDU (I, 244).

Penser, c'est réapprendre à voir, à être attentif, c'est diriger sa conscience, c'est faire de chaque idée et de chaque image, à la façon de Proust, un lieu privilégié.
— ALBERT CAMUS (LE MYTHE DE SISYPHE, p. 43).

EVERYONE is agreed that images are an extremely important aspect of Proust's style, and he himself, in discussing the style of Flaubert, declared:

> Pour des raisons qui seraient trop longues à développer ici, je crois que la métaphore seule peut donner une sorte d'éternité au style, et il n'y a peut-être pas dans tout Flaubert une seule belle métaphore. Bien plus, ses images sont généralement si faibles qu'elles ne s'élèvent guère au-dessus de celles que pourraient trouver ses personnages les plus insignifiants.[1]

Elsewhere, he criticized Balzac for consistently using images that are discordant, *qui expliquent au lieu de suggérer, qui ne se subordonnent à aucun but de beauté et d'harmonie.*[2] Proust felt that his own unique gift as a writer lay in the ability, so highly praised by Aristotle, *de découvrir un lien profond entre deux idées, deux sensations . . . [de] sentir entre deux impressions, entre deux idées, une harmonie très fine que d'autres ne sentent pas.*[3]

Many figures of speech are merely rhetorical devices. In Proust there are to be found numerous examples of the oxymoron (a form of antithesis combining opposites). Take, for instance, *mon remerciement, d'une ardeur réfrigérante* (III, 65) or *les préceptes orgueilleusement humbles d'un snobisme évangélique* (VIII, 59). Hyperbole is not infrequent (*La Joconde se serait trouvée là qu'elle n'eût pas fait plus de plaisir qu'une robe de chambre de Mme Swann, ou ses flacons de sels* (III, 126)), and zeugma

---

[1] 'A Propos du "Style" de Flaubert,' *Chroniques*, pp. 193–94.
[2] *Contre Sainte Beuve, suivi de nouveaux mélanges*, préface de Bernard de Fallois, Paris 1954), p. 208.
[3] Ibid., pp. 301–2.

is fairly common (an adjective or verb governs two nouns, one related logically, the other not), e.g. *la place réservée, non seulement dans ses armoires mais dans son imagination* (XII, 210).

Instances of other less well-known figures of speech can also be found in Proust's work, but the only types of images with which we shall be concerned are those in the simile-metaphor class. They are not difficult to recognize, for they involve comparisons or identifications from different fields. Proust himself, in the above quotation, seems to group together metaphors, similes and images, and it is an examination of these particular figures of speech that throws an interesting light on one aspect of Proust's literary methods.

Proust's images have of course been studied to some extent before. In an early monograph, Irma Tiedtke examined at some length the qualitative nature of a very few arbitrarily chosen images.[1] She was mainly concerned with the inner truths Proust discovers in outward appearance but her work is restricted in scope, repetitious and somewhat bombastic in style. Jean Mouton in a chapter on imagery has some penetrating remarks on Proust's purposes in using figures of speech.[2] With very few exceptions, however, Mouton selects his examples from the first part of *Du Côté de chez Swann*, and this is unfortunate, for it leads him into making generalizations that are not always true.[3] Stephen Ullmann, on the other hand, has a splendid chapter on Proust's synaesthetic images in his book on style in the French novel,[4] and in his more recent study of the image in the modern French novel,[5] even though he restricts himself to the metaphorical techniques involved in a few selected themes from *Du Côté de chez Swann*, he presents an admirable analysis of Proust's style. All of Professor Ullmann's conclusions are valid and his comments are always pertinent and helpful.

Emeric Fiser restricts his consideration of Proust's use of imagery to what is called the dynamic metaphor as illustrated by the instances of the operation of the involuntary memory.[6] Here, a present

---

[1] Irma Tiedtke, *Symbole und Bilder im Werke Marcel Prousts*, Hamburg (1936). Images selected include the mirror and its reflection, light and shade, the lighted window and Albertine, monocles (at great length), and the water lily in the Vivonne.

[2] Jean Mouton, *Le Style de Marcel Proust*, Paris (1948).

[3] See in particular, p. 77 where Mouton says that 'en tête de liste, s'inscrivent les comparaisons empruntées au monde des arts'. As we shall show later, figures drawn from this source are far from being the most numerous or the most interesting.

[4] Stephen Ullmann, *Style in the French Novel*, Cambridge (1957), pp. 189–209.

[5] Stephen Ullmann, *The Image in the Modern French Novel*, Cambridge (1960), pp. 124–238.

[6] Emeric Fiser, *La Théorie du Symbole littéraire et Marcel Proust*, Paris (1941).

experience is vividly linked with a past experience in a way that affects the aesthetic of the whole personality. This same specialized meaning is the one utilized by Pommier[1] and Dandieu,[2] and while all three writers have much of interest to say, their treatment of metaphor is very narrow. There are specialized studies of Proust's images drawn from science,[3] the theatre[4] and music,[5] as well as briefer articles on even more recondite aspects of his work.[6] Dr. H. C. R. Stockwell has a splendid article on a few specific images in Proust, showing their significance and their probable origin.[7] His method, however, is an ideal beyond the scope of a more general treatment.

A word or two, then, about the procedure used in this study and its purpose may not come amiss. The first step was to go carefully through the whole of *A la recherche du temps perdu*, indexing all relevant images. The word 'relevant' is used on purpose, because we are not actually concerned with what is usually called faded metaphor, even though Proust himself was much more likely than the average writer to be conscious of employing in ordinary speech figurative expressions that have lost their flavour. *Ennuyeuses comme la pluie* (I, 255) is no longer a fresh comparison nor is such an expression as *une âme d'acier* (X, 229). The only cases, then, in which individual images of this sort have been retained are those that are found in the conversational passages. These latter we shall examine separately.

From one point of view, of course, it is quite correct to say that very little of Proust's imagery is original. There is nothing new, for instance, about comparing young girls to flowers or love to an illness. It is just because of the infinitely varied way Proust does it, that we are made to realize the extent of the truth of the analogy. As a matter of fact, the frequency of occurrence of such images far

---

[1] Jean Pommier, *La Mystique de Marcel Proust*, Paris, Droz, 1939.

[2] A. Dandieu, '*La Signification de la Métaphore*', (Article extrait d'un ouvrage d' A. Dandieu sur Marcel Proust), *Bulletin Marcel Proust*, publié sous la direction de Louis Emie et Henri Bonnet, Paris, Le Rouge et le Noir, 1930.

[3] Reino Virtanen, 'Proust's Metaphors from the Natural and the Exact Sciences', *PMLA*, LXIX (1954), pp. 1038–59.

[4] J. G. Linn, 'Proust's Theatre Metaphors', *RR*, XLIX (1958), pp. 179–90.

[5] Florence Hier, *La Musique dans l'œuvre de Marcel Proust*, New York (1933), Ch. IV 'La Métaphore musicale'.

[6] See, for example, Georges Matoré, 'Les Images gustatives dans *Du Côté de chez Swann*', (*Annales Universitatis Saraviensis* vi, 1957); Vera L. Vance, 'Proust's Guermantes as Birds', *FR*, XXXV (1961–62), pp. 3–10.

[7] 'L'image dans l'œuvre de Marcel Proust,' XXVI (1944–45), pp. 10–15. *Modern Languages*.

exceeds the number any casual reader might be inclined to estimate.

One of the problems in connection with weighting figures of speech is knowing how to count them. If something relatively insignificant is compared in quick succession to three or four different things, how many images would that make as opposed to an extended metaphor covering a page or more? (e.g. the comparison of the restaurant at Rivebelle to the solar system (V, 58–59)). The only logical system would seem to be to count each comparison separately whether it is adjacent to another comparison or separated from it, and regardless of its length. This is the method which we have employed. It gives rise to certain anomalies, it is true, but it eliminates the subjective element in evaluation. Thus the lengthy comparison of the restaurant at Rivebelle to a universe has to be counted as one image because it is a development of one idea, whereas the following description of Charlus contains five complete figures:

> Il était raseur comme un savant qui ne voit rien au delà de sa spécialité, agaçant comme un renseigné qui tire vanité des secrets qu'il détient et brûle de divulguer, antipathique comme ceux qui, dès qu'il s'agit de leurs défauts, s'épanouissent sans s'apercevoir qu'ils déplaisent, assujetti comme un maniaque et irrésistiblement imprudent comme un coupable (XII, 127).

After the images were isolated, they were then analyzed from various points of view. It should be emphasized that all this was done *before* any totals were counted so that there would be as little influence as possible from any desire to twist figures to support a pre-conceived hypothesis. Much nonsense has been written about the frequency of images in Proust and what images he favors. Different critics, depending on the axe they have to grind, discover his most significant or most frequent source of images in the arts,[1] music,[2] science,[3] botany,[4] or even gustatory sensations.[5] It is our hope that we have been able to avoid unwarranted assumptions by making the processes of analysis as objective as possible.

[1] Jean Mouton, op. cit., p. 77.

[2] Benoist-Méchin, *La Musique et l'immortalité dans l'œuvre de Proust*, Paris (1926), pp. 40, 125, etc.

[3] *Hommage à Marcel Proust* (No. 1 of the series *Les Cahiers Marcel Proust*)—a reprint of a special number of the Nouvelle Revue Française, 1 Jan. (1923), p. 163.

[4] Samuel Beckett, *Proust*, London (1931), p. 68; Juliette Monnin-Hornung, *Proust et la peinture*, Genève (1951), p. 143.

[5] André Maurois, *A la recherche de Marcel Proust*, Paris (1949), p. 187.

The first thing to be done was to examine the context in which images occur. This may be most readily classified as conversational, descriptive or analytical. It turned out that sixty-nine per cent of Proust's images are to be found in analytical passages while twenty-eight per cent occur in description. Only three per cent are in conversation. In individual volumes, these percentages are maintained fairly well (See Appendix 1), except that the proportion of images in analytical contexts tends to be higher in the more abstract sections (*La Prisonnière, Albertine disparue*). The only volume in which descriptive images out-number analytical ones is *Du Côté de chez Swann* pt. 1, and the reason for this is the large occurrence of descriptions of nature in this section (the hawthorns, the Vivonne, the rural walks, etc.).

The next step was to compare the basic object or idea being treated with the secondary idea or object forming the term of comparison, in relation to their concreteness or abstractness. Proust sometimes takes a concrete thing and compares it to something else that is also concrete, e.g. *des tartes en bateaux, remplies de cerises comme des perles de corail* (X, 175). Much less often, he translates something concrete into abstract terms, e.g.

> En voyant ce corps insignifiant couché là [Albertine], je me demandais quelle table de logarithmes il constituait pour que toutes les actions auxquelles il avait pu être mêlé . . . pussent me causer . . . des angoisses si douloureuses (XII, 197).

More frequently, it is something abstract that he compares to something concrete, e.g.

> La zone de tristesse où je venais d'entrer était aussi distincte de la zone où je m'élançais avec joie il y avait un moment encore que dans certains ciels une bande rose est séparée comme par une ligne d'une bande verte ou d'une bande noire (I, 246).

The final possibility is the comparison of something abstract to something else abstract, e.g.

> De même que la pitié pour le malheur n'est peut-être pas très exacte, car par l'imagination nous recréons toute une douleur sur laquelle le malheureux obligé de lutter contre elle ne songe pas à s'attendrir, de même la méchanceté n'a probablement pas dans l'âme du méchant cette pure et voluptueuse cruauté qui nous fait si mal à imaginer (VI, 212).

B

Results showed that seventy-two per cent of Proust's images are concrete, i.e. a concrete object or person is compared to or identified with another concrete object or physical thing. Twenty-six per cent may be classified as abstract-concrete, i.e. an abstract idea is translated into tangible terms. Less than one per cent of the images are abstract or move from concrete to abstract (See Appendix 2).

Following this examination, the images were classified as either simile or metaphor. The division was not always as easy to make as one might think. Pure similes are easy enough to recognize because of the use of words like *comme, de même que, tout autant que, aussi . . . que*, etc. However, Proust very frequently omits these linking words and the comparison is reduced to analogy—the most rudimentary rhetorical device, e.g.

> Un homme a presque toujours la même manière de s'enrhumer, de tomber malade . . . il est naturel que quand il devient amoureux ce soit à propos d'un certain genre de femmes (XIII, 107).

In metaphor, no comparison is stated, but rather there is an identification of two things, a leaping-over the link between the two halves of an analogy, e.g. *Mon cœur, depuis que sa plaie se cicatrisait commençait à ne plus adhérer à celui de mon amie* (XI, 34). Similes and analogies form fifty-four per cent of the images examined, while metaphor accounts for the remaining forty-six per cent (See Appendix 3).

It was here, incidentally, that we were able to compute the total number of images on which this study is based. It came to 4,578, or an average of more than one per page throughout the whole of Proust. Naturally, there are passages which are particularly dense with images,[1] but there are other sections ranging up to six or seven pages in length where no images can be found.[2]

Proust originally planned *A la recherche du temps perdu* as a three volume work. Feuillerat, in his book on Proust, indicates the additions which were made by the author to the extant proofs of the second volume whose publication was delayed until after the war, and by analysis he tries to reconstitute the 500 original pages of the third and final volume which was never in proof.[3] His method is

---

[1] See especially VI, 90–94.
[2] We mean, of course, images which are not faded. Compare the following: I, 268–75; II, 44–53, 95–101, 162–68, 185–93; V, 25–30, 144–49; 178–83, 205–10; VI, 153–58; VII, 47–53, 61–66, 119–26; VIII, 100–105, 147–52; IX, 326–32; X, 35–40; XIV, 27–33, 85–91, 106–11, 138–46; XV, 161–67.
[3] Albert Feuillerat, *Comment Marcel Proust a composé son roman* (1934).

subjective and he says:

> Toutes les fois que l'auteur adopte une attitude passive, expectante, un tantinet naïve, ne retenant que des sensations et des impressions, qu'il s'exprime en un style chargé d'images et d'originales suggestions, souple et nuancé comme une étoffe de soie, on pourra être sûr qu'il s'agit d'un passage appartenant à la première version.[1]

There are other features to consider also, but with regard to the statement about images, it appeared to be of interest to compare the relative number of images in the parts Proust added to the proofs of the Grasset edition with the number in the parts we know belong to the original draft. These results are summarized in Appendix 4 and they completely disprove Feuillerat's suggestion, at least as far as the frequency of images is concerned. In the original edition there is a simile every 1.9 pages while in the additions there is one every 1.4 pages. In the original edition there is a metaphor every 2.6 pages: in the additions one every 2.1 pages. In other words, in the original edition there is a figure of one kind or another every 1.1 pages and in the additions there is one every .8 pages. Moreover there are several striking figures added in the new parts.[2]

From the above analysis, we were forced to conclude that one cannot determine from an examination of imagery when Proust wrote a given part of his work. His style is a metaphorical style, and it is just as much so in his maturity as it is at the beginning of his writing.[3]

The last preliminary analysis to be made was the classification of sources of images under the following heads: auditory, visual, kinaesthetic, synaesthetic, mental, gustatory and olfactory. These terms are all self-explanatory except perhaps for kinaesthetic and synaesthetic. Under the heading kinaesthetic were included all images drawing on bodily sensations apart from hearing, seeing, tasting and smelling, because it seemed pointless to subdivide such a class into tactile, visceral, caloric, etc. Under the heading synaesthetic were placed all images in which a stimulus in one sense calls forth a response in another.[4]

---

[1] Ibid., p. 135.
[2] See especially V, 58; VI, 91, 92, 161–63, 166, 213, 214, 216; VII, 23, 24, 26.
[3] This observation has already been made by Mouton, op. cit., p. 17.
[4] The commonest type of this phenomenon is what is called *audition colorée*. Here, a sound calls forth ideas of colour (see especially II, 230–32). There are other possible combinations, however.

This examination revealed very clearly the fundamentally visual quality of Proust's images. In the whole of *A la recherche du temps perdu*, sixty-two per cent of the images are visual. Nineteen per cent are mental (i.e. no specific physical field is involved). Nine per cent are kinaesthetic, while five per cent each are auditory and synaesthetic. Less than one per cent are gustatory and olfactory (See Appendix 5).[1]

Proust himself acknowledges the important rôle sight plays for him. He says: *Nos yeux ont plus de part qu'on ne croit dans cette exploration active du passé qu'on nomme le souvenir* (PM 213).[2] Moreover, the significance of the above figures can hardly be overestimated and their accuracy is borne out when we stop to examine individual images.

It is true, for instance, that Proust has one or two vivid descriptions of food that one tends to remember especially, but when one stops to examine them, the terms are almost always visual. The form of the *madeleine—petit coquillage de pâtisserie, si grassement sensuel sous son plissage sévère et dévot* (I, 68), the chicken cooked by Françoise *sa peau brodée d'or comme une chasuble et son jus précieux égoutté d'un ciboire*, (I, 167), the dinner prepared for Monsieur de Norpois where *. . . le bœuf froid aux carottes fit son apparition, couché par le Michel-Ange de notre cuisine sur d'énormes cristaux de gelée pareils à des blocs de quartz transparent* (III, 40)—all these are visual images. The same is true for the description of the peas (I, 166), the asparagus (I, 166), the fruit presented by Madame de Villeparisis to Marcel and his grandmother (IV, 122).

When one turns to auditory sensations, one is amazed that so many of them are translated into visual terms. A good example is the description of the bell on the gate at Combray,

> . . . non pas le grelot profus et criard qui arrosait, qui étourdissait au passage de son bruit ferrugineux, intarissable et glacé . . . mais le double tintement timide, ovale et doré de la clochette pour les étrangers (I, 25).[3]

Proper names almost always suggest colours or forms to Proust. Guermantes is represented by him as . . . *baignant comme dans un coucher*

[1] Pommier has been credited with proving that Proust's images are predominately gustatory. See André Maurois, *A la recherche de Marcel Proust*, Paris (1949), p. 187.

[2] Compare also 'Les mots nous présentent des choses une petite image claire et usuelle comme celles que l'on suspend aux murs des écoles', etc. (II, 229).

[3] Other examples of the same phenomenon are to be found at I, 116–17, 123; V, 200–1.

de soleil dans la lumière orangée qui émane de cette syllabe: 'antes' (I, 231–32). Palamède, the christian name of Charlus, is a *belle médaille de la Renaissance* (IV, 184).[1] Describing his own reactions, Marcel says that . . . *quand elle me disait 'Salon Arpajon' je voyais un papillon jaune, et 'Salon Swann' . . . un papillon noir aux ailes feutrées de neige* (IX, 192–93).

Undoubtedly Proust was a person of extraordinary sensitivity as far as all his perceptions are concerned, but until recently the fundamental importance with him of visual imagery has not been sufficiently emphasized.[2]

These preliminary examinations completed, there remained two major analyses to which chapters two and three are devoted. The first of them is a consideration of themes and the relation of them to imagery. One or two have been mentioned already and are well known: young girls as flowers and love as an illness. Others are less obvious but nonetheless striking when they are noticed. The second is a consideration of the sources of images, their relative weight and their significance. These two studies are, to a certain extent, complementary, but there is a distinct difference in emphasis. Even so, in concentrating attention first on the object of comparison and then on the term, it has been impossible to avoid a certain amount of repetition. If any precedent were needed, one could cite Proust himself since he keeps coming back to the same themes and the same images. By examining first one category and then the other, one can concentrate independently on the essential characteristics of each. The analysis only becomes truly useful, however, when the technique leads to a more accurate evaluation of the reconstituted elements.

[1] Compare also his remarks about Faffenheim (VII, 97), the *Faubourg St. Germain* (XV, 181).
[2] Recent studies to concentrate on this aspect of Proust's style include Howard Moss, *The Magic Lantern of Marcel Proust*, New York (1962); Harry Levin, *The Gates of Horn*, New York (1963), pp. 385 et seq. and Roger Shattuck, *Proust's Binoculars*, A Study of Memory, Time and Recognition in *A la recherche du temps perdu*, New York (1963).

IMAGERY RELATED TO THEMES

Le seul véritable voyage, le seul bain de Jouvence, ce ne serait pas d'aller vers de nouveaux paysages, mais d'avoir d'autres yeux, de voir l'univers avec les yeux d'un autre, de cent autres, de voir les cent univers que chacun d'eux voit, que chacun d'eux est.

—A LA RECHERCHE DU TEMPS PERDU (XII, 69).

ANY division of Proust's work into themes has to be more or less arbitrary. As in the case of the preliminary analyses, however, we have attempted to be as objective as possible, and the particular divisions selected are ones that were forced on us rather than ones that were set up in advance.

First of all, all conversational images were set aside, and we shall examine them independently. Then, the remaining images were classified into divisions as broad as possible from which there resulted four principal categories: Nature, Aesthetics, Society, Introspective Processes. We shall examine each of these in turn.

CONVERSATIONAL IMAGES

One of the criticisms Proust makes of Flaubert's style is that he introduces into conversations images that are inappropriate or out of character for the speaker concerned.[1] The same accusation can occasionally be made against Proust, though it would have to be agreed that the complexity of his images in descriptive and analytical contexts is much greater than in discourse. A strange case in point is the description of Marcel uttered by Céleste Albaret who appears in person in the book and who was, as we know, Proust's housekeeper. The comparisons, *joues amies et fraîches comme l'intérieur d'une amande, petites mains de satin tout pelucheux* (IX, 315), surely strike one as Proust and not as anyone else.

Generally speaking, the images used by Saint-Loup are just as banal as those employed by Cottard or Madame Verdurin or any of the other characters. He speaks of his *oncle Charlus . . . qui a eu*

[1] *Loc. cit.*, p. 194.

autant de femmes que don Juan, et qui à son âge ne dételle pas (IX, 120).
Vaugoubert is *une espèce de loque* and his wife *un grand cheval que tu
connais peut-être* (XIV, 72). There is one notable exception to this
manner, however, and that occurs when Saint-Loup is talking
military strategy (VI, 135–40). Here, his style is so different, his
sentences so long and involved and his manner so lofty in tone
that one has the impression of reading a text, or rather of reading an
exposition by Proust rather than a discussion by Saint-Loup. Take
the following for instance:

> Ce qui est récit confus pour le commun des lecteurs est pour
> toi un enchaînement aussi rationnel qu'un tableau pour l'amateur
> qui sait regarder ce que le personnage porte sur lui, tient dans les
> mains, tandis que le visiteur ahuri des musées se laisse étourdir et
> migrainer par de vagues couleurs. Mais, comme pour certains
> tableaux où il ne suffit pas de remarquer que le personnage tient un
> calice, mais où il faut savoir pourqoi le peintre lui a mis dans les
> mains un calice, ce qu'il symbolise par là, ces opérations militaires, en
> dehors même de leur but immédiat, sont habituellement, dans l'esprit
> du général qui dirige la campagne, calquées sur des batailles plus
> anciennes qui sont, si tu veux, comme le passé, comme la biblio-
> thèque, comme l'érudition, comme l'étymologie, comme l'aristo-
> cratie des batailles nouvelles (VI, 135).

In reading, one is perhaps not conscious of the incongruity of having
Saint-Loup talk this way, but one is forced to admit that here we
are listening not to Saint-Loup, but to the author himself.

The same accusation might be made in connection with Albertine's description of ice-cream moulds (XI, 160–61). Nowhere else
does she use imagery to any extent. She does call Marcel, in his
pyjamas, a *divinité du ciel déposée sur un lit* (XI, 20) and she compares
him to a dove, but this is all. Her use of imagery in picturing ice-
cream is supposed to illustrate the beneficial influence living with
Marcel has had on her intellect, but when she suddenly starts talking
about *colonnes votives* or about *pylônes élevés dans une allée à la
gloire de la Fraîcheur* (XI, 160), or when she says that

> . . . ces glaces au citron là sont tout de même des montagnes
> réduites à une échelle toute petite, mais l'imagination rétablit les
> proportions, comme pour ces petits arbres japonais nains qu'on sent
> très bien être tout de même des cèdres . . . si bien qu'en plaçant
> quelques-uns le long d'une petite rigole, dans ma chambre, j'aurais
> une immense forêt descendant vers un fleuve et où les petits enfants
> se perdraient (XI, 161),

we cannot but feel that there is more Proust here than just an influence.[1]

As one might expect, reported conversations of the narrator Marcel, with one exception, are identical in quality with that of the descriptive passages in the work, e.g.

> Certaines maisons nouvellement bâties . . . déchirent . . . l'air torride de midi en juillet . . . d'un cri aussi acide que l'odeur des cerises attendant que le déjeuner soit servie dans la salle à manger obscure, où les prismes de verre pour poser les couteaux projettent des feux multicolores et aussi beaux que les verrières de Chartres (XI, 207–8).

The exception is a curious case of mixed metaphor that is completely inconsistent with the rest of Proust's style: *Violà les Cambremer ancrés dans ce clan des Guermantes où ils n'espéraient pas pouvoir jamais planter leur tente* (XIII, 291). One might argue that here we are dealing with instances of faded metaphor, but the juxtaposition of two such incompatible images renders them again fully active, with the result that the passage seems stylistically defective.

Apart from these few exceptions, the images introduced by Proust into conversations are generally consistent with our impression of the characters concerned. We hardly need to be told that *'le temple secret où vous trônez serait envahi par la tourbe des lecteurs ignares'* (X, 303) is uttered by Bloch, or that it is Charlus who declares that

> . . . la notion du prodigieux personnage que je suis et du microscopique vibrion qu'il figure . . . ce petit âne peut braire autant qu'il lui plaît devant ma robe auguste d'évêque (IX, 21).

The speech of Françoise is filled with picturesque proverbial expressions:

> Il y a des jours où il est poli comme une porte de prison (IX, 244); voleur comme une pie (VI, 27); pauvre jeunesse qui sera fauchée comme un pré (I, 124); la vie, le seul cadeau que le bon Dieu ne fasse jamais deux fois (I, 124).

Brichot, in typical professorial style, speaks of *la chapelle mallarméenne, où notre nouvel ami, comme tous ceux de son âge, a dû servir la messe ésotérique* (X, 119). Madame de Guermantes displays the same

---

[1] Professor Ullmann also points out various instances where Legrandin also seems to be a parody of Proust. See S. Ullmann, *The Image in the Modern French Novel*, p. 222.

malicious wit in comparisons as in her *bons mots*. For her, Madame de Cambremer is *cette énorme herbivore* . . . *qui avait l'air d'une vache* (VII, 66), and unproductive writers are *les auteurs constipés qui pondent tous les quinze ans une pièce en un acte ou un sonnet* (VIII, 130).

By and large, the images we find in conversations in Proust are the same images we would find in life, and they serve a double function. They are consistent with the intellect of the person who utters them and they serve indirectly to strengthen and enlarge our conception of that character.

NATURE

Proust's love of nature is too well-known to need comment. The episode of his walk with Reynaldo Hahn when he stopped in rapt preoccupation to admire the hawthorn, sending his friend on in advance,[1] and anecdotes of his drives in hermetically sealed carriages where he might see the blossoms without suffering from hay fever[2] are familiar.

One of Proust's consistently recurring stylistic devices is to use what we may call reciprocal images. Young girls are compared to flowers, and flowers in turn are compared to young girls. He compares trees, waves, the moon and seasons to people and he compares humans to plants, flowers, or even a landscape. This has the effect of animating the inanimate and inanimating the animate. It emphasizes the unity of nature by showing that humans are no more free than plants and animals and that all orders of life partake of the same fundamental characteristics.

Flowers and Trees. The hawthorn is associated by Proust with the spring of the year, with May-day festivals and rural weddings (IX, 238). He usually compares it to an innocent young girl:

> Je l'imaginais comme si ç'avait été le mouvement de tête étourdi et rapide, au regard coquet, aux pupilles diminuées, d'une blanche jeune fille, distraite et vive (I, 155).

but he also associates it with manifestations of the spirit of spring. The blooms on the branches remind him of the *pompons qui enguir-*

---

[1] Compare the transcription of this incident in *A la recherche du temps perdu* at V, 191.
[2] NRF, *Hommage*, pp. 39–40.

landent une houlette rococo (I, 190) or the elaborate wedding train of a bride (I, 154).

Apple trees in bloom are like beautiful girls *en toilette de bal* (IX, 232; VI, 191), and the lilacs also remind him of young girls—*jeunes houris qui gardaient dans ce jardin français les tons vifs et purs des miniatures de la Perse* (I, 185).

The latter comparison is especially interesting, for it is a further illustration of another set of common reciprocal images. Proust frequently compares real life to art and art to real life.

The roses which Madame de Villeparisis is about to paint . . . *avaient l'air d'achalander le comptoir d'une fleuriste dans quelque estampe du XVIIIe siècle* (VII, 14). The chrysanthemums Odette is so fond of are *comme des feux arrachés par un grand coloriste à l'instabilité de l'atmosphère et du soleil* (III, 209), and the *boules de neige* have stalks *nues comme les arbustes linéaires des préraphaélites* (IV, 45). Even the humble buttercups have, with their bright yellow, *comme certaines de nos vieilles toiles peintes dans leur simplicité populaire, un poétique éclat d'orient* (I, 227). The hawthorn is Proust's special favourite, of course, and he returns to it again and again, *comme devant ces chefs-d'œuvre dont on croit qu'on saura mieux les voir quand on a cessé un moment de les regarder* (I, 189). In particular, he admires the pink hawthorn which seems more precious because of its rarity, like the rose-coloured biscuits sold at Camus's shop or cheese made pink by the addition of strawberries (I, 190).[1]

A second animating type of image is the comparison of flowers to insects. The acacias are covered with blossoms, *comme des colonies ailées et vibratiles de parasites précieux* (II, 268), and the hawthorn in certain shades seems to have kept *la virulence printanière, le pouvoir irritant, d'insectes aujourd'hui métamorphosés en fleurs* (I, 157).

Proust frequently compares anything mysterious or unattainable to stars or gods. The chrysanthemums are *ces astres éphémères qui s'allument dans les jours gris* (II, 10), and the fruit tree in bloom outside the rather disreputable quarter in which Rachel lives is like an angel, *un mystérieux voyageur, arrêté pour un jour dans la cité maudite* (VI, 196). He also has images about flowers in which he uses comparisons drawn from the sea. Just as the stars or gods are for him symbols of the remote or unattainable, the sea represents that which is eternal, mysterious in its unchanging quality and provocative because of it.

---

[1] For other examples of flowers and trees compared to art, see I, 189, 214, 274; II, 276; IV, 133.

La vue d'un seul coquelicot hissant au bout de son cordage et faisant cingler au vent sa flamme rouge, au-dessus de sa bouée graisseuse et noire, me faisait battre le cœur, comme au voyageur qui aperçoit sur une terre basse une première barque échouée que répare un calfat, et s'écrie, avant de l'avoir encore vue: 'La Mer!' (I, 189).

Some of the lilacs, in their unvarying cycle,

. . . effusaient encore en hauts lustres mauves les bulles délicates de leurs fleurs, mais dans bien des parties du feuillage où déferlait, il y avait seulement une semaine, leur mousse embaumée, se flétrissait, diminuée et noircie, une écume creuse (I, 185).

A final comparison which emphasizes the elusive quality of the beauty of flowers and its intangibility is that with music. Again, the mysterious quality of music which enables it to express emotions that cannot be articulated, makes it particularly suitable to compare with flowers.[1] The hawthorn, like certain musical intervals

. . . m'offraient indéfiniment le même charme avec une profusion inépuisable, mais sans me le laisser approfondir davantage, comme ces mélodies qu'on rejoue cent fois de suite sans descendre plus avant dans leur secret (I, 188).

Birds, etc. Proust admires the beauty of birds and he uses them extensively as a source of imagery. Actual figures of speech in which birds are themselves described with other terms of reference are few in number, but they follow Proust's usual traditions. Pigeons on the ground are compared to antique sculptures (II, 252). Because of their colour, no doubt, they are also compared to lilacs and antique enamel ornaments (II, 255). The flight of martins and swallows is compared to fountains and fireworks (V, 51) and birds near the sea are personified as Oceanides because of their song (X, 168). Gulls are compared to water lilies (IX, 265, 269).

Water (The Sea, Rivers, Pools, etc.) One of Proust's techniques in trying to suggest the infinite variety of something like the sea is to compare it to as many different things as possible. By using descriptive terms, by personifying it and by relating it to varied realms of experience, he succeeds in conveying the impression of the sea with its vast complexity and its manifold moods.

[1] On this aspect of music, see Susanne K. Langer, *Philosophy in a New Key*, New York (1942), pp. 81–82.

The surface of the water reminds him of enamel (X, 172), of agate (V, 150) or emerald (IV, 91). The sea itself is at times like a wayward Nereid playing on the sea-shore (IV, 130), with its waves *. . . qui s'élançaient l'un après l'autre comme des sauteurs sur un tremplin* (IV, 91). This personification is extended to the ships, and we see *un vaisseau qui s'éloignait comme un voyageur de nuit* (V, 50). At Venice, the sea caught between the gondolas and the marble curbs is like a startled steed (XIII, 261). The River Seine is like a huge stranded whale captive between its banks (II, 242), and the Vivonne, *dont les insectes irritaient perpétuellement le sommeil* (I, 187), no doubt dreams of some imaginary maelstrom.

Proust uses a category of reciprocal images in his description of the sea. He frequently compares it to the land and later, as we shall see, the land to the sea. His procedure is not without an element of paradox, but it opens our eyes to features of both that perhaps never struck us before. At Rivebelle *les îlots . . . donnaient à cette partie de la mer l'aspect nouveau . . . d'un plan en relief* (X, 44). The white caps on the waves are like the snowy summits of mountains (IV, 91), and from his window at Balbec Marcel looks out on the sea each morning, *comme au carreau d'une diligence dans laquelle on a dormi, pour voir si pendant la nuit s'est rapprochée ou éloignée une chaîne désirée* (IV, 91). The most lengthy comparison of this sort occurs at IX, 235–36, but the most extraordinary, without a doubt, is one in which the sea is compared not only to a glacier or a plain but to enamel, and a pail of milk in which the floating flies correspond to the little boats on the sea:

> La mer n'apparaissait plus . . . pareille aux ondulations de montagnes soulevées, mais, au contraire, comme apparaît d'un pic, ou d'une route qui contourne la montagne, un glacier bleuâtre, ou une plaine éblouissante, situés à une moindre altitude. Le déchiquetage des remous y semblait immobilisé et avoir dessiné pour toujours leurs cercles concentriques: l'émail même de la mer . . . prenait vers le fond de la baie . . . la blancheur bleue d'un lait où de petits bacs noirs qui n'avançaient pas semblaient empêtrés comme des mouches (X, 46).

As in the case of flowers, Proust often compares the real sea to artistic representations. At times, it is like the waves one sees in a stained glass window (VI, 177). At other times, there is:

> . . . une brume invisible qui n'était qu'un espace vide réservé autour de sa surface translucide rendue ainsi plus abrégée et plus

saisissante, comme ces déesses que le sculpteur détache sur le reste du bloc qu'il ne daigne pas dégrossir (IV, 130).[1]

At Balbec, the view Proust gets from the different windows of his room reminds him of an exhibition of Japanese prints (V, 51) or a showing of contemporary pastels framed behind glass (V, 52). At the same time it reminds him of the delicate sketches of Pisanello, *fixés par cet émail blanc, inaltérable et camaïeux qui figure une couche de neige dans les verreries de Gallé* (V, 49).[2]

When Proust says that

> . . . un petit papillon qui s'était endormi au bas de la fenêtre semblait apposer avec ses ailes, au bas de cette 'harmonie gris et rose' dans le goût de celles de Whistler, la signature favorite du maître de Chelsea (V, 52),

the juxtaposition of the butterfly and the sea is not accidental. For him, the butterfly represents the transitory (IX, 192) as opposed to the eternal quality of the sea, even though it may be beautiful and permanent as a species. In the case of the butterfly, however, one tends to regard only the ephemeral. Elsewhere, Proust compares the temporal ships which sail on the sea to butterflies:

> Les ailes immobiles des vaisseaux lointains et bleuâtres avaient l'air de papillons exotiques et nocturnes dans une vitrine (VI, 186).[3]

These two things, together with the conception of young girls as flowers, are combined symbolically in the following interesting metaphor:

> Me rendant bien compte, avec une satisfaction de botaniste, qu'il n'était pas possible de trouver réunies des espèces plus rares que celles de ces jeunes fleurs qui interrompaient en ce moment devant moi la ligne du flot de leur haie légère, pareille à un bosquet de roses de Pensylvanie, ornement d'un jardin sur la falaise, entre lesquelles tient tout le trajet de l'océan parcouru par quelque steamer, si lent à glisser sur le trait horizontal et bleu qui va d'une tige à l'autre, qu'un papillon paresseux, attardé au fond de la corolle que la coque du navire a depuis longtemps depassée, peut pour s'envoler en étant sûr d'arriver avant le vaisseau, attendre que rien qu'une seule parcelle azurée sépare encore la proue de celui-ci du premier pétale de la fleur vers laquelle il navigue (V, 43–44).

[1] Compare this style of sculpture with that of Rodin, about whom Proust must certainly have been thinking. (See p. 43 below.)
[2] For other comparisons of the sea to art, see I, 228–29 (Japanese cloisonné), IV, 91 (Tuscan primitives), 101 (picture in rich bachelor's apartment).
[3] Compare the same idea expressed in PJ, 238.

Landscape. Proust's technique in describing landscape does not differ from his method of describing the sea. The scenery reminds him at times of enamel (VI, 112), or, on occasion, *le lointain des bois paraissait plus bleu, comme peint dans ces camaïeux qui décorent les trumeaux des anciennes demeures* (I, 204). He personifies aspects of terrain,[1] and, as in the case of vessels on the sea, the villas and cities which one finds on the land.[2]

Just as Proust compares the different views of the sea from his window at the hotel at Balbec to an exhibition of paintings, he describes the various outlook points around the château of La Raspelière as uniting

> . . . les plus belles 'vues' des pays avoisinants, des plages ou des forêts, aperçus fort diminués par l'éloignement, comme Hadrien avait assemblé dans sa villa des réductions des monuments les plus célèbres des diverses contrées (X, 174).

The sea had reminded Proust of mountain scenery (see p. 16), and conversely, hill scenery, particularly at night and in the rain, makes him think of the sea:

> Des maisons isolées, accrochées au flanc d'une colline plongée dans la nuit et dans l'eau, brillaient comme des petits bateaux qui ont replié leurs voiles et sont immobiles au large pour toute la nuit (I, 206).[3]

Grass waving in the sunlight also reminds him of water:

> Ces prairies où, quand le soleil les rend réfléchissantes comme une mare, se dessinent les feuilles des pommiers (I, 249).

Occasionally, an effect of the sunlight makes him think that a whole scene has a submarine look:

> Quand un rayon de soleil dorait les plus hautes branches [des acacias], elles semblaient, trempées d'une humidité étincelante, émerger seules de l'atmosphère liquide et couleur d'émeraude, où la futaie tout entière était plongée comme sous la mer (II, 276).[4]

---

[1] Les seins bombés des premières falaises de Maineville (V, 204). Une maigre colline, dressant tout contre le quartier son dos déjà dépouillé d'ombre, grêle et rugueux (VI, 98) La campagne . . . emmitouflée encore dans sa douce et blanche robe, etc. (VI, 97–98).

[2] Un château . . . bien qu'il se blottisse vainement sous sa feuillée séculaire; ces cercles, de plus en plus rapprochés, que décrit l'automobile autour d'une ville fascinée qui fuit dans tous les sens pour échapper, et sur laquelle finalement elle fonce tout droit, à pic, au fond de la vallée où elle reste gisante à terre (X, 182).

[3] Compare also IV, 92; V, 89; VI, 85. [4] Compare also VIII, 14.

The land can also be compared to art, and as Marcel rides with his grandmother and Madame de Villeparisis:

> Comme la voiture gravissait une route montante entre des terres labourées, rendant les champs plus réels, leur ajoutant une marque d'authenticité, comme la précieuse fleurette dont certains maîtres anciens signaient leurs tableaux, quelques bleuets hésitants pareils à ceux de Combray suivaient notre voiture (IV, 137–38).

The analogy between the *précieuse fleurette* and the butterfly of Whistler which Proust associated with the seascapes at Balbec is significant, and while Proust may be thinking of a particular school of artists who used this method of identifying themselves, he could very easily just be thinking of Whistler.

Finally, either consciously or unconsciously, Proust associates with the conception of the permanency of landscape, the idea of the transitory quality of human existence. Speaking of a ride in a coach taken by Marcel and Gilberte long after their youth had passed, he says:

> Au moment de descendre dans le mystère d'une vallée parfaite et profonde que tapissait le clair de lune, nous nous arrêtâmes un instant, comme deux insectes qui vont s'enfoncer au cœur d'un calice bleuâtre (XIII, 328).

Light (Sun, moon, shadows, sky). We have already remarked on the significance with Proust of visual imagery, and, as we might expect, descriptions of the effects of light hold a very important place in his work. He is acutely conscious of the transforming power of different illuminations:

> La diversité de l'éclairage ne modifie pas moins l'orientation d'un lieu, ne dresse pas moins devant nous de nouveaux buts qu'il nous donne le désir d'atteindre, que ne ferait un trajet longuement et effectivement parcouru en voyage (IV, 92).

Notice the variety of effects achieved by rays of sunlight shining on the sea at Balbec:

> Celui qui en ce moment brûlait la mer comme une topaze, la faisait fermenter, devenir blonde et laiteuse comme de la bière, écumante comme du lait, tandis que par moments s'y promenaient çà et là de grandes ombres bleues, que quelque dieu semblait s'amuser à déplacer en bougeant un miroir dans le ciel (IV, 93).

In volume XI (pp. 11–13) Proust acknowledges how much the sun and sunlight mean to him. He says that there are different personages in him responsive to different seasons and he sums up his attitude to the sun and sunlight by saying:

> Je crois bien qu'à mon agonie, quand tous mes autres 'moi' seront morts, s'il vient à briller un rayon de soleil tandis que je pousserai mes derniers soupirs, le petit personnage barométrique se sentira bien aise, et ôtera son capuchon pour chanter: 'Ah! enfin, il fait beau.'

As is so often the case with Proust's imagery, none of the figures he uses in connection with light is fundamentally original. In particular, he utilizes two of the most common metaphors associated with it. One is its golden colour. The morning sidewalks (VI, 71; XV, 159), the balconies (II, 251; VII, 159), the leaves bathed in light (I, 198; XI, 11), a wall illuminated by the sun (V, 229), the snow (II, 241), lamps (V, 55), light seen through shutters (II, 78)—all these are compared in one way or another to gold. The other is the effect of a woven material which can be given by sunlight. Sometimes it is a dusty curtain of sunlight (II, 232) or the effect of muslin swaying between the balustrades of a balcony (VII, 159). The setting sun seems to weave impalpable golden silk under the leaves (I, 198), and the evening hours when one goes to a banquet and returns from it produce

> . . . la double écharpe sombre et singulière qu'avaient tissée . . . les heures nocturnes, champêtres et marines de l'aller et du retour (X, 294).

A dull day

> . . . tissait sans arrêt de transparents filets dans lesquels les promeneurs dominicaux semblaient s'argenter (VII, 211).

Sometimes the sun in penetrating into a room seems to put furniture covers on the sofa and the chairs (XII, 237) and when it strikes a serviette, *le soleil intercale un morceau de velours jaune* (V, 128).

The sun itself is not described very picturesquely. It is *un bloc rouge* (X, 217), *rond et rouge* (X, 218) or *la figure raide, géométrique* (V, 49). Sometimes Proust personifies it (VI, 98; VIII, 18), and here he finds one particularly felicitous metaphor:

> Le soleil était déjà installé sur les toits comme un couvreur matinal qui commence tôt son ouvrage et l'accomplit en silence pour ne pas réveiller la ville (IV, 87).

The personification is carried to the sun's rays and this form of animation is very striking. We may note two examples:

> Un rayon qui y avait commencé sa sieste et était déjà revenu la continuer l'instant d'après (II, 251).

> Les rayons du matin, appuyant, comme le jardinier, leurs barreaux au mur revêtu de capucines (I, 246).

The effect of illumination in a room is to make it appear now like a block of crystal (V, 87), now like a submarine chamber (X, 167).

Proust is equally sensitive to all degrees of light and shade. Dawn traces *dans l'obscurité, et comme à la craie, sa première raie blanche* (I, 251) and the early morning is a *tableau si transparent et si doux* (VI, 107). Dawn (X, 337) and a gray day (VII, 215) are compared to mother-of-pearl and the night to a *nacre opaline* (IV, 69). At Balbec, the rays of the setting sun, through the curtains . . . *laissaient se répandre sur le tapis comme un écarlate effeuillement d'anémones* (V, 228–29).

Again, Proust compares nature to art. In addition to the two examples in the preceding paragraph, he speaks of *les dernières aquarelles du jour . . . encore visibles au ciel* (XV, 13). The contrast of dark stairways with one or two objects in them illuminated by a golden amber light makes him think of Rembrandt (V, 46; VI, 117). The setting sun reflected in the glass bookcases of his room at Balbec reminds him of a series of paintings by an artist (V, 49), and the view from the window at that time is like a work of religious art set in precious stones and exposed on feast days to the veneration of the faithful (V, 48–49). At night, the columns of the *Palais de Gabriel* remind him of the setting for the opera *Orpheus* and, significantly, . . . *donnaient pour la première fois une impression de beauté* (III, 78).

The full moon is compared by Proust to a Chinese lantern (X, 129) or the face of a clock (XI, 217). When it is not full, it reminds him especially of the juicy section of an orange which is so satisfying to quench thirst (IX, 48, 62; X, 198–99). At the same time, because of its shape it also reminds him of a knife or a scimitar (XIV, 138). This in turn makes him think of the Orient and he uses the device to personify the moon and a nearby star:

> Une pauvre petite étoile allait servir d'unique compagne à la lune solitaire, tandis que celle-ci, tout en protégeant son amie, mais

C

plus hardie et allant de l'avant, brandirait comme une arme irrésistible, comme un symbole oriental, son ample et merveilleux croissant d'or (IX, 48).

Proust also compares the moon to an actress:

> La lune blanche comme une nuée, furtive, sans éclat, comme une actrice dont ce n'est pas l'heure de jouer et qui, de la salle, en toilette de ville, regarde un moment ses camarades, s'effaçant, ne voulant pas qu'on fasse attention à elle (I, 198–99).

The effect of moonlight on the ground is similar to that of snow (X, 141; XIV, 57) or fallen blossoms (XIV, 57), or it may unite the woods . . . *avec le firmament auquel il les avait assimilés, dans l'agate arborisée d'un seul azur* (XIII, 81). Sometimes it is like *un doux magnésium continu permettant de prendre une dernière fois des images nocturnes* (XIV, 131).

In connection with shadows in particular, Proust likes to use the device of animating the inanimate. Shadows are easily adapted to this procecdure since they are usually associated with people and have movement. The shadow of the iron work on a balcony is like a capricious vegetation (II, 240). The shadows of trees are *légères commes des âmes* (XIV, 56) and the shadows of the rocks in Elstir's painting . . . *nageant lentement sur les eaux comme des dauphins s'attachaient aux flancs de barques en promenade* (V, 166). The narrator speaks of himself, *laissant mon ombre derrière moi, comme une barque qui poursuit sa navigation à travers des étendues enchantées* (XIII, 326).

In describing the sky and clouds, Proust employs tactics with which we are fast becoming familiar. He compares them first to other objects. The sky at sunset is red, *comme, à cette heure, dans les cuisines les fourneaux qu'on allume* (XIII, 187). The clouds are like down or pastels (IV, 69) or steps made of turquoise (XIV, 84). The clouds are then personified: *dans le ciel férié flânait longuement un nuage oisif* (I, 230), and a very obvious comparison is made between the sky and the sea. For this purpose, the clouds are represented as sportive sea dogs in the eyes of Françoise (I, 223). Finally the sky is compared to art, both secular (IV, 69) and religious:

> Le ciel violet semblait stigmatisé per la figure raide, géométrique, passagère et fulgurante du soleil (pareille à la représentation de quelque signe miraculeux, de quelque apparition mystique), s'inclinait vers la mer sur la charnière de l'horizon comme un tableau religieux au-dessus du maître autel (V, 49).

Proust even goes so far as to compare an effect of the sky with rosy clouds to a blue wall-paper on which some prankster had scribbled *les tirebouchons d'un crayonnage rose* (VI, 116).

Seasons and Weather. Just as Proust describes with equal sensitivity all degrees of light and shade even though his particular delight is bright sunshine, he pictures graphically all kinds of weather, fog, rain or storm, despite the fact that it is the springtime he really loves (II, 232). The sequence of days is for him like turning the pages of a book, and he reads with equal interest if not delight the sombre pages as well as the bright ones:

> L'air vif tournait de lui-même les pages qu'il fallait, et je trouvais, tout indiqué devant moi, pour que je pusse le suivre de mon lit, l'évangile du jour (XI, 30).

Flowers symbolize spring, and the first day of spring is for Proust just like a flower,

> . . . irisé, imprévu comme une première jacinthe déchirant doucement son cœur nourricier pour qu'en jaillît, mauve et satinée, sa fleur sonore, faisant entrer comme une fenêtre ouverte, dans ma chambre encore fermée et noire, la tiédeur, l'éblouissement, la fatigue d'un premier beau jour (VI, 173).

Proust re-integrates the well-worn metaphor of the intoxication of spring but manages to distil from it new life and interest:

> Un printemps décanté, qui est réduit à son essence, et traduit . . . l'épanouissement graduel de ses jours par la fermentation progressive . . . d'une eau vierge et bleue (XII, 260).

The summer is personified as a lazy person reluctant to move (IX, 47) or a happy, smiling individual (II, 273). The simile which closes *A l'Ombre des jeunes filles en fleurs* is more striking, for when Françoise draws back the blinds,

> . . . le jour d'été qu'elle découvrait semblait aussi mort, aussi immémorial qu'une somptueuse et millénaire momie que notre vieille servante n'eût fait que précautionneusement désemmailloter de tous ses linges, avant de la faire apparaître, embaumée dans sa robe d'or (V, 230).

Summer holds within it the seeds of its own decay, and the gold-wrapped mummy which is so glorious to behold is only a relic of that which once had life. The joy is gone, for inevitable death is on its way.

The effect of rain, like a change in the illumination of a scene, is to alter completely the character of a locality which may be well known to us. Proust animates the stormy sky by comparing it to a wild beast (I, 250), and by a fantastic stretch of the imagination, he likens raindrops to migratory birds:

> Les gouttes d'eau, comme des oiseaux migrateurs qui prennent leur vol tous ensemble, descendaient à rangs pressés du ciel (I, 204).

When he is caught by a rainstorm out in the woods, it seems to him that he is actually beneath the sea. The dead leaves are like shells under his feet and the prickly chestnuts look just like small sea-urchins (VIII, 14). In addition, when Marcel is kept indoors by the howling storm, the building seems to be a ship driven before the wind (V, 226).[1]

The murmur of a gentle breeze reminds Proust of the sinuous phrases of Chopin's Nocturnes (X, 143), but the chill north wind which comes with the approach of winter is more like the frantic humming of some refrain composed by Fragson, Mayol or Paulus (XI, 70). The wilder storms with their mystery and grandeur remind him in particular of the eloquent opening of Beethoven's Fifth Symphony with its repeated blows (VII, 209).

Fog has the same gift as rain or light for transforming a scene. It makes Proust think he is a lonely traveller unable to find his way through danger to the inn he seeks (VIII, 26). At the same time, he associates it with Christmas (VIII, 24), and in the bright winter sunlight, it reminds him of spun sugar (VIII, 15). When it is illuminated by the entrance to a café, it seems to him to be a servant welcoming with joy the familiar guest (VIII, 28).

The winter can be a melancholy time for Proust (II, 243), but when the sun shines on the snow, the effect is so beautiful that he is lost in admiration. He overworks the old metaphor of the blanket or covering of snow (II, 241, 242), but the rose tints and the metallic lustre of the surface suggest to him a comparison with rich brocade that is very provocative (II, 241, 244).

---

[1] Compare the same image in PJ, 218.

and Lilies, which he translated. Elstir's work is *un royaume clos, aux frontières infranchissables* (VI, 152). A promising young author is *peut-être distrait de son génie, l'ayant laissé la clef sous la porte dans l'effervescence de passions juvéniles* (XIII, 232).

For Proust, the methods employed in the different arts are similar despite the fact that, on the surface, the media appear to be completely unrelated. The broad technique of La Berma in the theatre resembles that of the impressionistic painter who subjugates detail to the grand effect he desires (VI, 61). Her various characterizations are as recognizable for that reason as different works of the same painter (VI, 62).

In music, the technique of the composer is not dissimilar to that of the painter (XII, 65) or the architect (III, 129) who also construct on broad lines with the idea of the finished work in mind. Certain qualities in music are also to be found in art or even in literature, and Wagner, retrospectively reorganizing his operas into a vast cycle, did so in much the same spirit and for the same reasons as Balzac did when he saw the vision of *La Comédie humaine* (XI, 199).

In the pictorial field, Elstir utilizes techniques common to literature and painting. The transposition of sea and land effects so frequent in his pictures could be said to be *analogue à celle qu'en poésie on nomme métaphore* (V, 87). The balance or rhythm in his compositions is just like that to be found in music (V, 92–93).

When we come to literature itself, which is Proust's special interest, we find that he regards his own methods as not far different from those of the painter and the composer. The characters he portrays sit for him relatively long or short periods, just as they do for a painter (XV, 59). Style is like music (I, 130), and the writer labours to perfect his style in the same way the painter strives to render in all its beauty what may be a rather inconspicuous detail (XI, 232). At the same time, it is not the detail which counts, but the over-all effect, and it is this which both the composer and the writer have in mind even in their concentration on individual details. Any writer plays on the keyboard of his century (VIII, 48), but his work is destined for future generations, and like a great painting, must not be judged from too close up (III, 130).

Proust considers art to be the real religion: *L'art est ce qu'il y a de plus réel, la plus austère école de la vie, et le vrai Jugement dernier* (XV, 23). If there is any immortality for individuals, it is to be found in

the continuing existence of works of art which they have created
(XI, 233; XIII, 133).

The performance of art as in the theatre or at a concert is like the
celebration of religious rites. Albertine at the piano is a sort of St.
Cecilia or *ange musicien* (XII, 226). The stage on which Vinteuil's
music is re-created, as well as the theatre where La Berma re-creates
the great dramatic rôles of the past, become altars consecrated to art
(II, 181; III, 22; VI, 53). La Berma herself is like the Holy of Holies
hidden within the sanctuary before the curtain goes up (III, 21–22).

In writing literature, the novelist is like a priest or a theologian;
though essentially good, he familiarizes himself with all the sins of
humanity either directly or vicariously, and this enables him to
understand others and to arrive at moral conclusions (III, 163;
175–76). The novelist plays the rôle of the grain in the Biblical
parable, *car si le grain de froment ne meurt après qu'on l'a semé, il restera
seul, mais s'il meurt, il portera beaucoup de fruits* (XV, 227).

Works of art, like religious concepts, have been handed down to
us through the centuries, and the great creations of our generation
will become with them the legacy of future generations. Like
religion too, our impressions of them change and will continue to
change, since they appear to successive generations *sous le voile
sensible que leur ont tissé l'amour et la contemplation de tant d'adorateurs
pendant des siècles* (XV, 30).

Painting. Proust is always emphatic that our eyes are not merely
un simple appareil enregistreur qui prend des instantanés (VIII, 172).
There is far more to art than the mere reproduction of forms. When
Elstir paints a rose, for example, he transplants it into that inner
garden where we are all forced to remain, and the result is a variety
of roses we should never have known without him (X, 103). Elstir
is like a chemist experimenting with new products (V, 86). The
materials he uses are familiar or even indifferent to him (V, 107, 119),
but any object is thus, *par l'alchimie des impressions, transformée chez
lui en œuvres d'art* (XIV, 93). The quality of this subjective world of
the artist is as individual as the invalid's hallucinations (XIV, 38),
and his style is as consistent as the projections of a magic lantern
(VIII, 50).

The paintings of Elstir have the same element of surprise in
them as these same projections of the magic lantern, partly because
they are so unexpected. Elstir dissociates himself from the ordinary

connotations which intelligence and experience provide and he paints just what he sees. He is especially fond of the transposition which we noted in connection with Proust's own description of landscape and the sea, *i.e.* to compare the one with the other. In the famous description of Elstir's painting of the port (V, 87–90), Marcel tells how he mistakes the sea for the land (V, 87, 90) and the land for the sea (V, 89, 163). The boats are like high-spirited steeds controlled with difficulty by a gay youth (V, 90), and this intermingling of the two elements gives a unity to the scene which is new to our experience but convincing.

Another device common to Proust and Elstir is the comparison of living creatures to inanimate objects and vice versa. The sails of the boats are like butterflies (V, 92) and the shadows at the base of the rocks are like shy marine goddesses, living and ready to disappear in fright at the appearance of the light (V, 194). Conversely, the muses portrayed by Elstir look like fossils and the poets walking with them like some zoological specimens, each one . . . *caractérisée par une certaine insexualité* (VIII, 53).

Theatre. With painting, if our eyes are open, we cannot but see what the painter portrays for us, even though it may contravene our sense of propriety. With the theatre, not only must the performer arrive at his own interpretation of a rôle, but the spectator, in order to evaluate it, must rid himself of those connotations and prejudices which previous acquaintance with the work have built up. To a certain extent, we may say that every member of an audience sees a different play, even though it may be similar to the play which others see.[1]

The work of an artist like La Berma is just as homogeneous as that of an Elstir, and she has

> . . . ses chefs-d'œuvre à elle, et où on la reconnaissait comme, dans des portraits qu'il a peints d'après des modèles différents, on reconnaît un peintre (VI, 62).

She is in the peculiar position of being herself, a fictitious character and a part of a setting. Her face is no more than a single costume

---

[1] Je n'étais pas éloigné de croire que chaque spectateur [dans le théâtre] regardait comme dans un stéréoscope un décor qui n'était que pour lui, quoique semblable au millier d'autres que regardait, chacun pour soi, le reste des spectateurs (I, 104).

which must be modified to suit the rôle she plays (III, 75).[1] One
might go further and say that:

> Théâtre et public n'était pour elle [La Berma] qu'un second
> vêtement plus extérieur (III, 26).

The characters portrayed by an actress are on the one hand unreal,
since we know that they do not exist (they are like *les personnages d'un
vieux roman comique* (VI, 210)), and on the other hand eternally true.

> Ces individualités éphémères et vivaces que sont les personnages
> d'une pièce . . . font, comme celle d'un être aimé, douter de la réalité
> du moi et méditer sur le mystère de la mort (VI, 210–11).

The performer depends first on make-up to change herself into
the character she wishes to portray. The operation of this trans-
formation is similar in technique to that of the painter (VI, 126).
Then, she utilizes appropriate costume.[2] Her voice serves her in
the same way as a great violinist's instrument (VI, 57). It reminds
Proust at times of a nightingale (VI, 55) or a sylvan spring,

> . . . comme dans le paysage antique où à la place d'une nymphe
> disparue il y a une source inanimée, une intention discernable et
> concrète s'y était changée en quelque qualité du timbre, d'une
> limpidité étrange, appropriée et froide (VI, 57).

Finally, the actress has at her disposition, in order to achieve the
effect she desires, variety of gesture. Here too, Proust is reminded of
nature and of water because of

> . . . les bras de la Berma que les vers eux-mêmes . . . semblaient
> soulever sur sa poitrine, comme ces feuillages que l'eau déplace en
> s'échappant (VI, 57).

The over-all impression of La Berma's acting draws on the same
source of imagery:

> Comme le peintre dissout maison, charrette, personnages, dans
> quelque grand effet de lumière qui les fait homogènes, la Berma
> étendait de vastes nappes de terreur, de tendresse, sur les mots
> fondus également (VI, 61).

---

[1] Compare the description of the *wings* of Rachel's nose *tout comme le relief des décors*
(VI, 216).
[2] In the case of the part of Phèdre, it is . . . 'ces blancs voiles . . . filés par la souffrance
mi-païenne, mi-janséniste, autour de laquelle ils se contractaient comme un cocon
fragile et frileux' (VI, 58).

We have already noted that Proust likes to compare nature to art and vice versa. We have mentioned the fact that, as far as Proust is concerned, the sea represents the eternal, something mobile and full of moods and mystery but something constant and unchanging. It is not surprising then that Elstir's paintings should so often deal with the sea or that La Berma's acting should be compared to aspects of the sea or water. From them we get the impression of enduring truth, of variety and flexibility and of life. We also get the impression of rhythm and sound from those analogies drawn from springs or the sea, and this in turn leads Proust to compare the applause which greets a performance to a storm at sea.

> La force des applaudissements antérieurs comme dans une tempête, une fois que la mer a été suffisamment remuée, elle continue à grossir, même si le vent ne s'accroît plus (III, 31).

Many of Proust's images are suggested to him by the association of ideas. For example one speaks commonly of the star of a play— *l'étoile*. This figure is utilized by Proust in connection with La Berma (VI, 59), and he extends it to describe the three blows traditionally struck just before the raising of the curtain as *aussi émouvants que des signaux venus de la planète Mars* (III, 26). When he comes to describe the actress Rachel, her nose is like *un croissant de lune* (VI, 213) and her power of attraction like that of any one of the planets (VI, 214). She is radiant like a star (VI, 213) or the moon, except when one gets close to her. Then,

> . . . en revanche, comme si nous nous approchions de la lune et qu'elle cessât de nous paraître de rose et d'or, sur ce visage si uni tout à l'heure je ne distinguais plus que des protubérances, des taches, des fondrières (VI, 216).

Reciprocally, Proust has already compared the moon to an actress. (See pp. 21–22).

Literature and Language. As one might expect, images dealing with the aesthetics of writing are much more common in Proust than those dealing with any of the other art forms. That is because, personally, the narrator is most vitally interested in literature, not only as it is practised by Bergotte but as he hopes and tries to practise it himself.

Creative literature uses language, and Proust as a writer is particularly concerned with words and their function. We have already noticed that he associates visual imagery with words (II, 229). Vocabulary is a function of one's class background (VII, 223) and one's country of origin. The *patois* which Françoise employs is an interesting study in linguistic geography (IX, 166), and the conversation of the Guermantes clan is like a dictionary of archaisms (VIII, 205). The vocabulary of Madame de Guermantes is

> . . . savoureux comme ces plats possibles à découvrir dans les livres délicieux de Pampille, mais dans la réalité devenus si rares, où les gelées, le beurre, le jus, les quenelles sont authentiques, ne comportent aucun alliage, et même où on fait venir le sel des marais salants de Bretagne (VIII, 146–47).

Besides the individual element to be found in language, there is a universal quality. New expressions can pervade all levels of society (from a relatively insignificant beginning) just like an epidemic or a plague of weeds (VII, 72). Even puns have a sort of evolution similar to that of epidemics (X, 95), and,

> . . . de toutes les graines voyageuses, celle à qui sont attachées les ailes les plus solides qui lui permettent d'être disséminée à une plus grande distance de son lieu d'éclosion, c'est encore une plaisanterie (VII, 75).

This comparison of words to seeds or germs is not new, but it is treated in a new way by Proust.

Proper names are just as distinct as individuals (II, 229), and their effect is to call to mind, as it were, a *carte photographique d'identité* for the individual concerned (VI, 12). Proper names are almost invariably associated with colour (II, 229). Pont-Aven is the green and rose of spring blossoms (IV, 76); Parma is mauve (II, 229)[1]; Guermantes is amaranth (VI, 15), even though its last syllable alone is orange (I, 231–32); Brabant is yellow (I, 19) and Mortemart is conspicuous by contrast among so many bright colours because it is black (VIII, 192).[2] Names may change their colour when they correspond to living changing beings, or, because of the variety of colours associated with them at different periods, they may become almost a neutral gray. Then,

[1] Probably because of association with 'violettes de Parme'. See VIII, 59.
[2] Probably because of the association of black with mourning and death ('morte').

... nous sentons l'entité originale tressaillir et reprendre sa forme et sa ciselure au sein des syllabes mortes aujourd'hui, si dans le tourbillon vertigineux de la vie courante, où ils n'ont plus qu'un usage entièrement pratique, les noms ont perdu toute couleur comme une toupie prismatique qui tourne trop vite et qui semble grise (VI, 13).

In addition to their visual quality, words and names cause definite auditory impressions. When they date back a long way in history, their sound for us is very much like that of the contemporary musical instruments of the time, *violas da gamba* or *violes d'amour* (IV, 184–85). When their history is more recent, they are like recordings made at different periods in the immediate past, and sensations recalled for one reason or another can give us the exact reproduction of the quality a name had for us at that time (VI, 12).

The individual character of a proper name is most striking when it is first presented to us. It is then that its colour and its sound are most vivid and it seems, as it were, to have a quality of mystery and a life of its own. This spirit abiding in proper names of all kinds (cities, rivers, châteaux, family names) is similar to the lesser divinities thought by the Greeks to inhabit places. These nymphs or fairies are very elusive, however, and, like the colour of the name, disappear when the name becomes associated definitely with a person or a place (VI, 11–12).

When we turn to literature itself, we are faced with a great complexity of apparently contradictory ways of looking at the writer's art and his technique. When it is all sorted out, however, we see that as usual Proust desires to show us as many facets as possible of what is really a very involved creative process, and it is largely through the variety of the imagery he uses that he succeeds in making the account so realistic. There is no inherent contradiction.

For Proust, a book is an individual and a unique entity (I, 61; IV, 70–71). He utilizes the familiar concept that a book is the writer's offspring:

Les vrais livres doivent être les enfants non du grand jour et de la causerie mais de l'obscurité et du silence (XV, 46).

The works of Bergotte are like his impetuous daughters (III, 160–61; VII, 183), and, when Marcel feels himself near death, he has the same distracted interest in his book as a dying mother concerned about the welfare of her son:

> Elle l'aime peut-être encore, mais ne le sait plus que par le devoir excédant qu'elle a de s'occuper de lui (XV, 222).

An extension of this idea of offspring is the consideration of a writer's thoughts or works as his seed. When Bergotte extemporizes orally, the result is like beautiful flowers, which are however sterile, since they produce nothing (XIV, 91). His written words, on the other hand, are like seeds which propagate themselves all over the world (I, 132). Marcel nurtures within himself the seeds which feed the developing plant (XV, 48), and after it has grown he can die (XV, 227). The rich pasture thus provided for future readers constitutes

> ... l'herbe drue des œuvres fécondes, sur laquelle les générations viendront faire gaiement, sans souci de ceux qui dorment en dessous, leur 'déjeuner sur l'herbe' (XV, 218).

This sustenance will be assimilated without much thought of how it was produced.

> Ceux qui se nourriraient ensuite d'elle ignoreraient ce qui aurait été fait pour leur nourriture, comme ignorent ceux qui mangent les graines alimentaires que les riches substances qu'elles contiennent ont d'abord nourri la graine et permis sa maturation (XV, 48).

In addition to being like an offspring with a unique personality, or a plant or seed with nutritional value, the great book is also very much something consciously planned and constructed by its creator. Proust speaks of Racine's chisel (PM, 269), and he describes any writer's first works as similar in their primitive qualities to early airplanes that would not fly (XV, 39–40). He mentions his own *travaux d'architecte* (XV, 220), and, in accordance with his conception of the religious nature of art, it is most usual for him to consider a great work as a sort of temple (III, 150) or religious monument (XV, 210, 221). The various real people who have been incorporated one way or another into the book,

> ... les inconnues qui s'en doutaient le moins . . . ont apporté chacune leur pierre pour l'édification du monument qu'elles ne verront pas (XV, 54).

This makes of the work a sort of cemetery. The actual people there do not count for much:

> Un livre est un grand cimetière où sur la plupart des tombes on ne peut plus lire les noms effacés (XV, 53).[1]

A certain amount of the materials in a book is contributed by others, but the actual resources have to be assembled and arranged by the author himself. Proust thinks of his mind as a treasure house, (XV, 218) and he fears that he will not have time to pass on to others the precious object which is stored inside him (XV, 216). His brain is like a rich geological deposit which he alone is able to exploit (XV, 216).

An author is very much like a mirror in that he reflects in his works the truth which he as an individual sees (XIV, 37). By the same token, he provides his readers with an optical instrument which enables them to perceive things they might never have noticed on their own (XV, 62, 211). The process of reflection which the author instigates is not unselective, however, for he is a sort of diagnostician or anatomist. The expert clinician rarely encounters the perfectly normal organ (See PM 258), but he and the author can study anatomy just as well on the atypical specimen (XV, 26). From their generalizations, they can arrive at a description that is physiologically accurate (XV, 50).

In emphasizing the importance of generalizing from many instances, Proust compares the writer's technique to that of the artist who needs to see many churches in order to paint one (XV, 58), or the cook who enriches the characteristic flavour of her beef jelly with many different pieces of meat (XV, 213). Conversely, the individual who presents in himself generalities of a society of which he is not fully conscious is indispensable to the author.

These people,

> . . . répétant comme des perroquets ce que disent les gens de caractère semblable . . . s'étaient faits par là même les oiseaux prophètes (XV, 49).

What they say and do is not necessarily typical of them as individuals, but it reflects features of the times:

> Dans un ridicule l'artiste voit une belle généralité, il ne l'impute pas plus à grief à la personne observée que le chirurgien ne la

[1] For an effective elaboration of this image, compare PJ, 203.

mésestimerait d'être affectée d'un trouble assez fréquent de la circulation (XV, 50).

The author primarily seeks truth. Proust warns elsewhere against accepting uncritically any pronouncement of a writer, (PM, 254), but he feels that we intuitively respond to what is true. When Marcel encounters a page of Bergotte that coincides with his own thought and could pass as a collection of epigraphs for his letters (I, 133), he weeps, *comme dans les bras d'un père retrouvé* (I, 134).

In his search for truth and in his revelation of it, the author is like a god (I, 133). Bergotte walks among ordinary men like a god in disguise (I, 138–39). It is really *l'Esprit éternel* which is the author of Bergotte's books (III, 162).

The pursuit of truth and its promulgation is a very difficult business, and one might say that in the final analysis it is the quest of death. Proust believes that suffering alone produces a great work, and he compares the phenomenon in turn to intense heat which gives off light, lightning which ravages but produces enough illumination to photograph (XV, 57), and artesian wells whose flow is directly proportional to the depth to which they have been sunk (XV, 59). Bergotte is like a planet gradually cooling off (and produced, we may assume, in a moment of intense heat (XI, 228)). Bergotte, in his devotion to his art, is compared to a kleptomaniac (III, 162, 163), and he is thin as if the books he had produced were parts of himself removed during successive operations (VII, 186).

For Bergotte, art is more important than life, or perhaps we should say Art *is* life. When he is very ill, he goes to see a painting by Vermeer, despite the fact that it may be the death of him. He is particularly attracted by a beautifully painted bit of yellow wall which is like a precious Chinese work of art (XI, 231) or a bright golden butterfly (XI, 232).[1] He feels that his techniques with language and his purpose are not far different from those of the painter in his medium, and he has a vision of a heavenly balance with his own life on one side and on the other the bit of yellow wall (XI, 232).

The effect on a reader of a work like Bergotte's is similar in quality to that experienced by its creator. Contact with truth is shattering, whether we are the ones to lay it bare or the ones to acknowledge the truths others have discovered.

[1] Notice here that the butterfly is used to represent both the beautiful and that which is transient. Cf. p. 17.

Certains romans sont comme de grands deuils momentanés, abolissent l'habitude, nous remettent en contact avec la réalité de la vie, mais pour quelques heures seulement, comme un cauchemar (XIII, 176).

To the uninitiated, not only does the writer seem as far removed from the ordinary walks of life as a god, but he manages to accomplish marvellous feats of dexterity beyond the range of ordinary mortals. He is like a gymnast compared to a gauche child (VII, 184), or a sleight-of-hand artist confounding the credulous (III, 149). The narrator compares his own early efforts at writing to a sort of card trick in which he is the victim, being forced inevitably to choose a blank card (VI, 182).

Marcel describes his early attitude toward Bergotte as a love affair (I, 135). He does not at first realize that it is not just Bergotte he loves, so much as the craft, any more than a lover is aware that it is the experience which is important rather than the object to which it is directed (I, 130).

The important thing with any potential writer is the process of the awakening of his talent. Proust believes that talent is just as constitutional as good health (III, 190–91). He admits that certain faculties may assume the functions of others, *comme des gens dont l'estomac est incapable de digérer chargent de cette fonction leur intestin* (XV, 50), but no one without talent can find any substitute for it. Individual cases vary, but the moment of realization of one's possibilities is bound to come like a revelation, as in the narrator's case. We may compare his decision to write with the example of the young author for whom it appears that *quelque cataclysme physiologique avait éveillé en lui le génie assoupi comme la Belle au bois dormant* (XIII, 232).

We must not exaggerate either the influence of environment or the degree of consciousness of the individual author. Proust compares successive schools of literature and their reactions to the clever speculation of traders in response to the rise and fall of stocks at the Bourse (IX, 275). It is only retrospectively, as in the case of war, that we can prophesy what will happen (XV, 35). On the other hand, the individual writer is no more conscious where he is going than the group, but some deep-lying instinct leads him in the right direction: *Nous agissons à l'aveuglette, mais en choisissant comme les bêtes la plante qui nous est favorable* (XII, 17). Like the authors of the great epics, he may not realize the true value of his work (III, 103–4).

Proust insists that any author's work is a unity. If it appears

D

contradictory to us, it is only because we do not know all the aspects of his character. It is wrong of us to reconstruct the entire mental universe of Bergotte from the *découpure* which he has put in certain books (III, 175). The unity which Balzac saw in his work was retrospective (XI, 199), and Marcel himself, before his revelation, was like a painter

> . . . montant un chemin qui surplombe un lac dont un rideau de rochers et d'arbres lui cache la vue. Par une brèche il l'aperçoit, il l'a tout entier devant lui, il prend ses pinceaux (XV, 214).

The work of literature it only fully completed when it has an audience and critics:

> C'est une Vénus collective, dont on n'a qu'un membre mutilé si l'on s'en tient à la pensée de l'auteur, car elle ne se réalise complète que dans l'esprit de ses lecteurs (XIII, 190).

It is quite evident from the examination of images dealing with literature that Proust is here on very familiar ground. No longer does he seem to be theorising, as is often the case when he talks about painting and, indeed, music. His words have a ring of authenticity and he speaks with the authority of a master. In XV, 210–13 he sums up in a brilliant series of images his own uncompromising conception of the cult of literature. What he has to say is a *résumé* of almost all that has preceded with respect to Bergotte and himself. It is one of the most inspiring and idealistic statements of the aesthetic of the true writer. In order to do his task justice, he says, the author should

> . . . préparer son livre minutieusement, avec de perpétuels regroupements de forces, comme pour une offensive, le supporter comme une fatigue, l'accepter comme une règle, le construire comme une église, le suivre comme un régime, le vaincre comme un obstacle, le conquérir comme une amitié, le suralimenter comme un enfant, le créer comme un monde (XV, 211).

Music. When Proust comments that Bergotte is . . . *surtout un homme qui au fond n'aimait vraiment que certaines images et (comme une miniature au fond d'un coffret) que les composer et les peindre sous les mots* (III, 164), we may assume that he is not being entirely complimentary. At the same time, it must be admitted that Proust himself prefers to translate things into visual terms and of necessity into words. This is particularly noticeable when we come to music, and the result, as far as imagery is concerned, is to make the treatment seem rather superficial. To regard all types of musical composition as tone poems has never been considered aesthetically perspicacious; yet that is just what Proust tends to do.

Proust's sense of colour vision is very acute as we have seen. Auditory impressions such as proper names suggest certain shades to him (cf. p. 32), so it is not surprising then that music also should create definite visual colours. For Swann, the piano part of Vinteuil's sonata is like *la mauve agitation des flots que charme et bémolise le clair de lune* (I, 282). For the narrator himself, the Sonata of Vinteuil is white, while his septet, in contrast, is bright red (XII, 60, 65, 216; XV, 21). In it a joyous theme struggles with a melancholy one. This optimistic theme is a violent crimson and it tints the sky, *comme l'aurore, d'un espoir mystérieux* (XII, 60). It literally tears the air: . . . *aussi vif que la nuance écarlate dans laquelle le début était noyé, quelque chose comme un mystique chant de coq, un appel ineffable, mais suraigu, de l'éternel matin* (XII, 60). This vibrant, ecstatic theme, compared also to a scarlet angel blowing carmine notes on its trumpet (XII, 72–73), triumphs over its sombre counterpart. A page of Vinteuil's music played on the piano is clear and uniform like a beam of light, but when it is rendered by the full orchestra it is bright and varicoloured like the spectrum into which the ray of light can be decomposed (XII, 64–65).

Music also acts as an olfactory stimulus as far as Proust is concerned. Marcel admits to Legrandin's sister, Mme de Cambremer, that in a certain scene of Pelleas . . . *cette odeur de roses . . . est si forte, dans la partition, que, comme j'ai le hay-fever et la rose-fever, elle me faisait éternuer chaque fois que j'entendais cette scène* (IX, 272). The pleasure which Swann finds in Vinteuil's music is similar to the odour of roses (I, 282) or subtle perfumes which he tries to analyse (II, 32, 177).

Both Swann and Marcel personify the *petite phrase de Vinteuil*. For Swann, it is like an elfin creature perceived dancing beyond one of the doorways in a picture by Pieter de Hooch (I, 294) or a person one had seen but never dared hope to meet (I, 286). For Marcel, it is like a person who has become one's friend, a dancer, . . . *enveloppée, harnachée d'argent, toute ruisselante de sonorités brillantes, légères et douces comme des écharpes* (XII, 59), or a person walking outdoors amid magnificent natural surroundings (II, 67).

Proust likes to compare music to nature, just as he compared painting to nature. We have already noted how he relates natural sounds to music (p. 24), and it is not surprising that he should compare music in turn to bird-cries or the wind. The dialogue of piano and violin in the Sonata by Vinteuil is like two birds calling to each other from neighbouring trees (II, 180). The *petite phrase* is like a dove's cooing, while the opening of the septet reminds Marcel of the strident crowing of a cock. The music of Tristan is at times like a great storm at sea (XI, 208–9), while the theme of the hammer blows of Siegfried reminds Marcel of the roar of those mechanical birds, the airplanes he had heard at Balbec (XI, 200). When Marcel first hears the septet of Vinteuil, he finds himself in a strange land where he cannot find his way until he recognizes the familiar theme of the Sonata, like a well-known path (XII, 58–59).

The musician's medium is like a relatively unexplored land (II, 177) or even a separate little universe which every composer creates for himself (XII, 59). This universe is like a Paradise (XII, 70), whose themes are its dryads or domestic divinities (XII, 71), or like a supernatural world, the inhabitants of which we can recognize but not hold captive long among us (II, 178).

The particular universe which each musician creates for himself is constructed logically, *comme les prémisses dans la conclusion nécessaire* (II, 180), in just the same way as it was for the writer. It may be difficult at first impression for us to see the unity of a work. Indeed for Marcel himself, . . . *des phrases inaperçues chez Mme Verdurin, larves obscures alors indistinctes, devenaient d'éblouissantes architectures* (XII, 214). Early impressions are compared by him to structures crudely modelled or seen through a fog (XII, 212). The musician, however, is like any craftsman skilled in his trade, and he builds logically, adapting himself to the resistance of his medium:

> Wagner allait . . . mais en respectant toutefois son originalité première comme un huchier les fibres, l'essence particulière du bois qu'il sculpte (XI, 198).

It is up to us to discover the symmetry of the work, for music requires the intelligent participation of the audience just like any other art form. Otherwise, *la manifestation reste étouffée comme dans du coton* (XII, 22).

As in the case of literature, the individual creator of music is partly a product of the times, partly an original artist. Both Debussy and Vintueil owe something to Wagner. The former is spoken of as using some of the *armes conquises pour achever de s'affranchir de celui qu'on a momentanément vaincu* (IX, 274); and the latter's music is greeted by Marcel *avec le sourire qu'a l'ami d'une famille retrouvant quelque chose de l'aïeul dans une intonation, un geste du petit-fils qui ne l'a pas connu* (XI, 196). At the same time, each composer seems to Proust to create and inhabit a world of his own (XII, 68), which is as much a thing apart as any writer's world:

> Cet accent de Vinteuil, est séparé de l'accent des autres musiciens par une différence bien plus grande que celle que nous percevons entre la voix de deux personnes, même entre le beuglement et le cri de deux espèces animales (XII, 67).

The composer experimenting with new harmonies and advancing the limits of what it is possible to do in music is like a chemist, a Lavoisier or an Ampère, *découvrant les lois secrètes d'une force inconnue, menant à travers l'inexploré, vers le seul but possible* (II, 180). His notes are like hieroglyphics or difficult formulae which are almost impossible to decipher but which contain *la formule éternellement vraie* (XII, 75). This conception of the inevitability of the evolution of truths in music is similar to Proust's theory about literature. When we are presented with a completely new concept, we intuitively respond to it if it is true. For Swann, the *phrase de Vinteuil*, after a first hearing,

> . . . existait latente dans son esprit au même titre que certaines autres notions sans équivalent, comme les notions de la lumière, du son, du relief, de la volupté physique (II, 178).

Proust often uses imagery to elucidate the emotional states which are produced when one performs music or listens to it, but surprisingly enough, he never goes into the emotional experience required for the creative process itself, as he did in the case of literature.

With music, the performer stands between the composer and the listener as a sort of a re-creator and his movements are like those of the body of a medium in a seance (II, 180). When Morel plays his violin, he is like a skilled surgeon who must at all costs avoid upsetting experiences (XI, 244). A skilled pianist is as dexterous as an acrobat on the tight rope (II, 150). In group performances of music, the individual member is not so directly concerned with the fusion of himself with the music performed. It may very well be then that a 'cellist may resemble someone peeling a cabbage or a harpist an allegorical goddess plucking stars from the gold trellis of her little firmament (XII, 61).

The effect of great music on a listener seems to be similar to that of an anaesthetic or an intoxicating liquor (II, 32–33), or to partake of the quality of exaltation experienced during exceptionally fine weather or a night of opium, except that it is *une ivresse plus réelle, plus féconde* (XII, 215). The emotional excitement which results from it affects the whole organism so much that the hearer sometimes cannot distinguish a theme from a headache (XI, 197; XII, 72). As in all emotional tension, the viscera are affected as well as the intellect (XI, 197).

It is probably because of this fact that Proust associates music with love. The *petite phrase de Vinteuil* becomes by association the national anthem of Swann's love for Odette (I, 294; XII, 217). He desires it just as he desires her (I, 284), and later it becomes for him a sort of confidant of his love (II, 67). After the love is gone, the theme remains, like jewels or letters, as a keepsake or memento to remind him of the past (I, 295).

For the narrator, each motif in music, while being . . . *particulier comme une femme, ne réservait pas comme elle eût fait, pour quelque privilégié, le secret de volupté qu'il recélait* (V, 60). The great Septet of Vinteuil symbolizes his love for Albertine (XIII, 108), and just as Vinteuil's earlier works in relation to it were timid trials, Marcel's earlier loves, as compared to his love for Albertine, . . . *n'y avaient été que de minces et timides essais, des appels, qui préparaient ce plus vaste amour; l'amour pour Albertine* (XII, 62).

Architecture. What Proust has to say about buildings of one kind and another is not systematized around the personality of a creative artist, even though it is Elstir who awakens in him a sensitivity to the aesthetic qualities of architecture and of churches in particular. Most of the images used in connection with architecture are descriptive images and the techniques which Proust employs are much the same as those he used in dealing with painting.

Let us examine first of all the imagery associated with churches. For any rural town, like Combray, the church summarizes the community (I, 71). It is a living contact with the past, as unaffected by human history as the ocean or the Big Dipper, and produced as inevitably as *ces plantes frêles mais vivaces qui, quand c'est le printemps, étoilent çà et là la neige des pôles* (II, 225–26).

The church is a very natural part of the life of the French peasant and Proust compares it to the most familiar items of every-day rural life. Its outline in the light of the setting sun reminds him of a luscious ripening fruit (IV, 74) or a rose bush in bloom (X, 191). The church of St.-André-des-Champs is *rustique et dorée comme une meule* (I, 248), and its two steeples are *jaunissants et grumeleux, comme deux épis* (I, 198). The porch of the church at Combray is *noir, grêlé comme une écumoire* (I, 85), and its vault *puissamment nervurée comme la membrane d'une immense chauve-souris de pierre* (I, 89). The nave is like a fairy-like valley where the peasant sees indications in trees or pools of the presence of supernatural creatures (I, 88). The steeple is like a plough traversing the regular cloud furrows in the sky (I, 90) or a brown cushion against whose pressure the sky has yielded (I, 93), and the worn *bénitier* inside shows the same effect of wear over the centuries as the stone post daily rubbed by the passing cart (I, 85).

At Balbec, which is on the sea-coast, the churches reflect that scenery. Some are *escarpées et rugueuses comme des falaises* (II, 227). The towers of the church at Marcouville are salmon coloured, and, reflected against the watery blue of the sky, they resemble nothing quite so much as *de vieux poissons aigus, imbriqués d'écailles, moussus et roux* (X, 193). The steeple of an unidentified church, when seen between two ancient buildings, *n'en fait pas plus partie que de deux beaux galets unis, entre lesquels elle est prise sur la plage, la flèche purpurine et crénelée de quelque coquillage fuselé en tourelle et glacé d'émail* (I, 94).

In a more abstract vein, Proust sees in the church steeple the very finger of God raised before him (I, 95). The shape of the vaulted roof with its supporting buttresses is like hands posed in the gesture of prayer.[1] The steeple seen from an unfamiliar angle is *comme un solide surpris à un moment inconnu de sa révolution* (I, 95).

As usual, Proust personifies the Church. In the midst of the houses of the village, the church at Combray is like a shepherdess surrounded by her sheep (I, 71). The actual church whose basic shape is concealed by Gothic arcades is like a rather crude and roughly dressed youth shielded by his older sisters (I, 88–89). The steeple of a church in Paris makes Proust think of a member of holy orders, *levant la pointe de son bonnet ecclésiastique au coin d'une rue* (I, 95), and a church at Venice welcomes him with a smile (XIII, 257).

It is generally in connection with the statuary in churches that

---

[1] Rodin's sculpture 'La Cathédrale' on this same subject was first shown at the Exposition of 1909.

Proust uses his familiar comparison of art and real life, although on occasion the prospect of a scene with a lone church steeple the only man-made object in it reminds him of a painting (I, 91). The statues in the church seem like real people. Their expression may be fixed, like that of a corpse (IV, 74–75), but their forms are real, like those of buxom peasants with *le sein ferme et qui gonflait la draperie comme une grappe mûre dans un sac de crin* (I, 206). The little angels which are placed near God in the church at Balbec are recognized by Marcel as *des amours d'Herculanum* (VII, 220), and the confrontation of a young peasant girl and a statue in the church of St.-André-des-Champs, like a real leaf growing beside a carved one, merely permits one to judge of the veracity of the work of art (I, 206).

The beauty of stained glass windows also gives Proust the opportunity to compare effects of art with nature. In one window at Combray there appears to be a mountain of rose snow and the glass seems covered with sleet through which the dawn glows faintly (I, 86). From another, the light of the sun produces a vivid carpet of myosotis on the bare floor of the church (I, 87). Certain figures in the windows look like kings in a card game (I, 86; 86–87), and the beauty of the individual lozenges of coloured glass is similar to that of the jewels of an immense pectoral (I, 87). The overall effect is like that of a peacock's tail or a fairy grotto in which stalactites are mysteriously illuminated (I, 87).

When we turn to secular architecture, we find that Proust continues to associate buildings with their setting, just as he did with churches. The large glassed-in dining room at Balbec is like a huge swimming pool filled with clear water (II, 223; IV, 93), and when the door is opened, the fresh air coming in is like water from a reservoir (VII, 160). The crowd of curious outside it at night are like spectators in front of an illuminated aquarium (XIII, 130).[1] At Venice, the little restaurants near the canals resemble from the interior the hulls of ships (XI, 218).

From another point of view, the hotel at Balbec with its continually changing panorama of guests, each with a distinct and fascinating character, makes Proust think of a theatre. The *décor*, like that of old provincial theatres, is unchanging (XIII, 155), but the players are as startling and grotesque as those of a Guignol (IV, 83). The central hall reminds Proust of the narthex of a church, and the young grooms and valets who are stationed there like

[1] Proust also compares them to bees outside a glass hive (V, 53).

choristers make him think of Racine's *Esther* and *Athalie*, in particular, and the presentation of those plays by the *protégées* of Mme de
Maintenon at St. Cyr (IV, 131). This image is developed at great
length by him (See IX, 223–24, 309–11; X, 158). The Head Waiter
Aimé is the *metteur en scène et régisseur* (IX, 311), and the clients at the
hotel are both actors and spectators. The servants are appropriately
costumed (IX, 223), and the progress of the action is just like that
of a play (X, 158). Proust quotes extensively from Racine (IX, 223,
310; X, 158), and the association of the hotel with the Jewish
element in these plays has interesting implications as we shall see
when we come to the question of homosexuality.

Proust carries personification to rooms (VI, 100) and courtyards
(VI, 101). Shutterless windows are like sleepless eyes (VI, 102).
Even furniture is like creatures metamorphosized and imploring
pity and deliverance (III, 187).

Elsewhere Proust compares furniture and houses to living nature.
The Beauvais tapestries on chairs are like purple irises in a field of
buttercups (VII, 115), and tulle curtains have the consistency of the
fragile wings of June bugs (VII, 212). A single house in the distance
is like a bright poppy at the line of the horizon (XI, 216), and in
Paris, the light of the sun on rows of chimney pots transforms the
whole into a Dutch tulip garden (VIII, 230).

Proust compares the appearance of buildings and streets to art.
The different courtyards in Paris, seen at a great enough distance so
that noise is imperceptible, are like an exposition of Dutch paintings
(VIII, 231). The illusion of distance in these built-up quarters of a
metropolis makes one think of the Alps as portrayed in the paintings
of Turner or Elstir (VIII, 231). During the war, the arrival of
costumed Africans and Hindus makes Paris a sort of Constantinople
or Jerusalem, in the same way that Carpaccio utilized the *décor* of
the city where he lived to form the background of his most disparate
paintings (XIV, 85). The great stations such as St. Lazare are
murky and ominous like the skies in the Crucifixions of Mantegna
or Veronese (IV, 57).

Finally, in connection with Venice, Proust uses a great variety of
images to try to create as vividly as possible the atmosphere of that
exotic city. The water of its canals is sapphire (XIII, 256) and the
effect of the sight of its monuments is like that of a surprise package
(XIII, 260). There is something magical about its fairy-tale buildings, and in wandering about the city one feels like a character in a

tale from the Arabian Nights, mystified and delighted by a genie
(XIII, 259, 281). The whole effect is that of a fabulous garden of
stone fruits and birds (XII, 261), and the dwellings are more like
monuments or a chain of marble cliffs than human habitations
(XIII, 260).

SOCIETY

Under the general heading of society, we shall deal with all the
images Proust uses in connection with people, except those that
have to do with psychological phenomena such as memory, dreams,
the notion of reality, habit, etc. This will include the images
associated with particular characters, as well as those used in
discussing more general topics such as family relations, castes or the
Dreyfus Affair.

To begin with, let us examine some of the descriptive images
used by Proust in painting purely external appearance. He is a keen
observer of modes and those physical features such as eyes, laughs
and smiles which are most likely to reveal character.

Proust can be quite anatomical in his descriptions: there is a
sharp difference between the impression left by the eyes of a dancer
with their *gelée droite et grise* (VI, 217) and that of the eyes of the
Princesse de Guermantes, *taillés dans un diamant que semblaient bien
fluidifier . . . l'intelligence et l'amitié* (VI, 52). The comparison of eyes
to jewels is an old one, of course, and Proust uses it also in connection
with the Duc d'Aumale (VI, 47) and the Duchesse de Guermantes
(IX, 83). The eyes of Albertine, on the other hand, are a transparent
violet, like the sea on occasion (V, 220).

Spectacles and monocles are directly related in appearance to the
character of the wearer. Those of the scholar Brichot are like the
complicated mechanism of an astronomical instrument (XI, 246)[1] or
a microscope (XI, 246), and they are shiny, like the reflectors utilized
by laryngologists to illuminate the throats of their patients (X, 18).
The monocle of General de Froberville is like a shell splinter or a
wound (II, 148), and when he takes it off to wipe it, it is like changing
a dressing (II, 162). That of M. de Palancy (who looks like a big
clumsy carp) resembles a piece of the glass of his aquarium that he
carries ahead of him (II, 149). The monocle of the volatile Saint-

[1] For a similar image, compare PM 214.

Loup, on the other hand, flutters before him like a gay butterfly (IV, 160).

Smiles and laughs can be as omnibus and impersonal as a railway or a public moving van (X, 178). Bergotte's laugh, however, is distinctive and noisy as a trumpet (I, 126). The sound of Ski's laughter resembles bells ringing (XII, 107), and that of the military Duc Wladimir is like the re-echoing of a shell shot or thunder (IX, 77–78). The insincere smile of the Duchesse de Lambresac is like a feeble shooting star or the senile smirk of a doddering priest administering the blessing (IX, 107).

Hair and coiffures seem to fascinate Proust, and because of their change with age, they are particularly associated by him with evolution and heredity. His mother's dark hair is arranged like a tower constructed on her head (II, 251). The uneven outlines of Rachel's curled black hair make one think that her coiffure had been brushed on with *encre de Chine* (III, 186). The distinctive sort of hair that is hereditary in the Guermantes clan resembles lichens or a sort of cat fur (VIII, 72). Swann's hair is also like fur a little moth-eaten (IX, 119). Albertine's hair is like a narrow diadem (XII, 231) or an unknown but charming vegetable growth (V, 149); on certain occasions it is like a florescence or like waves (XI, 21), like wings or a mountainous terrain (XII, 226). Andrée's hair is smooth and deep as windswept sand, but her mother's hair by contrast is more like drifted snow (V, 218). White hair is like wool or cotton batting and the degree of whiteness varies directly as the length of time lived, just as the amount of snow on mountains varies according to their height (XV, 102–3).

The interest which Proust has in hair arrangement and the variety of suggestions which a coiffure can offer him are well illustrated in the following description of the hairdo of a young servant at the home of Mme de Saint-Euverte. It contains no less than six separate images:

> Une chevelure, par l'enroulement lisse et les becs aigus de ses boucles, ou dans la superposition du triple et fleurissant diadème de ses tresses, a l'air à la fois d'un paquet d'algues, d'une nichée de colombes, d'un bandeau de jacinthes et d'une torsade de serpents (II, 145).

When we turn to actual clothing and costume itself, we find that Proust regards creations of the world of the *couturier* in just the same

way as those of any of the creative arts. They can be masterpieces
(X, 244) and the result of long deliberation (XI, 39–40). Like any
rare book, the number of copies available is strictly limited (XIV,
43), and items of costume in contemporary photographs will have
as much interest for art-lovers in the future as those allegorical
figures in the paintings at the Arena in Padua (V, 149). A rich
woman surrounded by her dresses is like a spectator in a museum
(XI, 76). The ensemble of a dress with its overall lines and its
harmonizing detail is like that of a great musical composition or a
vast cathedral (IV, 49, 50).

Costume indicates rank just as clearly as the insignia of religious
orders. Also, there is something so ritualistic about a woman adorn-
ing herself that Proust likes to compare the results to various
aspects of religion. Odette dressing is like a high-priestess performing rites in accordance with a liturgy known only to her (IV, 49).
Her umbrella is compared to religious accessories (V, 165), and even
Mme de Cambremer, who is no fashion plate, wears a black mantle
similar to a dalmatic and a necklace which is like a pectoral (IX,
262–63, 265, 285). A dress by Fortuny is like a precious relic
exposed to the view of the faithful (XII, 209), and the sewing of the
inside seams and linings of one of Odette's jackets is just as carefully
executed as those parts of a cathedral which are not normally seen
by the eyes (IV, 50).

The exotic mystery of a woman's garments is conveyed by
Proust by comparing them to the Orient (V, 164) or Venice (XII,
209, 240–41) or some marvellous creation brought by the Ballet
Russe in their baggage (IX, 184). The materials from which they
are made are, in their elusive beauty, like a golden butterfly wing
(XI, 52) or a rainbow in the grey sky (X, 243). Albertine's house-
coat is deep blue, like the canals of Venice it reminds Proust of, and
it changes in the light into shimmering gold, *par ces mêmes trans-
mutations qui, devant les gondoles qui s'avancent, changent en métal flam-
boyant l'azur du grand canal* (XII, 241).

Cloth has a character of its own and Proust personifies it as well
as dresses. One chooses a dress as one chooses a friend (XII, 252),
and materials and colours clearly indicate moods:

> On aurait dit qu'il y avait soudain de la décision dans le velours
> bleu, une humeur facile dans le taffetas blanc, et qu'une sorte de
> réserve suprême ... avait ... revêtu l'apparence brillante du sourire
> des grands sacrifices, du crêpe de Chine noir (IV, 28).

From among the different characters in *A la recherche du temps perdu*, one can pick representatives of many varied classes. Françoise, the *fille de cuisine*, Aimé and the various valets and waiters represent the servant class; Bloch, Rachel, and, to a certain extent, Swann, represent Jews; the Guermantes clan, the Princesse de Luxembourg and Madame de Saint Euverte represent the upper class. In the following section, we shall consider in turn the various individuals with whom Proust associates different images grouping them as far as possible according to class and rank.

Servants, Peasants. The servant who is best known to Marcel and whom he describes at greatest length is, of course, Françoise. He uses an amazing variety of apparently contradictory images to highlight the different aspects of her character.

Françoise is, first and foremost, a representative of the French peasant class. Etymologically, this fact is suggested by her very name. As such, she has certain qualities shared by animals or lower orders of life. She works like a horse (I, 79), and her eyes looking at her masters are like those of a good dog (IV, 63; XIV, 67). When she is old, she is like an ancient, half-blind eagle (XII, 206). Like animals or primitive peoples, she acts by instinct, and some of her apparent knowledge seems quite astounding; it is like mind-reading (XI, 120). Her refined cruelty towards the *fille de cuisine* is as physiologically sure as the method used by the burrowing wasp to paralyze but not kill prey for its hatching larvae (I, 169). Her senses, like those of animals or savages, seem more acute than those of ordinary people (I, 45), and she immediately perceives the truth, like a blindfolded spiritist (XII, 204) or an African who has learned news by fire signals well before the mails have brought it to his more civilized European contemporaries (VI, 76). From her long association with the narrator's family, Françoise arrives at the point where she has for them

> . . . cette sorte de connaissance instinctive et presque divinatoire qu'a de la mer le matelot, du chasseur le gibier, et de la maladie, sinon le médecin, du moins souvent le malade. Tout ce qu'elle arrivait à savoir aurait pu stupéfier à aussi bon droit que l'état avancé de certaines connaissances chez les anciens, vu les moyens presque nuls d'information qu'ils possédaient (VII, 225).

All Françoise's knowledge is purely instinctive, however, and her conduct is ruled by an antique code at least as ancient as that of the early books of the Old Testament (I, 44, 45, 149). This code is illustrated in the bas-reliefs of the Church of Saint-André-des-Champs (XI, 18) and there is something about Françoise herself that is as unchanging as the statue of a saint (I, 77), a figure in a stained glass window (I, 167) or an illustration of Anne de Bretagne in a book of hours (IV, 63). Françoise is a creature of prejudice, as is shown by her attitude toward learning how to use the telephone; she avoids it like the plague (XI, 192) or vaccination (IX, 168; XI, 123).

To illustrate further that aspect of the nature of Françoise which we may call the living past in the present, Proust compares her to terrain. Her character is like a well-worn rustic path (V, 161), and certain inherited features resemble ancient mansions reminiscent of the past, which one finds almost swallowed up in a growing manufacturing city (I, 44–45). Françoise is practically a part of her native province, and Méséglise and Combray are old friends to her (VI, 29).

Certain surviving features in the vocabulary of Françoise are like those curious animals, the whale and the giraffe, which show us the states animal life has passed through (IX, 176), or certain stones, *présentant ainsi par endroit un défaut et qui projetait de l'obscurité jusque dans la pensée de Françoise* (VI, 26). Her method of expressing herself in order to get a point across obliquely reminds one of Tiresias or Tacitus (VII, 226).

The appearance of Françoise reminds Proust of art. Her righteous attitude is like that of a *'justice éclairant le Crime'* (VII, 227) or a majestic *entremetteuse* who completely overshadows the insignificant mistress and lover in ancient pictures (XI, 174). She is also like an actress in her ability to make every line of her clothes and face expressive of her feelings (IX, 174). She is conscious of the importance of her rôle in family affairs (VII, 178), and such events as the death of the grandmother seem to her to require a certain setting (VII, 190) and a certain appropriate routine. Françoise's entries into a room are often like those of a character coming on stage (I, 44; V, 160).

Above all, however, Marcel associates Françoise with food. He first knew her as his aunt's cook at Combray, and there he quite naturally associated her appearance with the delicious food she symbolized to him:

L'arome de cette chair [de poule] qu'elle savait rendre si onctueuse et si tendre n'étant pour moi que le propre parfum d'une de ses vertus (I, 167).

Even her house cap reminded him of biscuit (I, 79) or spun sugar (I, 77), and the very figures of speech which she uses conversationally are derived from cooking. She says that anyone could tell that Albertine's rings came from the same source: *Ça se reconnaît comme la cuisine d'une bonne cuisinière* (XIII, 61).

Later in life, however, Marcel continues to associate Françoise and food. When she knows a certain truth and represses it, indicating the fact only by a slight movement of her lips, it is *comme si elle avait encore la bouche pleine et finissait un bon morceau* (VI, 79). When the grandmother dies, Françoise repeats over and over:

'Cela me fait quelque chose,' du même ton dont elle disait, quand elle avait pris trop de soupe aux choux: 'J'ai comme un poids sur l'estomac' (VII, 201).

From the point of view of her cooking, Françoise is a great creative artist, and Proust compares her in turn to the sculptor, Michelangelo (III, 24, 40), a celebrated actress (III, 74), a great singer, and a fashion-conscious leader of society (III, 73). To leave anything on one's plate is to insult her as much as it would insult a composer to get up and leave before his composition was over (I, 102). The compliments of M. de Norpois on her food are transmitted to Françoise by Marcel's mother as a minister of war passes on to the officer in charge the compliments of a sovereign after a successful military review (III, 72). Françoise accepts them as an artist accepts tributes to his work (III, 72).

Proust regards food itself (and not always just the food prepared by Françoise) as products of art. A chocolate cream is *fugitive et légère comme une œuvre de circonstance* (I, 101) and a chocolate cake *gothiquement historié de sucre* (V, 169). Potatoes are like buttons of Japanese ivory (XIV, 25), and a fish like something in a ceramic of Bernard Palissy (VI, 143-44). Elsewhere, Proust compares the symmetrical anatomy of the fish to a vast polychrome cathedral (IV, 118). Cherries in a tart are similar to beads of coral (X, 175), and a golden roast chicken resembles a beautiful chasuble (I, 167). Even the shell of an oyster with a few drops of salty liquor in it makes him think of a *bénitier* (VI, 143). The azure crowns on asparagus remind the narrator of the band of flowers on the forehead and in the basket of the Virtue in the fresco at the Arena in Padua (I, 166).

Food also reminds Proust of nature and the seasons. Asparagus is coloured like the dawn sky, a rainbow or an evening sky (I, 166), and the marvellous basket of fruit which Madame de Villeparisis presents to Marcel and his grandmother contains plums round as the sea, grapes clear as an autumn day, and pears like an ultramarine sky with light rose clouds floating in it (IV, 122).

Compared to Françoise, the *fille de cuisine* is like Error in the presence of Virtue (I, 116). The outstanding feature about her is her unfortunate pregnancy, and Proust compares the revealing bulge beneath her smock to a mysterious basket (I, 113). Her attention is continually drawn to it as to an illness which will prove fatal (I, 115), and her deliverance is likened to the falling of a ripe fruit at night (I, 150). The inexpressive quality of her features recalls to Swann (and to the narrator) the allegorial figure of Charity in Giotto's fresco at Padua (I, 114). It is interesting here to note the association in Proust's mind between the *fille de cuisine* and the asparagus to which Françoise cruelly exposes her, knowing that it gives her hay-fever. The buds on the asparagus are compared to the flowers intertwined in the *corbeille* carried by one of the Virtues in Giotto's painting. The word '*corbeille*' is used in turn to describe the distended abdomen of the miserable *fille de cuisine* who herself resembles the figure of Charity in the same painting.

When we come to servants in general (and especially those of the Grand Hotel at Balbec) we find Proust emphasizing through images various aspects of their functions.

Servants spend a great deal of time standing around, and because of this, they remind Proust of plants (IV, 152–53) or bushes (IV, 131, 132; IX, 222). For the same reason, no doubt, they often appear to be like statues (II, 146–47; VII, 27; X, 194) or saints in their niches (II, 146). Since the best known works of sculpture are of Greek and Roman origin, Proust sometimes specifies that the particular style is Etruscan (X, 163), or he occasionally omits the reference to statuary altogether and simply compares servants to Greeks. The concierge at the Swanns' is changed into a *bienveillante Euménide* (III, 95), and the chasseur at Balbec is *beau comme Endymion* (IX, 245). The receptionists at the hotel make Marcel apprehensive by giving him *le regard de Minos, Eaque et Rhadamante* (IV, 80). As usual, Proust compares real life to art. The person whom he takes to be Albertine's governess is like the portrait of Jeffries by Hogarth

(V, 80). Aimé stands in a particular spot of the dining room at Balbec, like a hanging portrait of Prince Eugene (VI, 202). Other servants remind Proust of figures in paintings by Mantegna (II, 144), Goya (II, 146) and Breughel (VI, 119).

Servants are in a position of inferiority, and to a certain extent they are like domestic animals. A group of them is like a pack of hounds (II, 143), and one newly-entered into service is like a captive beast in the first few hours of domesticity (II, 144). The *patron* and the *maître d'hôtel* are like well trained horses (VIII, 36), though sometimes a young waiter in his excitement may want to take the bit between his teeth and bolt (X, 278). Servants can recognize each other just like animals or criminals (X, 160), and their costumes are uniform, like the markings of animals or exotic birds in the zoo (V, 58).

From another point of view, servants wield considerable power, since they control access to their masters. For this reason they are like unbending examiners (VIII, 29) or aloof academicians (VI, 205). Among them, there is a rigid hierarchy comparable to that which existed at Versailles (VI, 78) or that which we find in the church (VI, 201 et seq.). Françoise is flattered like a minor prince when a valet gives her a higher title than she deserves (VI, 28), and Marcel's mother feels the same indignation when a valet leaves as Saint-Simon when a noble who has no right to it takes the title of *Altesse* (X, 208). The *directeur* of the hotel is a sort of sovereign (V, 226) or commanding general (IV, 114), and the guardian of the public washrooms is a marquise (VII, 161). The servants in the hotel where Aimé serves after he leaves Balbec are like priests, curates and confessors (VI, 201) or lesser orders of angels (VI, 120, 205). The *directeur* himself carving a turkey is like a high priest, and this event is the starting point as it were of a new calendar (X, 279). The butcher's boy weighing meat is like a celestial power dividing the good from the evil in the Judgment Scales (XI, 170–71). Françoise and the other servants eating follow rites very similar to those of the mass (VI, 19).

Family, Family Relations. The outstanding feature about family relations as far as Proust is concerned is the mutual love of mother and child and the sacrificing love of wife for husband. Marcel's love for his own mother and her love for the grandmother illustrate the first, and the love Marcel's mother has for his father and the

E

love his grandmother has for the grandfather illustrate the second.

One of the important *leit-motifs* of the first volume of *A la recherche du temps perdu* is the good night kiss Marcel is in the habit of receiving from his mother. A study of this obsession involves a consideration of certain aspects of the mind of the narrator, but it seems logical to include it here. Marcel associates love for his mother with love of a mistress (I, 47, 48–49), but he regards it as much more satisfying and much superior (I, 249). The kiss itself is a religious experience, and the narrator compares receiving it to taking communion (I, 24) or the last sacrament (I, 43). To be without the kiss is like falling into an abyss (I, 38) or having a dreadful nightmare (I, 43). Marcel admits that his attitude about it is like that of a maniac (I, 37), and when his mother refuses to come to bid him goodnight the evening Swann is there, he compares his feelings in turn to those of a patient being operated on under a local anaesthetic (I, 39) and a dying man preparing himself for the tomb (I, 44). When he decides to wait up, the effect on him is like that of a powerful medicine (I, 49).

Caresses and embraces are freely exchanged by Marcel, his mother and his grandmother, and always there is something religious about the experience. Marcel's mother feels very humble towards her mother and she kisses her hand *comme celle de son Dieu* (VII, 174). When the grandmother looks after her daughter or her grandson, she wears a special costume, *sa blouse de servante et de garde, son habit de religieuse* (IV, 85).

Parents are particularly interested in the welfare of their children and they will go to any extremes to make them happy. Marcel's mother asks Gilberte to write to him in just the same way as she used to get the swimming instructor to place surprises under the water for him to find when he dived (III, 92–93). She and his father forget their dislike of Bergotte only when Marcel reports that the writer had thought him intelligent. This is the precious antidote to their instinctive antipathy (III, 182).

The narrator associates his grandmother particularly with nature and the out-of-doors. Her face is like a rosy cloud behind which shines her tenderness (IV, 85), and her cheeks are furrowed and dark like the ploughed fields of autumn (I, 23). She is as unperturbed by the furies of the elements as Saint Blandine thrown to the wild animals (IV, 94), and even her tastes in reading run to novels dealing with nature, like those of George Sand where *les grands souffles du génie* can exert a tonic influence on the spirit comparable to that of fresh air on the physique (I, 58, 60–61).

Both the grandmother and Marcel's mother devote themselves to their husbands. The grandmother is easily upset when her husband is tempted to drink, and, like an insect returning to a light, she gives up her cherished after-dinner walk in order to re-enter the salon when the liqueurs are brought out (I, 22). Marcel's mother feels it her duty to sustain her husband with sympathy just as much as with good food (III, 15). She is as much alert to news that would harm him as a diplomat watching over the interests of France (III, 49).

Bourgeois, The Verdurin Circle, The Cambremers. In all levels of society, Proust uses images drawn from those institutions which are particularly rigid in their distinctions of rank—the church, the army and royalty. In addition, he likes to regard the world of society as a stage where each individual plays a part. We have already seen examples of these images in connection with servants, and they are used again in more extended fashion in the *Salon Verdurin.*

The members of Madame Verdurin's salon are invariably referred to as *les fidèles* and the Verdurin circle is a sort of *petite église* (I, 255; XII, 53). Madame Verdurin is at the same time its grand inquisitor (II, 61), its pope (XI, 60) and its reigning divinity (XII, 138), whether that divinity be called a Norn (XII, 58) or a powerful fairy (IX, 184; XII, 43). She is most concerned about maintaining the orthodoxy of her followers (XII, 98), and when Elstir breaks with the salon, it amounts to a religious conversion (X, 99). The identity of outlook of *les fidèles* seems to surround their heads with a sort of halo that is perceptible to others when they appear in public in a group (X, 10).

For her followers, Madame Verdurin is a general or commanding officer (X, 12) whose invitations have as much force as a military order (X, 25). She is a keen military strategist (III, 215) and she lets the members of her circle know that she expects implicit obedience, just like the Kaiser or even Christ (X, 21). Saniette, in the presence of either Monsieur or Mme Verdurin is like a terrified recruit before a sergeant major (X, 91) or a general (X, 87).

Madame Verdurin is primarily interested in music, even though its power to sway her emotions gives her terrific headaches. These

countless migraines have deformed her temples just like rheumatism
(X, 57), so that they resemble two vast spheres (X, 57, 127, 136).
Music seems to affect her in the same way as an illness (XIV, 49) or
drug addiction (XII, 34), although Marcel cannot be sure what she
really experiences when listening to music, since she covers her
face like someone praying (X, 118) or repressing a laugh (I, 278), or
comme un enfant qui joue à cache-cache (X, 118).

Madame Verdurin's real ambition is to form an enviable salon
and all her activities are directed to this end:

> Mme Verdurin avait arraché petit à petit, comme l'oiseau fait son
> nid, les bribes successives, provisoirement inutilisables, de ce qui
> serait un jour son salon (XII, 43).[1]

A salon is a little world of its own (XIV, 96) and its members, as
well as being similar to the members of a sect, can be like primitive
head-hunters out for blood (X, 91–92) or argumentative members of
the *Reichstag* (I, 279). At the same time, the reputation of a salon is
a precious thing and as fragile as Venetian glass (X, 31). Its protocol
must be regulated as carefully as that of the official banquet of
Saint Charlemagne (XII, 43). Madame Verdurin, in order to avoid
unpleasant episodes which might destroy the spirit of her salon,
sometimes acts as impassively and unresponsively as a statue
(II, 20, 60). Her husband's attitude towards intransigent frequenters
of the salon is like that of a marauding spider in quest of flies
(XII, 35) or a recalcitrant public in the face of literary innovations
(II, 69).

Both Monsieur and Madame Verdurin conceal their true feelings
as efficiently as two theatre masks (II, 65). Madame Verdurin's
mannerisms are like those of a *marquise du Théâtre-Français* (X, 64)
and her voice is like that of *un premier prix du Conservatoire jouant du
Dumas fils* (X, 65). Her attitude is that of a *dramaturge hardi* (XII, 46),
and *les fidèles* listen to her as they would to a play cruelly realistic
(XII, 47). Madame Verdurin is furious when Charlus cuts her
rôle for his famous reception (XII, 93), and at the *soirée* itself, she
is no more than a theatre attendant (XII, 79).

Among the lesser members of the Verdurin *coterie*, the only ones
for whom Proust uses more than an isolated image or two are
Brichot, Saniette and Cottard. We have already noted (p. 46) that
the images used in connection with Brichot's spectacles are well

[1] Madame Verdurin is compared to a bird at I, 278.

suited to his scholarly occupation. The same is true of the other images used by Proust. For example, when describing Brichot's method of speaking, Proust compares him to an orator or university lecturer because of his manner of glancing around (X, 119) and judging the acoustics of the room (X, 112). Saniette, on the other hand, is the scape-goat of the salon, and besides being like a miserable subaltern (X, 91), he is like a helpless child (I, 275). He is always getting in wrong with either Monsieur or Madame Verdurin, and these periods of disfavour are referred to by Proust as *orages* (X, 91, 94; XII, 29). Cottard is particularly susceptible to the hierarchal nature of the salon. For him it is just as important and exclusive as the Academy (X, 24).

When we come to the Cambremer family, we have to consider not only the images associated with Madame de Cambremer and her son and daughter-in-law, but those associated with the latter's brother, Legrandin.

Both Legrandin and his sister are very proud and independent. When Legrandin encounters Marcel and his father, he pays no more attention to them than if they were away in the distance (I, 164). He refuses to give them his sister's name when he knows they are going to visit Balbec where she lives, and he goes to as much trouble to conceal her identity as that misguided forger who expended energy concocting false palimpsests when he could have earned a good living with a fraction of the talent employed to advantage (I, 181). He is jealous of the Guermantes' name, and this is revealed by the fact that when someone speaks of them, the pupils of his eyes dilate just as though they had been pierced by an arrow (I, 174). Like Saint Sebastian, he is a martyr to his pride (I, 174, 176). His snobbery is indicated by his attention to his figure (XIII, 302) and the arrogant way he wears his tie (I, 171–72).

Madame de Cambremer-Legrandin is just as haughty as her brother. When she meets Marcel, she is charming, and he may freely browse *dans le gros gâteau de miel que Madame de Cambremer était si rarement* (IX, 269). To the Verdurins and their followers, however, she is more like a *galette normande . . . dure comme un galet, ou les fidèles eussent en vain essayé de mettre la dent* (X, 68). She and her family regard the Verdurins who have rented the Cambremer château for the summer as enemy occupation troops (X, 68, 72). They resent their innovations as much as an ignorant curate the restorations of the architect of the diocese (X, 71–72). For Madame de Cambremer, snobbery is a real disease, congenital and morbid (X, 79–80).

The older Madame de Cambremer is interested in the arts and especially the music of Chopin. This would be self-evident even to a paralytic *atteint d'agraphie après une attaque et réduit à regarder les caractères comme un dessin, sans savoir les lire* (X, 106). Her physical reactions to aesthetic experiences are quite disgusting and remind the narrator of primitive savages (IX, 272), horses (IX, 277–78) or animals in rut (IX, 266). Even Madame de Cambremer's language is related by Proust to the musical scale (X, 283), and her reactions to nature and fresh air are compared to the reactions of the prisoners in Beethoven's *Fidelio* (IX, 277).[1]

There is little to say about Monsieur de Cambremer. For him, as for his wife and mother, Proust seems to emphasize vulgar, physical details. He is as pompous as a military officer (X, 71), and his eye, framed, as it were, like a bit of blue sky surrounded by clouds, is as unpleasant to look at, really, as an operation (X, 146–47). His character is summed up by his nose which seems to be his organ of perception.[2] It is *busqué, astiqué, luisant, flambant, neuf* (X, 66).

Monsieur de Norpois, Diplomats. Proust is not very fond of diplomats because of their authoritarian way of saying things and the emptiness or hypocrisy behind so much of what they do say. For him, Monsieur de Norpois symbolizes all that is good and bad about diplomats.

To begin with, Monsieur de Norpois looks very dignified and kindly. His great capacity for work and his ability to assimilate, float in their native element, as it were, in his watery blue eyes (III, 57) which in turn are drowned in his white beard (VII, 54). He reminds Marcel of Saint Louis dispensing justice under an oak (VIII, 178). Monsieur de Norpois keeps his face as expressionless as that of a statue (III, 33) or a musician in an orchestra (III, 37), but when he speaks, he is as peremptory in tone as an auctioneer or the Delphic Oracle (III, 33–34).

Monsieur de Norpois has an incredible memory for facts and dates, but Proust implies that most of his knowledge is of a useless

[1] For remarks on the religious character of Madame de Cambremer's clothing compare p. 48 above.
[2] Proust suggests that stupidity reveals itself first of all in the shape of a person's nose (X, 48).

kind. He compares the data which the diplomat has at his fingertips to such things as the exact list of hunters invited by Assourbanipal to his games ten centuries before Christ, which appears in an obscure book by Maspero (III, 65). Monsieur de Norpois treats other people much as a doctor treats ignorant patients (III, 34), and his official pronouncements on international affairs have the same ambiguity and caution as a medical bulletin which may, in fact, appear with optimistic comments after the patient is actually dead (XIII, 270).

The world of diplomacy is one set apart. Proust compares the subtle relations between different diplomats to the performance of a major work of music where each instrument or player has its own particular themes, its own particular qualities and techniques (XIII, 267, 268, 269). The diplomat has to be a sort of diagnostician for whom any one fact is merely a bit of evidence to be fitted into a larger pattern (VII, 78–79). In his attempts to achieve his own desires, he is like someone discreetly trying to open a door with a variety of keys (VII, 103–4); he may eventually find the right one or he may remain forever shut off from the attainment of his own ambition.

Jews, (Bloch, Rachel, etc.), L'Affaire Dreyfus. The imagery which Proust uses in connection with Bloch, Rachel, Swann, Monsieur Nissim Bernard and the other Jews, despite Proust's own Jewish blood and his attitude in the Dreyfus Case, is uniformly uncomplimentary. Jews are compared to jail-birds (VII, 86), misers (IV, 181–82), prostitutes (V, 15; XIII, 196), *'chasseurs' de Cercle* (V, 12) and hyenas (VII, 15; XV, 132). Bloch is ashamed of his Jewish blood (IV, 181) and both he and his father have a double scale to judge such qualities as the personality, value and interest of people (IV, 179). Bloch himself . . . *était d'un caractère lâche et vivant gaiement et paresseusement dans les mensonges, comme les méduses à fleur d'eau* (XIII, 37). Even the Jewish nose is regarded as a deformity like a hunch-back (XV, 84) or a comic make-up for Mascarille (VII, 15).

Proust associates Jews particularly with their Old Testament background and the near Orient. In a group, they are like a cortege (IV, 172) or figures in an Assyrian freize (IX, 136). Bloch's glove is held in his hand like a roll of papyrus (VII, 15), and the personality of Rachel is *mystérieusement enfermée dans un corps comme dans un Tabernacle* (VI, 192). The bearded M. Nissim Bernard is like the Assyrian king Sargon (V, 15), or something brought back from the palace of Darius (V, 14). He explores the corridors of the hotel at Balbec as though it were a seraglio (IX, 311–12) and he and the other Jews are like figures from illustrations for the Arabian Nights (IV, 172). Jews are so little of this world that they remind one of figures materialized by a medium (VII, 16–17).

All Jews are bound by the chains of Israel (XV, 83), and with the passage of time their rôle on the stage of society becomes either that of *un mufle* or *un prophète* (IX, 118). Bloch becomes a grasping, selfish Shylock (XV, 132, 172), and even Swann, who remains so long a man of society and a refined intellectual, eventually reaches *l'âge du prophète* (IX, 118)—a state of isolation and misunderstanding, if not vilification. As a matter of fact, the history of Swann's life epitomizes that of the Jewish race *depuis le snobisme le plus naïf et la plus grossière goujaterie, jusqu'à la plus fine politesse* (III, 8).

The incident which brought about the distinct social cleavage over the whole question of Jews was, of course, the Dreyfus Case. Proust compares it to a great storm at sea (VII, 146) or a cyclone over the ocean (VII, 15); the waves continue to grow even after the wind has begun to drop (IX, 105). The attitude of most people toward the case is one of prejudice. Military personnel are as united in their views as members of a Catholic order, financiers (VIII, 140–41) or graduates of the Schola Cantorum (VI, 130). The comments of a typical café owner concerning the case are about as varied and original as the repertoire of a teacher of elocution (VIII, 35).

Relations between friends and groups are strained by differences of opinion over the Dreyfus Case, and anti-Dreyfusards tend to regard those on the opposite side as more obnoxious than Jews themselves. Madame Sazerat treats Marcel's mother as an estranged fiancée (VII, 182) and she greets his father as though he were a criminal, a reprobate, an outlaw or one involved in a divorce suit (VI, 184–85). The Duc de Guermantes considers Swann a sort of wastrel son for whom one had made great sacrifices (IX, 104–5). Scandal is eventually forgotten, however, and with the Dreyfus Case it is just the same as with the marriage of Swann and Odette or the disgrace brought on a young girl by a crime committed by her father (XIV, 45–46).

Odette. We have already had occasion to mention some imagery used in connection with Odette under the general heading of clothing and costume (p. 48 above). We can here elaborate on this aspect of her character.

Odette dressing herself is like the Creator forming the universe (IV, 48) or a high-priestess following the intricate rites of a service known only to her (IV, 49). When she appears in public, she is like a queen (II, 277), a majestic sovereign (IV, 50), an angel (II, 129) or a goddess (IV, 50). Other people around her are no more important than the frame of a window in which she appears (IV, 47–48), the mechanism of a clock (IV, 52) or those secondary characters on the stage of life whom one takes for granted—the park attendants in the Bois de Boulogne, the boatman, or even the ducks on the pond (II, 272).

Odette's various costumes remind Proust of living nature and the seasons. Her ermines and her white peignoir are like snow (III, 208; IV, 45). Other house-coats are flowing and foamy as water and Odette almost seems to be taking a refreshing bath in them (IV, 23,) like a voluptuous siren (IV, 26). Certain materials remind him of strewn rose petals (III, 208), lilies of the valley or carnations (V, 103–4). The bows and ribbons on Odette's bodice are like little living creatures (IV, 48), and her umbrella is similar to a bouquet of violets (IV, 48) or another, nearer, round blue sky (IV, 49).

Odette walking in the Bois de Boulogne is herself like a beautiful blooming flower, although in her old age she is more like a sterilized rose (XV, 112) or a museum specimen (XV, 108). Her expression is sometimes like that of a gray cloudy landscape, but when a generous impulse strikes her, her appearance changes like the landscape transformed by the setting sun (II, 131). For Swann, she is like the moon with its mysterious pervading rays (II, 31).

Proust compares the real-life Odette to art, for she reminds Swann of the paintings of Botticelli (II, 27). He also uses the theatre figure when he speaks of her as playing certain stellar rôles. There is a certain contradiction inherent at this point, however, for Proust in the early volumes compares Odette to the great actress La Berma (II, 271), and at the end of *A la recherche du temps perdu*, he makes this extraordinary statement about her various metamorphoses:

> Elle était médiocre dans ce rôle comme dans tous les autres. Non pas que la vie ne lui en eût souvent donné de beaux, mais elle ne savait pas les jouer (XV, 196).

It is part of Proust's technique to illustrate the various facets of a personality with apparently conflicting categories of images, but when one comes across contradictory images within a class, one is forced to attribute their co-existence to a stylistic lapse of some sort. Odette in her old age is unattractive. She is compared by Proust to a mechanical doll (XV, 109) as well as a sterile rose or a biological specimen but there is no excuse for introducing an image which is so sweeping in its general condemnation that it contradicts previous images.

Les Jeunes Filles (Gilberte, Albertine, etc.). When we come to a consideration of the images allied to the narrator's elaboration of his relations with Gilberte, Albertine and her friends and the many anonymous young girls who at one time or another attracted his attention, we enter one of the major fields of image patterns. Proust's techniques remain the same, but the number of different sources from which he draws images to describe the various objects of his love is greatly expanded, and the diverse sources themselves are inter-related and linked in such a way that it becomes very difficult to analyse them in logical progression. The resulting artistic harmony as far as Proust is concerned is the most outstanding example we have met yet of the 'unity which lies below the level of plot and character'.[1]

To begin with, of course, Volumes III, IV, and V bear the metaphorical title '*A l'Ombre des jeunes filles en fleurs*'. The actual form of the noun *fleurs*, with its plural, has sometimes been the subject of dispute, but the explanation is quite simple; for Proust the expression can be used in the singular or its optional plural form'[2]

We have already noted that Proust frequently compares flowers to young girls.[3] There is nothing new about this comparison or about the reciprocal form of comparing young girls to flowers. Proust himself quotes no less than two examples of the latter practice from his predecessors, and the list of precedents could no doubt be extended indefinitely. In the first one, the narrator in

---

[1] See p. vi above.
[2] See *Correspondance générale*, V, p. 235; letter to Marie Scheikevitch summarizing the parts of *A la recherche du temps perdu* at that time unpublished. Concerning Albertine he says 'Vous la verrez quand elle n'est encore qu'une 'jeune fille en fleurs' à l'ombre de laquelle je passe de si bonnes heures à Balbec.'
[3] See p. 14 above. Compare also PJ, 174.

the Guermantes salon, surrounded by young girls who reminded him of flowers, thinks that he is like Parsifal *au milieu des filles fleurs* (VIII, 54–55). The second one is an actual quotation from Racine's *Esther* (I, i, 102–4), and although it refers to young girls as flowers, it is introduced by Proust, significantly, into a section on homosexuality involving conversations between Vaugoubert and Charlus (IX, 87). We find

> . . . de filles de Sion,
> Jeunes et tendres fleurs par le sort agitées,
> Sous un ciel étranger comme moi transplantées.

It would not be profitable to count the number of times Proust refers to *jeunes filles en fleurs*. Sometimes he compares them to flowers without naming any particular variety.[1] His favourite procedure, probably because of the rosy colour of their cheeks, is to compare them to roses,[2] although occasionally he utilizes other reddish flowers such as the colaeus (IX, 304) or the geranium (V, 219). Andrée, who is rather pale, reminds him of a camellia (V, 219), and another unidentified girl has skin like magnolia blossoms (X, 28).

Marcel seems quite fascinated by the luscious curves of cheeks. He compares them specifically to roses with a waxy surface (V, 151), to rose wax itself (V, 220; XI, 93), and to geraniums (V, 33) and the ruddy hearts of white water-lilies (IV, 110–11). He also compares them to the rose enamel of the cheeks of a miniature (V, 220), the sky at dawn (V, 149), or the rose illumination of granite in the morning sun (V, 201). He seems impelled to kiss the cheeks, and the figure he uses is that of desiring to taste the rose (VII, 231–32) or the rosy fruit (III, 84; V, 205). Indeed, by the same analogy no doubt, whole faces are compared by him to food and especially cake (V, 112), honey (V, 156) or syrup (XI, 74).

The general comparison of young girls to flowers and of certain aspects of their cheeks or breasts (XI, 96) to flowers or fruit is part of a wider plan. Proust utilizes the briefer cycles of flower, fruit, seed; spring, summer, winter; and dawn, midday, evening to make more vivid the slower cycle of human life moving from youth through middle-age to death. We shall have a good deal more to say

[1] See especially I, 213; IV, 138; V, 54–55; VI, 71; VII, 227; IX, 242; XI, 83, 84, 237.
[2] See the following: V, 43–44, 154, 170, 217, 219; VII, 216, 217; IX, 171; XI, 82; XV, 156.

about the later aspects of these cycles when we come to a consideration of heredity, evolution and the progress from youth to old age
and death. For that reason, it is probably enough to notice here that
the young girls are spoken of as being at the rosy dawn of life (V,
171, 201, 220) or the spring, where they are but beautiful blooming
flowers. Even so,

> . . . dans la fleur la plus fraîche on peut distinguer les points
> imperceptibles qui pour l'esprit averti dessinent déjà ce qui sera, par
> la dessiccation ou la fructification des chairs aujourd'hui en fleur, la
> forme immuable et déjà prédestinée de la graine (V, 154).

The band of young girls to which Albertine belongs is a very
homogeneous and exclusive society, as Marcel notices before he
manages to introduce himself to its members. In the group, the
individuals are as indistinguishable and as unimportant as polyps
(V, 73), minnows (V, 74) zoophytes (V, 75, 111, 183) or separate
grapes in a bunch (V, 73-74). It is the organization as a whole that
counts and it has the unity and solidarity of a single shadow (V, 38),
a flock of birds (V, 36, 225), a machine (V, 35), a pagan society
(V, 40, 81) or a commercial firm such as a publishing house (XI,
222). The movements of the group are as well regulated and
predictable (though remote) as those of a constellation (V, 73, 83)
or a comet (V, 35). Like all the above-named agglomerations, the
band of young girls is completely oblivious to other people and
motivated entirely by considerations known only to its members.
For this reason, there is something as mysterious about its appearances as the sudden apparitions of Mephistopheles (V, 111) or any
exotic and unfamiliar thing (V, 39, 224).

The beauty of the young girls reminds Proust of art and especially
of sculpture. Their figures silhouetted against the sea suggest a
Greek frieze (V, 35, 40, 222-23). Individually, they are like little
statues of different moods (V, 171), or models for a sculptor (VIII,
15; IX, 336-37). Albertine is said to be a *bacchante à bicyclette* or *la
muse orgiaque du golf* (V, 133).

The fact that Marcel first encounters the band of young girls by
the sea is significant as far as the imagery associated with them is
concerned. They are like flowers, it is true, but their colour is that
of *la rose carnation d'une fleur de plage* (IX, 171) or *un géranium au bord
de la mer ensoleillée* (V, 219). Of them he says: *Ces jeunes filles, tiges de
roses dont le principal charme était de se détacher sur la mer* (V, 217).

In a group, it is marine specimens that they remind him of—zoophytes, madrepores, polyps and minnows. In addition, he often compares them to seabirds such as gulls (V, 31; IX, 214; XIV, 186), or migratory birds assembling on the shore before they fly (V, 36, 225; X, 331).

The related imagery of the sea and birds pervades all of Marcel's relations with Albertine. She is said to have hair like a bird's wing (XI, 94; XII, 226) or a gleaming wet chicken (V, 153), and her eyelashes surround *les globes de ses paupières comme un doux nid d'alcyon* (XI, 86). Her legs, when she lies on the bed, are like a swan's neck (XI, 96; XIII, 138), and when she is about to leave, the symbol of her rebellion is the furious opening of a window she had been forbidden to touch. The sound it makes is like the hoarse cry of a screech owl (XII, 248), and Marcel, in his worry over what she will do, is himself like a caged bird pacing back and forth (XII, 247). The birds on her Fortuny robe the last time he sees her are the birds of Venice—symbols of death and resurrection (XII, 245). Even the Septet of Vinteuil, which is the national anthem of Marcel's love for Albertine, opens with a passage like the sound of a cock crowing (XII, 232), and the strange rings which Albertine wears and which rouse Marcel's jealousy after she inadvertently leaves them behind, are carved in the shape of an eagle (XIII, 63). In thinking of the departed Albertine, Marcel is like the enchanted bird which could only repeat monotonously the name of its beloved (XIII, 23).

The implications of the bird imagery as it is associated with the sea imagery are far-reaching. The sea gull is itself a bird of ill omen (XII, 248), and it is aesthetically fitting that Albertine, who causes Marcel so much grief, should be primarily associated with that bird. Then too, birds are elusive creatures and Marcel never feels that he fully possesses or understands Albertine even when she is a captive in his house (XI, 113, 213, 214). Symbolically, the bird represents the soul,[1] and since it is Albertine's soul that Marcel wants to possess and not just her body, the imagery is appropriate here too.[2] The fact that most of the birds are water birds (gulls, kingfisher, swan, sea swallows, a *wet* hen) links the two important and related fields of imagery.

The symbolic significance of the sea imagery is clearly indicated

[1] See Bayley, *The Lost Language of Symbolism*, II, pp. 117, 301.
[2] Compare here the use of bird imagery in connection with the Guermantes family, p. 71.

by the following quotations. Marcel regards love as a vast ocean and consequently as something infinite and imponderable. His love is bigger than Albertine, *l'enveloppant, ne la connaissant pas, comme une marée autour d'un mince brisant* (XIII, 109). Even so, he can exclaim about their affair: *quelle large étendue de mer avait été réservée dans mon amour . . . pour Albertine* (XIV, 176). The relation of the really inconsequential object of the affections to the eternal and overwhelming passion is summed up in the following passage where Proust describes Marcel's feelings as he strokes Albertine's head:

> Je pouvais la caresser, passer longuement mes mains sur elle, mais, comme si j'eusse manié une pierre qui enferme la saline des océans immémoriaux ou le rayon d'une étoile je sentais que je touchais seulement l'enveloppe close d'un être qui, par l'intérieur, accédait à l'infini (XII, 230).

Here the sea clearly represents the eternal and the infinite, and imagery drawn from the sea is very rightly applied to Marcel's love affairs[1] and in particular to his great love affair with Albertine.

Proust admits that he consciously associates Albertine with the sea (V, 81, 221; XI, 83). For him, her nose is like a little wave (V, 154), and her hair seems to be transposed into waves (XI, 21). Her eyes are fluid like the sea (XI, 21), and even her cheeks when flushed with joy are bathed in . . . *une clarté si mobile que la peau [devient] fluide et vague* (V, 220). Her peignoir reminds him of Venice and its canals (XII, 209–11, 240–41). When she leaves him, it is as though he had lost a sea shell which he never valued at its true worth until it was no longer his (XIII, 49). In the famous description of her sleep (XI, 84–89), Proust extends the metaphor; her breath is a sea-breeze or the sound of waves, her pearls like the chain holding a boat at anchor, Marcel's leg against hers like an oar dragging in the water, etc., etc. After Albertine has left Marcel, she continues to be associated with water imagery. He imagines her bathing with other young girls (XIII, 138), and conflicting ideas about her beat back and forth in his mind like ocean waves (XIII, 145). When he receives her letters after her death, it is as though he saw *la même place de sa chambre occupée par un canapé et par une grotte* (XIII, 77).

---

[1] We might just point out in passing that one sea-image is used in connection with Gilberte: *Sa figure, devenue presque livide, ressemblait alors à ces plages ennuyeuses où la mer retirée très loin vous fatigue d'un reflet toujours pareil que cerne un horizon immuable et borné* (III, 194–95). For sea images connected with Mme de Guermantes, cf. p. 71.

Marcel is obsessed by Albertine's eyes, for he knows that *le petit rayon qui les irise ou les grains de brillant qui les font étinceler sont tout ce que nous pouvons voir d'une pensée* (XI, 212). He compares them to the sea because of their mystery and their depth (V, 220). He also uses the familiar comparison of precious stones (XI, 212; XII, 226),[1] and he compares both them and the eyes to azure butterfly wings mounted under glass (V, 220; XII, 226). The butterfly, we have seen, is a symbol of the ephemeral, and the juxtaposition of butterfly wings and the sea contrasts as vividly as possible the difference between the transitory and the eternal.[2] This distinction, which is also the distinction between reflection and penetration of depth and the impossibility of our ever fully comprehending the thoughts in the mind of another are both high-lighted by Marcel's account of his presentation to Albertine:

> Dans les yeux situés à l'infini . . . le regard conscient, la pensée inconnaissable que nous cherchions, vient d'être miraculeusement et tout simplement remplacée par notre propre image peinte comme au fond d'un miroir qui sourirait (V, 132).

One of Proust's favourite devices is closely to associate individuals with the geography of their place of origin. Albertine is associated by Marcel with the sea because that is where he first met her, but behind all that she also represents a particular locale, the locale of her birthplace. She is an incarnation of the French peasant in the carvings of Saint-André-des-Champs (VII, 236), but she also reflects the customs and landscape of Austria where she was brought up (X, 323-34). Her coiffure is like mountainous scenery (XII, 226), and a lock displaced reminds Proust of the effects of perspective given to moonlit trees in the background of a picture (XI, 86). The image of Albertine is associated with the moon (V, 113, 195) and her figure is said to resemble the sky—stormy when she is angry (V, 113), calm and peaceful at other times (XI, 96).

From one point of view, Albertine is like an actress playing a rôle on the seashore at Balbec (V, 115; XI, 82, 214). This image is related by Proust to the bird image (XI, 214) and one can assume that the actress, like the bird, represents for Proust the unattainable and the mysterious. On the other hand, Albertine is often very childlike and transparent in her actions (XI, 86; XII, 257), and Marcel then has no difficulty in penetrating her lies and pretenses

[1] See p. 46 above.   [2] Compare p. 17 above.

(XI, 189). One may sum up the relation by saying that when Marcel does not possess Albertine, she seems to him remote and exotic like a brilliantly coloured bird (II, 214), an inhabitant of another planet (V, 38), a character in a fairy tale (V, 39; XII, 230) or a mythological figure (XIII, 90). When she is his prisoner, she is colourless (XI, 214), dull and cumbersome as the parts of his body (XII, 157), as though some quite prosaic thing had been substituted for the provocative one by a sleight-of-hand trick (V, 135).

When Albertine is made captive by Marcel, she is compared most frequently to common-place domesticated animals. This emphasizes the uninspiring side of her nature to the narrator under these circumstances, for even though one may pet animals and be charmed by their unassuming grace, nothing could be less exotic or less remote. Before she is tamed, Albertine is like a wild horse (V, 80) or a wild animal (XIII, 237). When she is domesticated, her spirit is thoroughly subdued (XII, 225) and she becomes as ordinary and easy-going as a house-cat or a dog (XI, 16; XV, 60). Proust likes especially to compare her little pink nose to that of a cat (V, 220; IX, 294; X, 243, 336; XI, 93).

The whole pattern of sea and bird imagery, together with the all-important distinction between Marcel's attitude toward *Albertine libre* and *Albertine prisonnière*, is summed up by Proust in one wonderfully provocative image:

> Le vent de la mer ne gonflait plus ses vêtements; parce que, surtout, je lui avais coupé les ailes, qu'elle avait cessé d'être une Victoire, qu'elle était une pesante esclave dont j'aurais voulu me débarrasser (XII, 212).

The adjective *pesante* indicates that Proust is undoubtedly thinking here of the Winged Victory of Samothrace. The identification of the bird, the human, the superhuman and Greek culture is suggested by means rarely equalled. This is a magnificent image and one of Proust's finest.

The Guermantes Clan. The various members of the Guermantes family represent for Proust the aristocracy. Above them and associated with them are those fabulous individuals entitled to be addressed as *altesse*, but the social prestige of such a person as the Duchesse de Guermantes is actually the higher. For this reason, the imagery which Proust uses in connection with the Duke and

Duchess is designed especially to emphasize their exalted position. They are compared to gold, to birds and Olympian gods, and their noble lineage with all the traditional rights associated with it is continually stressed.

Madame de Guermantes is a mysterious name to Marcel long before he ever meets her. He associates her with the magic lantern slides he has of her ancestor, Geneviève de Brabant, and with the stained glass window in the church at Combray which portrays Gilbert le Mauvais, a descendant of Geneviève and likewise an ancestor of Madame de Guermantes. Perhaps the colours of the slides and the stained glass windows influenced Marcel in the choice of colours he associated with the name Guermantes and Madame de Guermantes. At any rate, he constantly associates the name Guermantes with the colours of flame—red, yellow and orange, which one sees in the candle of the magic lantern or the setting sun which illuminates most brilliantly stained glass windows.

The name is said to have golden syllables (XV, 181), like sunlight (VII, 32), autumn woods (VII, 39), or a yellow tower (VI, 14). It has about it the emanation of mysterious rays (XIII, 193), and it is described at times as orange and brilliant (VI, 35), at others as amaranth, a deep red or reddish purple (VI, 15). Its final syllable— *antes* is also said to be orange or amaranth in colour (I, 231–32; VII, 38).

Gold or flame colour is associated with individual members of the Guermantes clan. They are all said to have

> . . . une certaine blondeur quasi éclairante des cheveux délicats, même chez les hommes, massés en touffes dorées et douces (VIII, 72).

This colour of hair is also compared to light (VIII, 72) or the colour of golden rays in jasper, onyx (VIII, 72) or opals (IV, 160). Madame de Guermantes (whose first name is *Oriane*) has fine hair on her arms, *comme une vapeur dorée* (VII, 244), and a golden voice (VII, 33; XIII, 211). Saint-Loup's skin and hair are *aussi dorés que s'ils avaient absorbé tous les rayons du soleil* (IV, 159; cf. XIV, 16).

Flame-colour, burning, fire and lightning are also extensively used in figures connected with Guermantes personalities. The Jupiterian Duke, who is like the gold statue by Phidias (VII, 131), is frequently angry at the Duchess and under the circumstances he is said to be hurling thunderbolts (XV, 199). We see him in his rage,

F

les yeux flambant de colère et d'étonnement, ses cheveux crespelés semblant sortir d'un cratère (IX, 109). The Duchess is fond of red or flame-coloured clothes, and her skin, surprisingly enough, is the same colour (VI, 33, 42, 74; VIII, 244; IX, 82; XV, 82). Before the narrator had even met her, he used to imagine her taking him around the garden of her estate pointing out unknown red and purple flowers and naming them for him (I, 233). Her arrival at the home of the Princesse d'Epinay is noticed from a distance, *telles les premières lueurs d'un inoffensif incendie* (VIII, 100).

The Princesse de Guermantes has incandescent eyes (IX, 50) which Marcel first notices when she is at the theatre:

> Mes regards se sentirent croisés par l'incandescence involontaire et les feux des yeux de la princesse, laquelle les avait fait entrer à son insu en conflagration rien qu'en les bougeant pour chercher à voir à qui sa cousine venait de dire bonjour, et celle-ci, qui m'avait reconnu, fit pleuvoir sur moi l'averse étincelante et céleste de son sourire (VI, 70).

Mythologically, the sun or fire is the first god, and there remains in it an element of mystery and glory that makes Proust's use of imagery drawn from this source particularly appropriate for the Guermantes clan. Later, we shall have more to say about the etymology of proper names and its influence on Proust's choice of imagery, but it is worth noting here that the name *Guermantes* is said by Proust to be German (the German ancestry and sympathies of Charlus are quite evident during the war). Now the probable origin of the root *Germ* or *Guerm* is a Celtic form of the Indo-European *$gh^{w}erm$* which gives Greek *thermos* and English *warm*, etc. Knowing Proust's interest in philology, and in the light of evidence to be presented later, it is not unreasonable to suggest that we have here the motivating cause for the particular choice of imagery drawn from heat or flame.[1]

The various members of the Guermantes clan are consistently compared to gods and in particular the Greek gods. The Duc de Guermantes is as handsome as a Greek god (VII, 57) and as impressive as Hercules (VIII, 122) or Jupiter (VII, 131; VIII, 153; IX, 109; XI, 49, 50; XV, 195, 199). The Princesse de Guermantes is *belle et légère comme Diane* (VI, 67), and in the famous extended figure at the theatre (VI, 45, 69), she and her cousin, together with the other members of their set, are compared to marine deities.[2]

[1] Cf. pp. 244–45 below.
[2] For other references to this figure, see XIII, 214; XV, 179–81.

It is paradoxical that Proust should associate both fire and water imagery with the Guermantes clan. The extended figure referred to above perhaps owes its origin to the term *baignoire* and (as Proust himself suggests) the fact that the draperies in the theatre were purplish (VII, 41). However, this does not explain references to Madame de Guermantes as a fish (XV, 82), a rose-coloured shell (VI, 42; XV, 96) or a wave opposed to the cliff which Monsieur de Guermantes becomes for his wife (VIII, 156). Monsieur de Guermantes is also described as a fish (VII, 56–57), and the genius of the family is referred to as water or vapour:

> Quand les Guermantes me furent devenus indifférents et que la gouttelette de leur originalité ne fut plus vaporisée par mon imagination, je pus la recueillir, tout impondérable qu'elle fût (VIII, 46).

When Charlus is angry, his face resembles the stormy sea (VIII, 209, 213), and his manner of smiling or talking is compared to the rising and falling of the tide (X, 134; XIV, 204–5). The Guermantes nose is shaped like a wave (XIII, 73). The mystery of Madame de Guermantes is like a separate parcel of water which does not evaporate or change but is merely displaced, *protégé par une cloison, enfermé dans un vase, au milieu de flots de la vie de tous* (VI, 42). In earlier years, she is associated by Marcel with the magic lantern and the stained glass window at Combray, but when this dream begins to lose its colours, *des rêves tout autres l'imprégnèrent de l'écumeuse humidité des torrents* (VI, 11).

The context of the last quotation abounds in water images of one kind and another and it may be that Proust is simply referring to the theatre scene and preparing for it. On the other hand, since the context also introduces Françoise reminiscing about Combray (VI, 25–31), near which the Guermantes had their ancestral seat, Proust may very well have had a more profound motive in mind. Combray means *confluent* (a fact Proust was well aware of (XV, 134, 135)), and since the ways of Swann and Guermantes meet in Combray and lead back there, he expressly associates water imagery with both names.

The Guermantes family, in addition to the distinguishing colour of their hair, are said to have something ornithological about their appearance (VI, 97).[1] Their eyes are piercing and their noses aquiline (VI, 74; XV, 143). Madame de Guermantes has a nose like the beak of a falcon (VI, 97) or a vulture (VI, 75). In the description of the Duchesse de Guermantes and her cousin the Princesse at

[1] Cf. Vera L. Vance, 'Proust's Guermantes as Birds', FR, XXXV (1961–62), pp. 3–10.

the theatre, their costumes are compared to the plumage of birds of paradise and peacocks (VI, 69).[1] Madame de Guermantes is loved by Marcel, and it is significant that both she and Albertine are compared by him to birds. In particular, the swan image is associated with both of them.[2]

Here again, we have an obvious connection with mythology, since birds are divinities to many primitive peoples, *e.g.* the Egyptians (VI, 74). In his emphasis on their mystery and their genealogy, Proust declares the Guermantes to be a product . . . *aux âges de la mythologie, de l'union d'une déesse et d'un oiseau* (VI, 97).

As members of the aristocracy, the Guermantes family are traditionally associated with noble pastimes—duelling, hunting, court ceremonies. Imagery drawn from these sources is used extensively by Proust. The eyes of the Duc de Guermantes are like targets perforated by perfect bullseyes (VII, 56), and when angry at the Duchess, *ses yeux de chasseur avaient l'air de deux pistolets chargés* (VIII, 133). Conversely, when the Duchess is trying to stand up to his intimidating looks, it is she who is the huntress (cf. VIII, 68) and he a sort of wild beast (VIII, 152; IX, 97). When the Duke is old and broken, he is like a weary old lion at the zoo (XV, 195). Saint-Loup has a glance that perforates like cold steel and he shakes hands like a fencer handing over a foil (VIII, 79). His manoeuvering in the famous walk along the backs of the restaurant seats reminds Proust of a skilled jumper at a horse-show (VIII, 41, 44).

The obscure formalities of polite society which the Guermantes family follow closely remind Proust of the stylized mannerisms of the ballet. Gestures are not spontaneous (VI, 42, 51), and salutations, though correct and in some cases elaborate, resemble nothing quite so much as dance steps (VII, 198; VIII, 81-82). The inherent distinction of manners of the Duchess (VI, 175–76), the Princesse de Guermantes (IX, 53) or Saint-Loup (IV, 160–61) is like the grace of a star performer in the field of one of the arts.

Both the Duc and the Duchesse de Guermantes are living prototypes of French nobility. In them, on the one hand, we see the manners and customs of the Court of Louis XIV (VIII, 55, 69, 70–71) or Louis XV, though certain vulgarities of the husband are more reminiscent of Louis-Philippe (VIII, 173). This visible connection between the current holders of the Guermantes titles and

---

[1] Compare the development of this bird image in PJ, 74–75.
[2] For Albertine, see p. 65 above. For Madame de Guermantes, see VI, 34–35.

their remote ancestors makes Marcel think of genealogical trees (Christ in particular (VIII, 195)), and the present geographical setting of famous past events (VIII, 70–71). On the other hand, the Duke and particularly the Duchess have, in their conversation and their manners, residua of language and customs that are as old as France itself (VIII, 47). The effect of the conversation of the Duchess is to unroll before the eyes *une carté historique et géographique de l'histoire de France* (XI, 42). Her speech is also compared to a museum (XI, 42), an archive (VI, 16; VIII, 203), an ancient folk-song (VIII, 138), a book in an old French dialect (XI, 40), such as a book of hours (XIII, 208), an ancient recipe (VIII, 146), or a venerable dwelling full of authentic works of art (VIII, 187). From this point of view, the Duchess has a side to her which has much in common with that of a peasant like Françoise (VIII, 127).[1]

Images connected with Madame de Guermantes, because of her intellectual pretensions, often contain references to literature and academic pursuits. She is clever, but only in the manner of a dictionary (VIII, 88) or a literary critic (VIII, 109). Her contemporaries have the same respect for her as for a great creative writer (VIII, 107) or a literary masterpiece (VI, 71, 176–77). Her decisions and actions seem as abstract and mysterious to them as the philosophical speculations of Kant (VIII, 118) or Leibniz (VIII, 120). For Marcel, before he knows her, she is like a theoretical treatise on geometry (VI, 96).

Both the Duke and the Duchess are compared to art and to the theatre. The Duchess uses her voice like a Réjane or a Jeanne Granier (VIII, 137), and the Duke in his old age is more like a pitiful Géronte than Jupiter (XV, 195). The Duke in his prime is dignified and unctuous like Rembrandt's Bourgmestre de Six (IX, 104) while the Duchess is more like a fine bit of Dresden (VI, 17; XIII, 325).

The eyes of the Duchess call for special comment. They are blue as the afternoon sky (I, 239, VII, 32) or the sunlit sea (IX, 90). Proust also compares them to flowers such as the periwinkle (I, 240; VI, 13) and the violet (XIII, 211),[2] and he says that they are blue,

---

[1] Compare p. 50 above.

[2] In contrast to the number of comparisons of Albertine to flowers, there are only four figures of speech relating Madame de Guermantes to plants—the two just named, one in which her mouth is compared to a flower (II, 155) and one in which her posture as she stands up is compared to a bush resuming its natural position after having been bent down (VII, 95).

comme un rayon de soleil qui aurait traversé le vitrail de Gilbert le Mauvais (I, 239). This latter comparison is probably the one Proust has in mind when he speaks of Madame de Guermantes's eyes as emitting a flood of blue light (VII, 95), or shining brilliantly (IX, 82, 111). Incidentally, this hypothesis, based on the above quotation, lends support to the theory that the gold colour of the Guermantes name and colouring comes from the setting sun or stained glass windows illuminated by the sun.

In connection with the Verdurin circle, we have already seen how Proust uses imagery drawn from the hierarchy of rank to emphasize class distinctions. The Guermantes clan, being at the top of the ladder, is quite naturally compared to the Olympian circle of the gods, but Madame de Guermantes is also compared to a sovereign (II, 153; VI, 34; XV, 177, 199) or, in the hierarchy of religion, to a saint, Moses, Christ (XV, 175–76) or the Creator himself (VIII, 105). The Duke can be like an inquisitor in his imperious attitude towards others (VIII, 240), but in his old age, he resembles rather a venerable archbishop (XV, 229).

Imagery drawn from religion is used only to a limited extent in connection with the Duke and Duchess, but it becomes extremely important when we come to consider Charlus, the Duke's brother. We shall leave him for separate consideration, since his personality is inextricably involved with the question of homosexuality, but we should remember that he, too, is a member of the Guermantes clan. Madame de Marsantes, a sister of the Duke and Charlus, and the mother of Saint-Loup, is spoken of in religious terms. In contrast to the Duke, she is said to be a saint, incorporating (as in the *chansons de geste*) all the graces and virtues which her fierce brother lacks (VII, 89–90).

The gatherings in the salon of Madame de Guermantes are thought by Marcel to be as exclusive as the reunion of the Apostles in the Sainte-Chapelle. When he is admitted to them, he discovers that the members

> . . . se réunissaient là en effet, comme les premiers Chrétiens, non pour partager seulement une nourriture matérielle, d'ailleurs exquise, mais dans une sorte de Cène sociale (VIII, 158–59).

This comparison of social intercourse to food or wine is exploited further by Proust. A *bon mot* of Madame de Guermantes is like spiritual sustenance and when it is repeated to others, it is as though *le 'mot' se mangeait encore froid le lendemain à déjeuner* (VIII, 105). The 'At Home's' of Madame de Guermantes are forbidden fruit to many (VIII, 157), and she saves her most scintillating comments for those who are able to *taste* them (VIII, 112). Even the Duke, making idle conversation, is like someone passing little cakes (VIII, 197). Any salon or social group soon acquires a reputation like wines of a given year (XV, 176) or pastry makers (XV, 177).

The Social Hierarchy. It is certainly very difficult to classify Proust's general images on society without appearing to oversimplify what is for him an extremely complex subject. The relations of the individual to society, and of the class to which he at the moment belongs to those above and below are continually changing, and it is almost impossible to capture in images at any one instant the volatile essence of social identity.

The sense of unity and continual change in the realm of society is suggested by Proust by comparing the social hierarchy to the open sea (III, 179–80) or a kaleidoscope (III, 112, 113, 116; VII, 15), both of which present a single impression despite their continual movement and the infinite variety of their constantly changing detail.

Each wave in the ocean and each little coloured lozenge in the kaleidoscope might be said to represent a social group as it comes to the surface and rises or falls. Its sense of perspective is derived only from those entities immediately above or below it, while those which are more remote might just as well be lost in the sky (III, 55; XII, 36) or across a bay on the opposite shore (IV, 129). Such great distances are overwhelming, and they represent the fact that a social group which can appraise what is near it in prestige, is completely unable to seize subtle distinctions in what is far above it or far below it. Ideas in a group are propagated with the same irresistible force as the tide or great waves (X, 8; XV, 100). The Princesse de Parme, exposed to the daring unorthodoxy of Madame de Guermantes, is like a bather prudently trying to enter the stinging but refreshing waves of the ocean (VIII, 95, 109–10, 120, 140).

Proust emphasizes repeatedly the homogeneity and, as it were, exclusiveness of those social groups which are sealed off into what we may call salons. They are compared by him to a tropical island in the vast sea (VI, 37) or a verdant oasis (VI, 36–37), and the camaraderie among members of the same set is compared to that which reigned in Noah's Ark (VIII, 35–36). Each salon or group is like a little universe obeying its own inevitable laws and following its own orbit, which bears a certain mathematical relation to the orbits of other similar constellations (I, 264; V, 58, 130). These salons are like heavily-walled buildings almost impossible to enter (VIII, 94, 188) but easy enough to leave (I, 261). They have the diplomatic immunity of embassies abroad (IV, 99), and their interests are as narrow and specialized as those of Latin scholars (X, 260; XIV, 62).

Proust compares the mystery and the apparently magic trans-forming powers of salons and their members to the metamorphoses which can be accomplished by fairies (IV, 105, 164; IX, 186–87, 192; XIV, 198–99).We have already noted that he compares the gatherings of the members of Madame de Guermantes' salon to a communion service (p. 74 above). He uses this figure extensively in referring to the salons of Madame de Guermantes, the now socially-prominent Odette and Madame Verdurin (cf. p. 55 above). A salon is like a church, *i.e.* it is not only a building but a gathering of the faithful (VI, 16; XI, 252). Its members are compared to the apostles (VIII, 158–59) or the columns supporting the temple (VI, 36). They assemble there in order to partake of social communion (VI, 35) following the strict ordinances of the true church (VIII, 195; IX, 101), and the uninitiated (like Marcel) who are fortunate enough to gain entrance must follow the rites

> . . . avec cet air naturel d'un libre-penseur dans une église, lequel ne connaît pas la messe, mais se lève quand tout le monde se lève et se met à genoux un peu après que tout le monde s'est mis à genoux (III, 152).

Proust consistently relates the activities of a salon to the par-taking of food. It may be communion, as above, or the conversation may just be spoken of as additional courses in a meal (III, 40–41) or little cakes passed around (VIII, 197). Individuals in a salon are compared to foods to be eaten (II, 151; IV, 97; IX, 74) or table decorations (VIII, 94). A new combination of guests is as exciting as a variation in the sauce of a recipe (III, 117–18).

The latter comparisons which obliterate, as it were, the person-ality of individual members of social groups are not very flattering. Proust never fails to underline the slavish conformity of those who follow uncritically the dictates of their social milieu. They are as unthinking as plants (VIII, 196–97) or trees (II, 151–52), and Proust compares them in turn to fish (II, 149; IV, 101–2; V, 61), rabbits

(VIII, 99) and kittens (VIII, 77). They treat their superiors with a deference as unquestioning as that accorded the Pope (III, 143; VIII, 91, 197; IX, 132).

The members of the nobility and the salon leaders are not dealt with any more kindly, since they are unable to appreciate the feelings of others. Leaders of salons, with their industrious but autocratic cultivation of the elements constituting their group, are compared by Proust to busy worker bees methodically passing from flower to flower collecting pollen (III, 111; IX, 94). They are also likened to generals or commanding officers preparing their troops for review (IX, 92, 241) or for battle (IX, 93). The Princesse de Luxembourg who treats Marcel and his grandmother as little children (IV, 123, 124) or animals in the zoo (IV, 124; VIII, 57), and Madame de Ville-parisis who treats her nieces like servants (VII, 46–47) are in turn compared by Proust to animals (VIII, 57) and the lower orders of life. Monsieur de Guermantes, because of his inability to under-stand the sentiments of others, is likened by Proust to an undertaker or a doctor (VII, 198).

The social hierarchy is consistently spoken of by Proust as *le théâtre du monde* (IX, 332). Individuals in all ranks of life are said to be playing a part (cf. p. 56) or several parts, either consecutively like Odette (cf. p. 61), or simultaneously like Saint-Loup, who,

> . . . comme un parfait comédien . . . pouvait dans sa vie de régiment, dans sa vie mondaine, jouer l'un après l'autre des rôles différents (VI, 215).

The arrival of a society queen at a *fête* creates the same effect as the unexpected presence of Sarah Bernhardt at a *soirée de théâtre* (XV, 123–24). Marcel meets Bergotte in the Swann salon *comme quelqu'un qui, au lieu de faire la queue avec tout le monde pour avoir une mauvaise place, gagne les meilleures, ayant passé par un couloir fermé aux autres* (III, 180). Those who promenade on the boulevards or the esplanade at Balbec are actors, while those who watch are the critics (V, 32).

In the realm of higher society, Proust satirizes members of the upper classes by comparing the rôles they play to comedy parts. The encounter of Madame de Villeparisis and Marcel's grandmother (IV, 117) and the insistent monologuing of Charlus and Monsieur de Sidonia (IX, 54) are compared to the artificial stylized actions of characters in a play by Molière. The Duc de Guermantes, when old, is *un risible Géronte* (XV, 195), and Madame d'Argencourt is a *mori-*

bond-bouffe d'un Regnard exagéré par Labiche (XV, 76). Society queens *jouent à la reine . . . comme les reines dans Sardou* (VIII, 58). Monsieur de Norpois is associated with Voisenon, Crébillon fils (VII, 119) and Augier (III, 71), and even Saint-Loup's attitude toward his father is compared to the attitude towards their fathers of a son of Boieldieu or Labiche (IV, 165).

The whole question of the relation of the individual to society and of the group to which he belongs to those above and below it is treated ironically by Proust. At Combray, *chacun est à jamais classé suivant les revenus qu'on lui connaît, comme dans une caste indienne* (XIII, 273). In this world of society, social prestige is a sort of income or financial power utilized in speculation by its possessors (I, 259; IV, 153–54). The privileges associated with social power are akin to those of royalty (III, 103; VIII, 221), and obeisance is given unquestioningly to those who possess it, even if they are ugly and stupid (I, 203). Like the kaleidoscope or the sea, however, prestige is subject to change, and when a person is unpopular, it is practically impossible for him to alter his situation (III, 107). *C'est de la même façon que le peuple chasse ou acclame les rois* (X, 92). Weddings are arranged solely on the basis of social prestige (IV, 129), and the final damning touch is added by Proust when he compares the social relations of those in the upper classes to those that exist in a barber shop:

> Comme un coiffeur voyant un officier qu'il sert avec une considération particulière, reconnaître un client qui vient d'entrer et entamer un bout de causette avec lui, se réjouit en comprenant qu'ils sont du même monde et ne peut s'empêcher de sourire en allant chercher le bol de savon, car il sait que dans son établissement, aux besognes vulgaires du simple salon de coiffure, s'ajoutent des plaisirs sociaux, voire aristocratiques, tel Aimé, voyant que Mme de Villeparisis avait retrouvé en nous d'anciennes relations, s'en allait chercher nos rince-bouches avec le même sourire orgueilleusement modeste et savamment discret de maîtresse de maison qui sait se retirer à propos. On eût dit aussi un père heureux et attendri qui veille sans le troubler sur le bonheur de fiançailles qui se sont nouées à sa table (IV, 118).

Charlus and Homosexuality. The character of Charlus is perhaps the most complex in the whole of *A la recherche du temps perdu*, but it resolves itself fundamentally into the curious paradox which results from the exalted social position of Charlus on the one hand, and his inferior rating as an inveterate and promiscuous homosexual on the other. Almost all the imagery used in connection with Charlus can be related to this dualism in his nature.

As one of the noblest members of the Guermantes clan, Charlus is compared, like the rest of them, to the Greek gods (XI, 57; IX, 55, 135) and Apollo in particular (VIII, 210). His position in relation to his brother, the Duke, is similar to that of Monsieur to Louis XIV (IX, 78), or the noble dukes to Queen Marie-Amélie or the Duc d'Orléans (VII, 251), and he can be most regal and haughty in manner (IX, 72; X, 263, 265; XII, 36). Like the Duke, Charlus is as inconsiderate of the feelings of others and as imperious as a busy doctor (XII, 41, 46, 116; VIII, 208). He treats inferiors like Cottard much as a squire treats his horses (X, 264). His Christian name "Palamède" is like a *belle médaille de la Renaissance* (IV, 184), and his laugh has the same ancient and authentic quality as the 16th-century trumpets Bach had had in mind when he wrote his works (X, 101– 102).[1] In the social hierarchy, his position is comparable to that of a high ecclesiastic in the church, and Charlus actually goes so far as to speak of his own *robe auguste d'évêque* (IX, 21).

We have previously noticed how fond Proust is of using images drawn from religion to emphasize social and class distinctions. The combination of religious imagery and homosexuality emphasizes one facet of the basic paradox in the character of Charlus, even though one does not need to look far for literary precedents. The theory that celibates in the church commonly practice sodomy is, of course, widely held. Vautrin, in Balzac's novel *Les Illusions perdues* (which is a favourite both of Charlus and of Proust himself), is disguised as a Spanish priest when his infatuation with Lucien de Rubempré begins.

Proust does not limit the use of religious imagery in connection with homosexuality to Charlus alone. The very terms Sodom and Gomorrha are Biblical in origin, and homosexuals turning to admire attractive youths are like Lot's wife turning to look back on the city of destruction (IX, 45). Morel is compared by Proust to the young David (IX, 334) and Lazarus (X, 274), and the chauffeur, who is probably a homosexual because of his association with Charlus, is spoken of as a *jeune évangéliste*, a *jeune apôtre* (X, 209), and *le charmant mécanicien apostolique* (XI, 165).

[1] Proust consistently speaks of the musical quality of the voice of Charlus. It varies from *pianissimo* (XIV, 204) or a graceful *scherzo* when he is pleased to a fierce *appassionato* when he is angry (VIII, 216). Its range is quite remarkable (VIII, 211), but when Charlus is old it as though *la voix . . . était fausse encore et aurait eu besoin de l'accordeur* (XIV, 128).

Charlus has a peculiar manner of speaking which resembles chanting in the church (IX, 127; X, 261), and his habit of continually keeping his eyes downcast causes Proust to refer to his *paupières d'ecclésiastique* (X, 221, 254; XII, 9, 109). He sometimes holds his hands as if he were praying (VII, 135), and when he shakes hands, it is almost as though he were wearing a bishop's ring which he expected to be kissed (VII, 114).

It is a commonplace to refer to the progressive degradation of Charlus during the course of the novel, but the paradox only becomes more startling when it is pointed out that the religious imagery which Proust uses in this connection becomes correspondingly more and more exalted. This has the effect of making the position of Charlus appear completely abject, but it seems also to give to him some of the qualities of a tragic hero.

When Marcel first meets Charlus, his appearance is compared. to that of a hypocrite (IV, 189). Later his expression is said to resemble that of an inquisitor (X, 221; XII, 9) or a prophet (XII, 57). He is identified in turn with the Pope (IX, 65; XII, 44, 150), an apostle (XII, 157), the prophet Daniel, and the Archangel Raphael himself (XII, 150). In the culminating phase of his jealousy of Morel, he is said to be *au terme de son calvaire* (X, 273) and he speaks of himself socially as able to "perform miracles" (XII, 90).

In the final sections of *A la recherche du temps perdu*, Charlus is also compared to the legendary tragic heroes Prometheus (XIV, 146, 174), Oedipus (XIV, 202–3) and King Lear (XV, 76). Elsewhere Proust identifies Charlus with Don Quixote (IX, 72) whose Dulcinea is Morel (XII, 96), and it is significant that these four figures, even though they are crushed by fate and apparently failures, remain symbols of the tragic greatness that is in man. It is not the intention here to argue that Proust admires Charlus, who is the victim of his own unconquerable vice, but it does seem from these images that Proust feels a certain sympathy for him that has not been sufficiently emphasized.

When we turn to the position of homosexuals in society, we find that the images Proust selects are uncompromisingly condemnatory. Individuals belonging to this class are compared to wild animals (IV, 197; IX, 36, 60, 61) or savage cannibals (X, 264; XI, 254). They are like oppressed minority groups such as the negroes (IX, 36) or the Jews (IX, 25–26, 86–87; X, 241; XII, 12). They are like tradesmen (IX, 127; X, 75), but since they traffic in illicit goods they are compared to black-marketeers (IV, 197; VII,

113) or downright criminals (IX, 26, 153; X, 236; XII, 127). Homo-sexuals are like spies (IV, 187; XIII, 137), exiles (XII, 12) or pirates (XIV, 168), and because of their obsession they resemble madmen (IV, 187; XII, 8–9, 126–27, 175) or drug addicts (IX, 31–32; XIV, 112). Proust speaks of homosexuality as an illness which is congenital (IX, 27; XI, 26) and irremediable (IX, 37; XI, 253; XII, 13; XIV, 173). To the initiated, this illness is as clearly apparent as any incipient disease would be to a competent diagnostician (X, 132; IX, 85, 86; XII, 13), or the evidence of guilt to an efficient judge (X, 132). Charlus in his later years is consistently spoken of as an invalid (X, 222, XII, 9–10, 24; XIV, 112, 127, 202). The disease is often most revolting, to be compared in its effects to a malady of the liver or a skin ailment (XII, 9–10).

Another facet of the paradox inherent in the nature of Charlus (and of all homosexuals) is the fact that even though the body is of one sex, the mind is of the other (X, 132). Proust sees this ambival-ence in Mlle de Vinteuil, who has the physical mannerisms now of a timid virgin, now of a brash youth (I, 156, 218). Morel's relations to Charlus are said to be like those of a morganatic wife (X, 290) or a concubine (X, 249), and Albertine looks away from an avowed Lesbian *avec le même genre de discrétion qu'un homme qui voit son ancienne maîtresse avec un autre amant* (IX, 319). The homosexual tailor Jupien, whose very name suggests not only his trade but his sexual nature, is compared to a *coquette* (IX, 18) or a Juliet whose Romeo is Charlus (IX, 40–41). In his establishment, the young homosexuals are described as a harem (XIV, 157), and Charlus himself is likened to an apparently devoted and modest matron (X, 221) who may not actually be so (IV, 203; X, 75). The physical mannerisms of Charlus remind Marcel of the Duchesse de Guermantes (X, 76, 263–64), and his voice under emotion reveals itself like hers (XII, 95) or like that of a giddy school-girl or a *coquette* (IV, 202–3).[1]

Despite the fact that Charlus is feminine in desiring relations with other men, in these relations it is he who takes the aggressive or masculine rôle. This leads to a certain protectiveness which causes Proust to compare the relation of Charlus to Morel to that of a father towards his son (XII, 50), or better, towards his daughter (X, 241). When Morel proves ungrateful, he is said to be like a spoiled but recalcitrant child (X, 251).

[1] For other comparisons of Charlus to women, see particularly IX, 23; X, 58–59, 61; XI, 224; XII, 142.

Curiously enough, when Charlus grows old and helpless, it is Jupien who adopts the rôle of the parent. He tenderly watches over his charge and takes care of him *comme d'un enfant* (XIV, 202, 203).

Homosexuals are a strange minority group. They are like members of the same school (IX, 99) or amateurs of chamber music (IX, 30) or collectors of rare and unusual items (IX, 29). More than any other members of society, they must hide their true nature by playing a rôle that does not come naturally to them. Charlus is said to wear a mask (IV, 199; XII, 11, 109). He and his like are in disguise (IV, 199; IX, 32, 99) and it is only by the eyes that he and other homosexuals reveal their character. Their eyes are as active as those of a painter sketching (XI, 185) or a hungry animal (XIV, 171), and the signals they emit to another of their kind are as conspicuous as those of phosphorescent insects (IX, 39), a light-house (IX, 318–19) or a star (IX, 319–20). The intensity of such glances makes them seem almost corrosive (XI, 185).

The homosexual trying to assess one whose true nature is not self-evident, or the normal person trying to decide if someone else is abnormal or not, is faced with a real cryptogram. Proust compares the necessary deciphering to the difficulty of reading an almost incomprehensible manuscript (IV, 198), a message enciphered by transposition of letters (IX, 24), or the solution of a problem in algebra (IX, 116–17; XI, 201; XIII, 138).

Since homosexuals vary a great deal in type within the framework of their rarity as a species, the successful encounter of two compatible individuals is as fortuitous as the fecundation of an exotic bloom by the very insect necessary for the process. This image is developed at length by Proust when Jupien and Charlus meet (IX, 11–64 but especially IX, 39–45). Jupien is the orchid (IX, 11–12, 43, 45), *Primula veris* (IX, 42), or *Lythrum salicoria* (IX, 41), and Charlus is the efficacious bee who pollenates the flower (IX, 11–12, 43, 45). The symbolism of this imagery is made the more emphatic since the encounter between Charlus and Jupien takes place in a courtyard where the Duchesse de Guermantes has exposed to the open air a rare plant of hers, in the hope that it may be fertilized by a vagrant insect:

> Au même instant où M. de Charlus avait passé la porte en sifflant comme un gros bourdon, un autre, un vrai celui-là, entrait dans la cour. Qui sait si ce n'était pas celui attendu depuis si longtemps par

l'orchidée, et qui venait lui apporter le pollen si rare sans lequel elle resterait vierge? (IX, 14).

Proust also compares homosexuals to hermaphrodite types like the snail (IX, 43) or the jelly fish (IX, 39), and parasitic plants which need to grow clinging to another plant (IX, 33). Charlus is described as a sort of centaur (IX, 23–24).

Still another facet of the paradox in the nature of Charlus is brought out by his imperious military bearing. This rather effeminate homosexual manages to conceal his true nature (except at times of emotional strain) under a façade of military sternness. It is fitting that a noble member of the Guermantes clan should have associated with him imagery emphasizing his aristocratic background, but it is ironic that Charlus, who is so feminine underneath, should be made to appear so masculine. When Marcel first meets him, the sharp glance he receives is *comme un dernier coup que l'on tire au moment de prendre la fuite* (IV, 187). Charlus' face sometimes has *un air de vieux mousquetaire Louis XIII* (X, 306), and in insisting on having his say, he is like an aviator who must drop his bombs even if they land in an open field where they are not effective (XIV, 126). When Charlus squeezes Marcel's shoulder, it hurts him as much as the recoil of a '76' (XIV, 137–38). In quarrels, in particular, Charlus is like a military commander. When he wins, he dictates the conditions of peace (X, 258), and when he loses, it is because he was without his arms (XII, 141). Even the vice of Charlus, which is known far afield but not to his own circle, is *comme certains coups de canon qu'on n'entend qu'après l'interférence d'une zone silencieuse* (X, 53).

Saint-Loup and Friendship. Just as Charlus and homosexuality are inseparable, so are Saint-Loup and friendship. It is true that Saint-Loup later also becomes a homosexual, but this does not affect his relations with the narrator. Moreover, Saint-Loup is the only close friend Marcel has, and around him he concentrates his remarks on friendship, as opposed to love.

Saint-Loup is first and foremost a member of the Guermantes clan, and images relating him to the other individuals in that group have already been examined. The Guermantes family is represented by a yellowing feudal tower (VI, 14), but it is only with Saint-Loup that this tower resumes its military character (XIV, 180). Saint-Loup is the only soldier in the Guermantes clan, and the fact that he

exposes himself to danger as he does, adds to the tender quality of
the solicitude Marcel feels for him. He regards Saint-Loup as one
does an invalid who has not long to live (XIV, 76, 77).

It is paradoxical that Marcel in turn feels himself an invalid
whose doctor and restorer is Saint-Loup (VI, 88, 109). Despite all
that Proust has to say against doctors, the relations between them
and their patients are apparently best suited to symbolize friendship.

The anxious care one feels for a friend is also compared by
Proust to that of a mother for her *débutante* daughter (VI, 125) or a
spectator for a tight rope artist (VI, 130). This is the attitude of
Saint-Loup towards Marcel when he so much desires him to succeed
in front of others. Saint-Loup is a sort of orchestral conductor who
silences with a rap of his baton those players who are making
distracting noises (VI, 129).

When a rude journalist refuses to put out a cigar because the smoke
bothers Marcel, Saint-Loup administers him a beating. As he raises
his arm before he strikes the culprit, he again resembles the conductor of an orchestra whose violent movements correspond to the
agitated quality of the music he directs (VI, 220). The blows themselves are like stones hurled from a sling, ovoid astral bodies in an
unstable constellation, or fire-works (VI, 222–23).

Proust has not nearly as much to say about friendship as about
love and there is a certain contradiction inherent in what he does
say. He describes the mutual sympathy which is instantly felt by
Marcel and another acquaintance of Saint-Loup's as a beautiful
flower opening, and he says that the two of them are *protégés des
autres par les voiles magnifiques d'une de ces sympathies entre hommes* (VI,
127). Compared to love, however, friendship partakes of *une qualité
si médiocre qu'elle ressemblait à quelque chose d'intermédiaire entre la
fatigue et l'ennui* (VIII, 22). Friendship has its place, and a man who
despises friendship can be the best friend in the world, *de même qu'un
artiste portant en lui un chef-d'œuvre . . . donne sa vie pour une cause inutile*
(VIII, 21).

Finally, in connection with friendship, Proust introduces in
juxtaposition two faded metaphors with the result that each has
restored to it its original force and colour so that we get a curious
stylistic effect. Of friendship versus love, he says: *Il n'est breuvage si
funeste qui ne puisse à certaines heures devenir précieux et réconfortant en
nous apportant le coup de fouet qui nous était nécessaire* (VIII, 22).

INTROSPECTIVE PROCESSES

It has already been emphasized that any division of themes in Proust is bound to be arbitrary. More than that, a certain overlapping is unavoidable, and this applies particularly to an examination of psychological processes. We were forced to include some of Proust's own reactions to art in the section on aesthetics, and in our consideration of introspective processes, we shall have to include images associated with characters other than the narrator himself when these images are directly related to themes that are fundamentally introspective, *e.g.* love, habit, dreams, time.

Love and Jealousy. As far as themes go, this one has associated with it by far the largest number of images of any theme in the whole of *A la recherche du temps perdu.* This is not perhaps surprising, since as a theme love plays such a predominant part in Proust's work. He compares love to a cathedral in the midst of a town; it is difficult to judge its relative importance amid the routine of life, but from a distance its true perspective stands out clearly (XIII, 97). Proust would be ready to agree with Stendhal who called love *la plus grande affaire de la vie, ou plutôt la seule.*

We have already had occasion several times to draw attention to the fact that the sea represents the eternal for Proust. In his work, we find images drawn from the sea closely associated with love and not just with Marcel's love for Albertine. Any lover is like a swimmer who, *entraîné sans s'en apercevoir, bien vite perd de vue la terre* (X, 166). The loved one is a sort of magnetic pole which gives direction to the inner compass of the lover (III, 196; IX, 177–78), whose actions, nevertheless,

> ... ne sont pas en rapport étroit et nécessaire avec la femme aimée, mais passent à côté d'elle, l'éclaboussent, la circonviennent comme le flux qui se jette le long des rochers (IX, 291).

The eyes of a jealous or disappointed lover reveal great depths, like those to which a diver may attain (VII, 114) or from which a bubble may rise to break on the surface (IX, 149). A woman who rejects us is like a person lost at sea; we never cease to hope that she may some day return to us safe and sound (III, 203).

Proust uses many marine images in connection with Albertine (cf. p. 65). He actually calls her a sea, because of her complex elusiveness (VII, 232; XI, 129), but he also refers to Marcel's own

G

love as a vast sea, greater and more important than the object to which it is directed (XIV, 176; XIII, 109). When Albertine eludes Marcel, the days are like the unending procession of waves on the sea (V, 199), and after he loses her, he feels that he is lost on a vast and barren beach (XIII, 129, 147).

Fundamentally, love (or desire) is an appetite. It and jealousy are like a burning thirst that demands assuaging (V, 39; VI, 149; XI, 104).[1] Love is also like famished hunger (V, 196), and the objects it seeks, *i.e.* kisses and carnal satisfaction and the young girls who provide these things, are all compared to food or fruits (X, 200; V, 98, 177; XI, 69–70; VII, 236; XII, 232; XIV, 172).[2] Proust emphasizes the animal side of the appetite by comparing the urge to the instinct of a snake to seize a bird (XII, 131), a wild beast to devour its prey (II, 34), or a butterfly to light on a flower (IX, 140). Desire satisfied is like the deep sleep which follows long walks out-of-doors (XI, 116–17).

Since love is an appetite, the particular object which satisfies it is of relatively little importance. We may think we love a certain young girl, but in truth, *nous n'aimons, hélas! en elle que cette aurore dont son visage reflète momentanément la rougeur* (XIII, 279). The different women desired by Marcel are as insignificant and as multiform as the pictures on a calendar (XV, 158). They are nothing more or less than items to be collected, like antique lorgnettes (VII, 218) or paintings (XIII, 274). Marcel compares his interest in women to his interest in different countries (XI, 177) or perfumes (IX, 305), or the interest of zoologists in the habits of fish or birds. They capture specimens and leave an identifying mark *avant de leur rendre la liberté, sous le ventre des oiseaux ou des poissons dont ils veulent pouvoir identifier les migrations* (XI, 171). Women themselves do not count; they are *comme des instruments interchangeables d'un plaisir toujours identique* (I, 213), and their only merit is that they put their lovers in contact with truths that are unattainable otherwise (X, 333): *Il n'y en a pas une seule [femme] dont la possession soit aussi précieuse que celle des vérités qu'elle nous découvre en nous faisant souffrir* (XIII, 100).

For Proust, the keynote of love is suffering (XIII, 125). Images related to this aspect of the theme number at least 133, and anyone who has ever read *A la recherche du temps perdu* knows without its being drawn to his attention that for Marcel love is an illness,

[1] Have we here another reason why Albertine is constantly associated with water imagery?

[2] Compare also p. 63.

jealousy a disease, a poison or a noxious drug. The only thing a reader might not realize is the extent to which Proust elaborates on this image.

As we mentioned earlier, there is nothing new about comparing love to an illness or a wound. The legend of Cupid and his piercing arrows dates far back in mythology (cf. PJ, 134; IV, 140), and the symptoms of the malady of love were recognized long before the Greeks and Romans. Proust is, of course, a hypochondriac by nature, and we shall see later how important a rôle images drawn from illness play in his work as a whole. With respect to love, however, it might be argued that one of the reasons why illness is so constantly suggested to him is that his own particular kind of homosexual love was unnatural and morbid. This may be so, but at any rate the meeting ground of love and illness is one of the most fertile cultivated by Proust.

The course of love differs slightly from individual to individual, just as one's method of catching cold or falling ill (XI, 34; XIII, 16, 107). Love is above all a sort of chronic illness which recurs inexplicably at the slightest pretext (IX, 260; XI, 25). The germs which cause it are as insignificant in size as those causing cholera (II, 169). It has the symptoms of a fever (II, 21; IV, 37), but it behaves like eczema (II, 87), rheumatism (XI, 104; XIII, 136) or asthma (XI, 34–35; XIV, 176). It is strictly nervous in origin (IX, 253; IV, 15, 43–44), and while it may almost disappear at times (II, 119, 127, 136), leaving its victim in a state of convalescence (II, 35), it can recur very suddenly (XI, 186). It is a sort of intoxication (VI, 199; X, 328) or insanity (IX, 294; XIII, 30) in which the mind is not entirely normal. One of the few consolations about suffering from it is that others are also affected by the same malady (XIII, 29; IX, 148).

Love (and especially jealousy) is also like a wound delivered by an enemy (II, 197), or by the object of one's affections (VI, 145; IX, 257). Words are like the knife which inflicts the wound (II, 200) or, after the original cut, they are like a jostle to the wound (II, 82, 196) which causes it to re-open (II, 199), or a painful change of dressings (XIII, 19).

Following the time-hallowed tradition, Proust most often speaks of the heart as being the member affected in love. Sometimes it is a real wound to the heart (II, 195; XI, 34, 178, 319–20; XIII, 88, 101; X, 326), sometimes heart disease (XI, 118; XIII, 40; XV, 55; III, 93). When Saint-Loup considers breaking with Rachel, the very thought of the separation is *pareille à ce cœur qu'on arrache à un malade et qui continue à battre, séparé du reste du corps* (VI, 149).

The effects of love and jealousy are like the effects of powerful drugs or poisons. The woman who is the object of the affections is a combination of seductive beauty and deadly poison, like certain flowers (XIII, 238) or an apparition of Gustave Moreau (II, 71). She is like morphine (XIV, 151), to which one can so easily become addicted (II, 123), and her ruses have the same effect on us as depriving a drug addict of his morphine (IV, 15, 29). We can absorb tremendous quantities of the poison of suspicions about a loved one of whom we are jealous, but the result is that we become hypersensitive and then a small virulent dose may prove fatal (III, 188; XI, 103–4, 211). The curious result of this state of affairs is that the woman who is a drug or a poison also becomes, because of that fact, its only remedy or effective antidote (II, 195–96; IV, 41; X, 323; XIII, 73). After Albertine has left Marcel, her memory occasionally provides the calming drug he needs (XIII, 43), but more often his unsatisfied suspicions act on him like a violent stimulant (XIII, 62, 83–84).[1] From another point of view, love is a self-inoculated malady (IX, 260) and its victim is like a doctor experimenting on himself with full consciousness of the potential hazards (II, 113; XV, 55). Masochistically, the victim cannot help palping the very organ that is paining him (II, 200; V, 158; XII, 247–48), but if he is ever to get well, he must remember that *ceux qui souffrent par l'amour sont, comme on dit de certains malades, leur propre médecin* (IV, 41). This is like asking the drug addict to cure himself. Theoretically, it is the ideal method, but practically, it seldom works.

Proust compares love and jealousy to intense physical pain like toothache (XII, 27–28) or breaking bones (XII, 168). He compares it to the most excruciating torture (XI, 127, 135; II, 83), and he even calls it martyrdom (X, 321; XI, 117) or condemnation to hell (XI, 187; II, 200; XIII, 14, 126). It is the loved one who sometimes acts as torturer or inquisitor (II, 205).

Despite its grave symptoms, the malady of love never proves fatal, like cancer (XIII, 278). Recovery may be dependent on an operation—a cutting away of the infected part of the body (XII, 239), or it may come about naturally. In either case, no one ever dies from love, even though there may be a long period of convalescence

---

[1] In a reciprocal image, Proust compares the taking of drugs to the nervous excitement of a new love affair. *Le cœur bat comme à un premier rendez-vous* (XI, 231).

(XIII, 218, 278). The *amputé* suffers from climate variations (XIII, 94) but hemiplegics learn to read again (XIII, 85) and cripples to go without crutches (XIII, 44).

The individual suffering from love may feel as though he is dying (XIII, 149–50) but actually what really dies for him is the loved one. The loved one is the cause of the illness (VI, 146) or the illness itself, and when it is cured, it is as though the illness or the loved one were dead. In Albertine's case, it is a physical fact that she dies, but for Marcel, her death dates from the moment she leaves him rather than from her actual demise.[1] Thoughts of death are associated by Saint-Loup with Rachel (VI, 149), and when Swann is determined to break off with Odette, it is she whom he regards as the dying one (II, 182, 200).

The relations between lovers then are never happy. Love is a painful illness which culminates either in a rupture from which recovery is slow and tedious or in the death of the love. In either case, the connotations suggested by Proust are unpleasant. Love is an integral part of life and it teaches us important truths just as illness and death teach us truths, but the overall tone of the theme is sombre and tragic.

The old idea of the enmity between the sexes is exploited by Proust. He compares Marcel's ruses with Gilberte (IV, 13) and Albertine (XII, 190, 191), and Albertine's ruses with him (XIII, 25; XII, 199, 200, 201), with the feints of a general in a military manoeuvre. Rivals are like enemy soldiers (X, 324–25) and the hapless lover is like a soldier exposed to fire (IX, 297). The force of Marcel's attraction to an unknown beauty is like that of a soldier's charge (XI, 33), and when he learns from Mlle de Stermaria that she cannot meet him, the envelope and the card which bore the fatal message fall at his feet, *comme la bourre d'une arme à feu quand le coup est parti* (VIII, 18).

In love, quarrels and misunderstandings constantly arise. Proust compares these disturbances to the periodic upheavals of a volcano (XI, 97; XIII, 313) or violent atmospheric storms (XIII, 90). Forebodings of these storms can be seen in the negligent dress a mistress adopts (XI, 127), the gathering clouds on a jealous face

[1] There are many premonitions of her death beginning with her trunks like coffins (XI, 14; XIII, 21), her corpse-like appearance when asleep (XII, 197), her instinctive stubbornness like that of animals about to die (XII, 245), and including also the many thoughts of death suggested to Marcel by reflections on Albertine as his prisoner (XI, 208; XII, 192, 206; XIII, 122).

(VI, 206) or the intensifying murmur of heated conversations (XII, 196). Sometimes the storm never breaks but is only felt inside the lover (III, 196; XII, 28, 201, 249). When the quarrels or suspicions which gave rise to it dissipate, the relief is similar to that after a violent thunderstorm (X, 200; XI, 238) when the sun comes out warm and brilliant (XI, 194, 195; XIII, 88).

In quarrels or jealousy, the one party tends to regard the other as a criminal (XI, 221; III, 195) and himself as a sort of lawyer (XI, 109), detective (XI, 28), or judge (XI, 69). Sometimes he is himself the criminal because of his ruthless treatment and the punishment he brings on himself (II, 168; XIII, 22, 130). In the presence of Madame de Guermantes, Marcel trembles like a criminal (VI, 175).

Love runs its course like the seasons of the year. The early quarrels are like the first frosts in autumn (III, 194), but when there is nothing left of desire but quarrels and jealousy, we seem to have the short days (XI, 138) and long nights of winter (X, 29). The lover himself shivers with the cold (XII, 194) and the object of his love is shrouded in snow and ice like a rock in the middle of the snow or a fountain sheeted in ice (XIII, 31–32).

This is also another way of saying that when love obscures our vision, we cannot really see the object which first inspired our passion. These objects are consistently referred to by Proust as goddesses, whether they are Albertine (XI, 188; XIII, 132), Madame de Guermantes (cf. p. 70) or unidentified young girls (XI, 172–73, 207, 210; XIII, 86). Their dwellings and their possessions seem to him to be like magnificent Christmas parcels (III, 124) or enchanted things (III, 96, 104). To the lover, his beloved is like a precious treasure (II, 108; XIII, 98) or a beautiful ancient marble (XI, 172; XV, 158). Any woman who inspires desire is like an alluring statue (XI, 208; IV, 140), but it is important to notice that it is we who are the sculptors: *Nous voulons obtenir d'une femme une statue entièrement différente de celle qu'elle nous a présentée* (XI, 175).

Proust likes to stress the fact that love and jealousy are really creations of our own minds (IV, 16; X, 319; II, 247). He compares the effort and thought that go into them to the industry necessary to produce any creative work, whether it be a painting (IV, 35), a poem (II, 192), a novel (XII, 186, 188; XIII, 45) or a work of history for which research is necessary (XI, 181–82). Love has a beginning, a middle, and an end, just like any composition of music or literature (I, 266; XIII, 105), and the narrator imposes the sentiments which love or jealousy inspire in him on the work of art he is absorbed in at the moment (XI, 67). It is for that reason that the phrase from Vinteuil's sonata becomes the theme of Swann's love for Odette (II, 33, 175) (and, to a certain extent, Marcel's love for Odette's daughter Gilberte (XIII, 108)) and the same composer's Septet the theme of Marcel's love for Albertine (XII, 63). The various stages in love resemble music in particular, with the parallel development (IX, 13), repeated phrases (VI, 207), and recapitulation (XIII, 105). It is interesting to note that Albertine grows more and more skilful as a musician (XII, 225). She becomes a veritable Saint Cecilia.

Love also resembles another art form—drama. Proust compares Gilberte to the starring actress with whom he is infatuated (III, 127), and his quarrels with her (and with Albertine later on) have an element of pretense that makes them seem like artificially staged misunderstandings or comedies (XII, 196, 198–99, 204). Proust declares however that the same course is followed by him (and by all men) in every love affair. In the *Jeu de l'amour*, he says:

> Quelle que fût la nouvelle 'étoile' que j'appelais à créer ou à reprendre le rôle, le scénario, les péripéties, le texte même, gardaient une forme *ne varietur* (V, 153).

In love we find something of the relationship which exists between parent and child.[1] When we speak of the kindness of the one we love, we are probably only projecting into her the feelings of pleasure which her appearance gives us, *comme les enfants quand ils disent 'Mon cher petit lit, mon cher petit oreiller, mes chères aubépines'* (XIII, 100). When Marcel kisses Albertine, it is he who is the child, and he derives the same sense of satisfaction from the experience as when his mother used to kiss him good-night (X, 329; XIII, 102; XI, 94).[2] On the other hand when he looks at Albertine asleep, he becomes the protective mother while she is the child (XI, 142). After he loses her, he is like an old father who continues to ask news of the son who has long since died (XIV, 18). In the relations between Swann and Odette and Saint-Loup and Rachel, it is always the women who are regarded as the children (II, 27, 43; VI, 147).

There is something about the satisfactions which love can afford that make the experience similar to religious exaltation. The good-

---

[1] Compare the relations of Charlus and Morel, pp. 81–82.
[2] Compare also I, 48–49. These examples are used by Charles Briand, op. cit., to prove that Proust's mentality at least was incestuous.

night kisses which Albertine regularly gives Marcel are said to be holy (XIII, 102), *comme un pain quotidien* (XI, 10), or like the communion wafer, *don du Saint-Esprit* (XI, 94). Albertine so preoccupies the mind of Marcel that one might almost call her his god:

> Je déposais mes doutes en elle, je les lui remettais pour qu'elle m'en déchargeât, dans l'abdication d'un croyant qui fait sa prière (XI, 93).

When they quarrel and finally separate, it is as though Marcel had lost his god (XIII, 26) or become an atheist (XII, 227–28); and after he hears the news of Albertine's death, he likes to imagine that at the last she (also an atheist because of her rejection of him) had perhaps called on him mentally, *de se confesser enfin à lui, de mourir en lui* (XIII, 114).

For Proust, the woman we love is not the real woman as she appears to an impartial observer, but the modified image of her which we carry inside us. Just how and at what moment this image is incorporated in our heart is a matter of chance, and the 'Open Sesame' which accomplishes it may be quite an insignificant combination of words (X, 334). At any rate, when we fall in love, it is as though we had formed a knot (IX, 294) or the first link of a chain (XI, 216) which joins us to our beloved and continues to grow (XI, 33, 240). This chain hampers the loved one (XI, 220) but it also restricts the lover (IV, 34), and it is this aggravating interference with liberty which causes Marcel to think he wants Albertine to leave him.

The disparity between the loved one as she actually is and the image which we carry in our own hearts leads Proust to use metaphors suggesting that our vision is based on a different sort of optics than the normal (III, 198; VII, 229). Women are, as it were, the negatives of our sensitivity (V, 158), or reflectors which redirect towards us the sentiments which we in the first place direct towards them (IV, 14). Or, when we see a woman, it is as though we took a photograph which we develop at leisure (IX, 252) and which we can examine under our own personal stereoscope (VII, 230).

There remains in women an element of mystery and intangibility similar to that of philosophic speculations (II, 108) or algebraic problems (IV, 140; XII, 197). They have about them the charm of strange cities (XI, 211), or the particular province or country of their origin (II, 44; XIII, 313; IX, 170). For this reason, love is like a journey (II, 27, 71, 111, 199). Jealousy especially is similar to a sojourn in a foreign land (II, 213–14).

Love is compared by Proust to electrical and chemical phenomena. The emotions of love penetrate one's body with the rapidity of electric currents (X, 333; XIII, 70; II, 18) and sometimes they are as devastating as lightning (XI, 173; XIII, 14). In quarrels, the electrical forces in the two lovers repel each other with sparks and heat (XI, 111), and jealousy and separation burn the heart unmercifully with electricity (XIII, 138, 150). Our relations with a lover are like those of an experimenting chemist (II, 70), and in quarrels or jealousy, suspicions are always ready to crystallize (XI, 187; II, 134; XIII, 94, 122): *On a toujours l'amour dans son cœur en état d'équilibre instable* (XII, 28).

It is clear from the examples quoted in this section that Proust regarded love as an infinitely complicated phenomenon. By a juxtaposition of the groups of images he used in connection with love, we can perceive how intangible it is and we see to what lengths Proust went to express something of its variety and complexity.

Heredity, Evolution. Influenced no doubt by Mendel and Darwin, to whom he makes a number of references, Proust reveals himself as a staunch believer in the cyclical nature of life and the inevitableness of the influence of heredity. The most interesting case he considers is Gilberte who is a product of the strange union between Swann and Odette. This match is a Mendelian case of cross breeding (III, 55), and Gilberte combines in a curious fashion traits of both parents (III, 171). She is like a new variety of white lilac beside her mother (III, 170–71).

To make more vivid the apparently startling metamorphoses through which human beings logically pass, Proust compares their evolution to that of plants, insects and animals (XV, 79).

In the section on the *Jeunes Filles en fleurs* (p. 62), we have already noted how consistent is the identification of these youthful specimens on the branch of life with spring blossoms of every sort. As they age, however, the flowers wither and hard fruits or seeds are formed:

> Comme sur un plant où les fleurs mûrissent à des époques différentes, je les avais vues, en de vieilles dames, sur cette plage de Balbec, ces dures graines, ces mous tubercules, que mes amies seraient un jour (V, 155).

These fruits or seeds bear a definite relation to the flowers that produced them:

Notre esprit possède d'avance comme certain cryptogame, comme telle graminée, les particularités que nous croyons choisir (V, 155).[1]

Distinguishing inherited physical traits, such as moles or birthmarks, are like the unusual but consistent features of certain families of flowers (IX, 281). People who do not go white with age are like ripening hedge berries which harden and wither without changing colour (X, 23; XV, 94), or lichens and mosses which do not change their appearance as winter approaches (XV, 92). Others, who seem completely altered at different stages of their life, are like trees which change their whole appearance when the colour of their leaves changes (XV, 95). One's development is as firmly regulated as the development of trees (V, 173).

Proust also compares the well-defined progression of human evolution to the stages of development of certain insects (XV, 76–77). The term chrysalis is used in describing the temporary stability of certain phases of change (II, 103), as well as old age (XV, 92) or the preparation for death (I, 195).

The *Jeunes Filles*, besides being compared to flowers, are also said to be like young birds, especially by reason of their immature voices (V, 174–75). These voices develop to be like those of their forbears, and Albertine is like a young finch modelling her accent after that of her aunt, Madame Bontemps (VII, 223).

The unformed features of young girls are like embryos beginning to grow (III, 171), and certain distinguishing family traits are like animal characteristics (pointed muzzle, etc.) (II, 247; X, 142). In old age especially, the grosser features and hardened characteristics remind Proust of haggard animals (VIII, 241; IX, 230), mangy old lions (XV, 195), or almost prehistoric specimens, like the whale (XV, 102).

The cycle from birth to death is like the cycle through spring, summer and autumn to winter. Again, the *Jeunes Filles* are *spring* blossoms (hawthorn, lilacs, fruit trees) and matrons are summer and fall fruits or seeds. Older people are like trees beginning to change their colour and lose their leaves (XV, 81; V, 171), and the illness and death which terminate old age are like the winter storms which whip the last leaves from the trees (XII, 249–50; XV, 229). White

[1] Compare also XV, 108; VII, 12.

hair and pale complexions make Proust think of snow and cold (XV, 74, 76, 81; V, 218) and ice (IX, 118–19, 217; XI, 247–48).

Another cycle which resembles that of life is the cycle from dawn to sunset. The *Jeunes Filles* are rosy like the dawn (XIII, 279), and their features are unexaggerated and delicate, like sea waves in the morning (V, 154). Older women are in the sunset of life when the last rays of light are disappearing (X, 335–36; XV, 107).

The consistent feature which Proust stresses in most of the imagery he uses in connection with the evolution of humans from youth to old age is the process of solidification (*cristallisation*) which takes place; the soft petals of flowers disappear and a hard fruit or seed replaces them; insects form for themselves a hard chrysalis; water freezes into snow or ice; trees lose their decorative leaves and animals conform to the rigid pattern of type: *L'adolescence est antérieure à la solidification complète* (V, 172). He elaborates on this idea by comparing the various stages in the development of an individual to geological periods (XV, 99; XIV, 201) and by comparing youth to wood carving (III, 170) or clay modelling (V, 171). As mature age arrives, the lines of the sculpture take on a fixity and rigidity that cannot be altered (XV, 103).

The comparison of people to statues is one that is used very extensively by Proust. The *coup de ciseau* which determines the exact line a feature will take is a result of heredity (III, 170); nature is the great sculptor who repeats the same line in different generations of the same family (XV, 210). Or, from another point of view, it is the parents who are the sculptors in transmitting features to their children (V, 98; VI, 159). Beautiful women are like wonderful marble statues (VIII, 124; IX, 71, 113), but as they grow old (exposed to the air and the elements), they weather badly (XV, 101, 105; VII, 26) or acquire lichens (VII, 30), until they are more like rough rock (VII, 180–81).[1]

In old age, individuals who have lost their youthful colour are like statues of funereal gods (XV, 91) or monuments on a tomb (IX, 10; XV, 106). They are like embalmed corpses (XV, 147) and their expressions are as grotesque as those of hideous plaster masks (XV, 168) or theatre masks (XV, 107).

The various metamorphoses through which individuals pass are like costumed rôles in a play where accoutrements for the new impersonations are waiting in the wings ready to be donned before

---

[1] Compare also the description of the Duc de Guermantes in old age (XV, 192–93).

the next entry is made (V, 155). If in her early years a young girl
plays with skill the *ingénue*, there is waiting for her later on the rôle
of *douairière* (XV, 98). Her voice alters to suit the part (XV, 107),
and it seems that *il est nécessaire que, dans le divertissement final d'une
pièce, les êtres fussent travestis à ne pas les reconnaître* (XV, 81).

Sickness, Death. When one remembers the number of images
drawn from illness and death that Proust uses in connection with
love, it is surprising to note how very few images he uses when
talking about sickness and death themselves.

Sickness and death are both personified by Proust. The illness
which strikes down his grandmother is described as a stranger (VII,
171–72) or a traveller (VII, 191) who lodges in her body. Death is
said to be a powerful angel who wrestles with her or a sculptor who
finally immobilizes her (VII, 207). It is also like an actor who makes
his entrance onto the stage at the psychological moment (VII, 199).

The struggle for victory which Death wages within the body of
an invalid makes of that individual a sort of soldier in action (III, 85–
86). The doctor who is Death's opponent is like a military strategist
planning the most tactically sound course of action (VII, 179).

We have previously noted how fond Proust is of using reversible
or reciprocal images. A subject drawing images from one field
becomes in turn a source of imagery when that field itself comes up
for discussion. We see examples of this phenomenon in Proust's
treatment of illness and love. Love is like an illness, etc. Curiously
enough, when we come to illness, we find that doctors are compared
to lovers and death to love:

   1. Le médecin consultant, soumis à la question, comme une
   maîtresse adorée, répond par des serments tel jour crus, tel jour mis
   en doute (VII, 172).
   2. Cette idée de la mort s'installa définitivement en moi comme
   fait un amour . . . après y avoir songé sans doute de temps en temps,
   comme à une femme qu'on n'aime pas encore (XV, 223).

Sleep, Waking, Dreams. A la recherche du temps perdu opens with a
discussion of sleeping and waking. Proust is very sensitive to the
difference between the two and particularly to that nebulous region
which lies between them, where one hovers in a state of suspension
not really knowing whether one is asleep or awake. The imagery
he uses makes very vivid the two worlds of consciousness.

Because of the loss of certain areas of sensibility, sleep seems to be a descent (in English we talk about 'falling' asleep) and Proust speaks of the difficulty of remounting the stairs to consciousness (XI, 90) or being pulled out of the pit (VI, 106) or the vacuum (I, 14) where one has sunk. For the same reason, sleep is a sort of petrification or immobilization, and Proust compares it to the chrysalis stage in insects (VI, 107). More picturesquely, he says:

> Près de la grille est la carrière où les sommeils profonds viennent chercher des substances qui imprègnent la tête d'enduits si durs que, pour éveiller le dormeur, sa propre volonté est obligée, même dans un matin d'or, de frapper à grands coups de hache, comme un jeune Siegfried (VI, 105–6).

In sleep, the higher centres of the brain have ceased to function and we more or or less revert to the state of primitive men, animals (I, 14) or even jelly fish (XI, 152).

Because of the different world we appear to enter, the phenomenon of going to sleep can be compared to taking a journey (I, 13, 14; XI, 151; XIII, 95) or a voyage (X, 153; V, 71; XI, 99). It is probably the rhythm of sleep with its resonant and regular breathing that makes Proust think of the sea in connection with it (VII, 195; VI, 103). Or again, it could be the reversion to a primitive state— that of marine life from which all life has sprung.

Sleep can even be regarded as a temporary sort of death, and this together with almost all the above ideas is strikingly expressed in the following interesting metaphor:

> Pour y parcourir les artères de la cité souterraine, nous nous sommes embarqués sur les flots noirs de notre propre sang comme sur un Léthé intérieur aux sextuples replis (IX, 206).[1]

The world to which sleep introduces us is a magic, fairy-tale sort of world (I, 14; VI, 111; XI, 141). Time means nothing there (VI, 103; X, 150, 154), and people exchange heads or faces as easily as faulty statues pieced together by incompetent restorers (IV, 39). Inanimate objects take on life and human beings change sex at will, like the mythical hermaphrodites who are supposed to have been the first semi-divine humans (X, 150).[2] Nightmares are like fantastic albums (VI, 106).

[1] Compare also IX, 208.
[2] The change of sex in dreams along with associated sensations of flying (X, 150) would be interpreted as sexually significant by psycho-analysts.

Proust realizes that dreams often have a logical explanation and, where possible, he seeks to discover it. *Quelquefois, comme Eve naquit d'une côte d'Adam, une femme naissait pendant mon sommeil d'une fausse position de ma cuisse* (I, 13). In his usual introspective fashion, he says that . . . *à la fois Joseph et Pharaon, je me mis à interpréter mon rêve* (IV, 39).[1]

Sleep is very precious because of its restorative powers. It erases the trivial cares of the day like a sponge on a blackboard (XI, 150), but it is volatile and it eludes us if we seek it too eagerly. *Il ressemble à la jeunesse et aux amours, on ne le retrouve plus* (XI, 155). Proust is fascinated by Albertine asleep and he compares the rhythmic sound of her breathing to musical effects (XI, 140, 150, 155). The association of sleep with love and music reveals how precious Proust considers it to be.

In apparently contradictory vein, and perhaps partly because of the fact that he so often needed to resort to artificial means to induce sleep, Proust compares the state of normal sleep to vertigo (VI, 110), drunkenness (V, 70), hypnotism (X, 154; VII, 240–41), amnesia (XI, 150), paralysis (XI, 152) and drug addiction (X, 154; V, 71). The difficulty of waking is just as great, he says, as the difficulty of returning to normal after any one of the above states.

Proust describes the nature of sleep induced by drugs, and he compares the effects of the different narcotics to the aromas of different flowers in an exotic garden (VI, 105). He uses the same comparison to illustrate the different varieties of sleep we experience (XI, 143, 153).

Sleep is partly a change of vision or the method of seeing. Dreams are one sort of lighting (II, 217; V, 123–24) or magic lantern or movie projection (I, 16; VI, 104; XIII, 151–52), and waking is another. When we wake, we have to adjust ourselves to our surroundings, with the result that walls may seem to move about us (I, 15) in a darkness which is like a kaleidoscope in motion (I, 12–13) until we are able to fix it.

Habit. When the narrator first enters a new environment, the lack of any fixed pattern of routine terrifies him. He feels the qualms of one about to dive into cold water (IV, 98). The objects surrounding him seem hostile (IV, 83–84). Each new door has its guardian dragon to be killed by habit (IX, 211), and a strange room

[1] Compare also II, 217.

is as frightening as a doctor's waiting room (IV, 81), a torture chamber (IV, 83) or a lower level in Dante's Hell (IV, 80). Even unfamiliar place-names are disturbing until they have been assimilated (X, 313).

On occasion, Proust regards habit as a beneficial influence. It is like a soothing nurse (I, 159) or a reliable servant whom one puts to work and then leaves unsupervised (XIII, 148). It has the effect of an analgesia (IV, 89) or an anaesthetic (I, 20), and it allows us to exist amid our surroundings in a state of tranquillity and ease (IV, 84).

Habit grows both wider and stronger. It is like a sculptor moulding and fashioning our lives (XI, 81) or a plant which can take root on the most barren rock (VI, 149). It is also like a net (X, 152) woven strand by strand (II, 172), and only by cutting through its cords (V, 56) or lifting its heavy fabric (XIII, 157) can we break away from its encumbrance. The protective barrier of habit can become an immovable wall (IV, 99) and the harmless plant an uncontrollable weed (XV, 56). In our persistence in following the meaningless pattern of habit, we sometimes act like maniacs (XI, 53).

Habit is like aphasia (II, 262) or the progressive death of certain parts of our sensibility (IV, 89–90). It is *une divinité redoutable* (XIII, 9), and even though Marcel is very much upset in a new environment, he later looks back with nostalgia to the freshness and the novelty of the initial sensations just as he remembers the advent of spring (XIII, 157). Habit conceals change from us (I, 32; III, 9), and the effort to break its power is more difficult than turning back an eyelid (IX, 210–11).

The Mind of Marcel. This sub-heading unavoidably appears ambiguous and pretentious, since the whole of *A la recherche du temps perdu* might very well be subtitled 'The Mind of Marcel'. It should be made clear at the outset that what we intend to deal with in this section are images associated with certain mental processes such as the search for truth, the impact of reality on anticipation, reverie, imagination and introspection, etc. Various aspects of the mind of Marcel have already been examined under aesthetics, love and jealousy, and habit, and others will be deferred until the concluding sections of this chapter on personality, memory and time. Uncharitably, one might say that the topics dealt with here consist of those which could not very well be fitted in anywhere else.

In the first instance, it should be noted that Proust consistently stresses the dualism of mind and body. One's mental equipment, unfortunately, is confined within the body, *semblable pour nous à un vase où notre spiritualité serait enclose* (IX, 201). The body is like an antagonistic foreigner (VII, 147) or a being of a lower order of life (VII, 146). Our bodies are as insensitive to pity for us as an octopus (VII, 147), and the animal side of their nature is apparent especially in love (cf. p. 86), sleep (cf. p. 97) and illness (cf. p. 117). They are much like machines (V, 229; XI, 31) or spinning tops (I, 209).

It is impossible for us to see our own bodies objectively as we would see a tree or a house or a passer-by (XIII, 99). Although we are able to get some idea of the nature of our body from a mirror (VI, 126), the real truth is borne home to us by a more faithful mirror—those individuals who are like us in trying to fool other people as well as themselves into thinking that they are different than they are (XV, 86).

Our bodies are our prisons, but when they die, they take with them to destruction our minds (XIII, 220). The only measure of freedom we can achieve while living comes through our minds (I, 121), *comme un fluide qui n'a de dimensions que celles du vase qu'on lui fournit* (III, 61). Indeed, it may be possible that our intelligence is merely a part or a function of the one universal intelligence,

> . . . dont tout le monde est co-locataire, une intelligence sur laquelle chacun, du fond de son corps particulier, porte ses regards, comme au théâtre, où si chacun a sa place, en revanche, il n'y a qu'une seule scène (III, 175).

The various emotions are associated by Proust with the body, even though he admits that *il en est du chagrin comme du désir des femmes, qu'on grandit en y pensant* (XIII, 218). Conversely, one can suppress sorrow by drowning its faint convent bell with the noise of busy life, but when calm returns, sorrow is again audible (I, 55). Proust likes to think of emotions as inner music (VIII, 23; XI, 29–30; XIII, 37) which is perceived by the ear, *exercée, comme le diapason d'un accordeur* (IX, 85). Both joy and sorrow are compared by Proust to drunkenness (VIII, 201; XIII, 126), and the effects of drugs (I, 49; cf. also p. 88).

Joy and sorrow are also said to be like natural phenomena. Joy is like sunshine (I, 246), an opening flower (XIII, 146) or fresh bubbling water (V, 177, 186, 204). Sorrow is like shadow (I, 246) or storms (XV, 45).

Proust delights especially in the exercise of his mental faculties. He compares the action of the mind and the memory to electrical phenomena. A stimulus to the memory is like a magnetized pen which calls up a chain of associated incidents (VIII, 203; XV, 29). The connection between two ideas is an electrical one (XIV, 50, 144), and the analysis which one person must make of another's statements is a process of electrolysis (XI, 108). In his observance of others, Proust makes of himself a sensitive plate (VI, 52). His mind is like a pile developing its electricity (VI, 53), and sudden intuitions are similar to bolts of lightning (IX, 205, 333; XIII, 156). The 'light' of intelligence is itself a sort of elaborate and perfected system of illumination by electricity (II, 73, 74).

The great purpose of the intelligence is to discover truth or reality (X, 332). To this end, our minds are like old Proteus who refuses to be in any sense a slave (XI, 252). Once new truths are attained, we feel impelled to pass them on to others even if we are dying (XI, 180–81).

Tout événement est comme un moule d'une forme particulière (XIII, 115). We may pause to reflect in our journey in pursuit of truth, but we have no assurance that we shall succeed any better thus (XI, 183). The impact of reality or truth generally comes as a shock (XI, 203). It always causes pain (XII, 234; X, 317; XV, 61) or vertigo (XI, 112; XIII, 77), and it benefits from the element of surprise (XI, 203; X, 234).

In trying to penetrate to truth, we have to reject the attracted particles of confusion or error (XI, 29) and the tissue of lies which it may be in others' interest to deceive us with (X, 70; XII, 233). The deciphering of a truth may be difficult (XV, 22), but in analyzing the final result, our intuition, like the ear of a musician (XI, 221) or the response to atmospheric change (VI, 79–80), is infallible. A truth may be like the pale white moon in a cloudy afternoon sky, but its consistency is completely different to the initiated observer (XIII, 227). There is a joy in penetrating to truth that varies directly as the depth to which we had to go to reach it (XV, 46, 47).

The method on which Proust relies to discover truth is that of introspection. To this end, he is a scholar or a chemist, and the truth he arrives at a precipitate which tears his heart since it is formed in pain (XIII, 8).

Proust emphasizes the difficulty of impartial introspection. It is like climbing a steep slope (XIII, 64) or swimming against the current

H

(III, 189). In contrast to it he places the imagination which he compares to a downward grade (XIII, 64). The imagination is a sort of *orgue de Barbarie détraqué qui joue toujours autre chose que l'air indiqué* (VI, 50). It is like a painter in representing what it *sees* and not what it *knows* (VIII, 225). It is fictional (II, 216), and its constitution, *restée rudimentaire, simpliste . . . ne nous permet de voir que fort peu de choses à la fois* (XIII, 94–95). The imagination is nourished easily (VIII, 176), but introspection needs solitude, and the effort required to withdraw into oneself and to penetrate through the surface appearance of objects to the truth they contain is certainly very great (IV, 79–80; I, 241–42). We have to undo the wrapping which hides the real object from view (XIII, 161) or develop in private the photograph of which our eyes have taken the exposure (V, 131).

The little verse about man 'always wanting what is not, never satisfied with what he's got' could be used to summarize one part of the narrator's attitude toward life. His sense of anticipation is very keen, and as a result he is almost always disappointed by actuality. He compares his frantic preparation for his mother's good-night kiss to the preparation for painting of an artist whose sittings are rigorously curtailed (I, 42). His emotion as he awaits an expected event is much like the sense of fear which we have *quand on sait que quelqu'un va entrer pour vous effrayer par une porte qui est encore fermée* (VII, 158). As a result, he is always disappointed, just as *on ne trouve jamais aussi hauts qu'on les avait espérés une cathédrale, une vague dans la tempête, le bond d'un danseur* (III, 126).

Even when Marcel thinks he is about to have his desire satisfied, he turns away in indifference, *comme un baigneur qui va recevoir la lame* (V, 111). The knowledge that he can have the *femme de chambre* of Madame Putbus when he wishes is like having a sleeping powder near at hand; its availability dispenses with the need actually to take it (IX, 159–60). It is only when desire is disappointed that it regains its elastic force (V, 112). Marcel cannot adjust himself to his failure and continues in his route, *comme un élève refusé à un examen voudrait répondre à une question de plus* (VIII, 18).

Personality of Marcel and Others. Proust's theory of the nature of one's personality is very closely linked to his theory of memory and it also relates to his ideas on heredity and evolution. He believes that all individuals are continuously changing and, while this process cannot be evaluated from day to day, over a longer period of time the alteration is quite remarkable. It is a biological process (I, 120), and we are like plants which grow and change completely, even though the pattern of evolution is fixed and determined by our heredity, just as it is for plants (XI, 133–34).

Proust thinks of the successive stages in personality as something applied over a fundamental core (IV, 56). He compares the super-posed and hardened layers of our nature to insect chrysales (IX, 217), shells (VII, 129) or geological stratification (XIII, 158; I, 248, 250–51). Growing older is a sort of progressive death (XV, 15). To penetrate to our former selves is like sounding the depths of the sea (VI, 209; I, 67).

The only connecting link between our successive personalities is the memory (XV, 129) or the will (V, 129–30). Proust allows himself here to get caught in a seemingly glaring contradiction, for in the first of these references he speaks of *notre personnalité identique* (XV, 129), whereas in the other he mentions *nos personnalités successives* (V, 129). The discrepancy, however, may only be an apparent one. We are, after all, unique individuals despite the sometimes startling alteration in our personalities. The various changes are linked or threaded together and under the influence of memory they can reappear individually or simultaneously (XV, 139). We are like an actor playing a variety of rôles (III, 208; V, 70). They are assumed and rejected in turn, but there is always the same person behind the different disguises.

The fact that we are constantly changing and that other people are also developing in their own way and at their own speed accounts for the difficulty we have in understanding others and arriving at any final analysis of their character. Their real nature and our conception of their nature are like two discs (I, 237) or an object and its reflector (VI, 45) which we seldom manoeuvre so that they coincide exactly. When we happen to meet people at a stage in their development where they mirror and faithfully reflect our own habits, friendship springs up (IV, 152). We make our great mistake in forgetting that others are fluid like ourselves. We only receive one impression of them at a time, each like a photograph (XIII, 78; XI, 184; XV, 129) and some apparently contradictory, but our intelligence must sort out those essential to the real action of the drama of life and discard the others (VI, 171). Other people play different rôles, just as we do ourselves (XV, 75, 77, 90, 140), and their different appearances are as varied as those of a dancer under different coloured lights (V, 221) or the many heads of one Indian god (V, 184; VII, 233).

Before we meet people, we build up pre-conceived notions of what they will be like, similar in their detail to paintings (XI, 83) or stalactites (III, 150). Reality forces us to re-edit completely our conception (II, 150), and we then continue to preserve that one until forced into a new one. This has the result of making these different conceptions of individuals as distinct as if they were real metamorphoses (IV, 191; V, 133), different family portraits (I, 32–33) or people from different planets (XV, 160). Also, *ces modifications de la notion qu'on a d'une personne ont l'instantanéité d'une réaction chimique* (V, 99).

When we first meet new people, their appearance has the enigmatic quality of a puzzle (X, 40) or an examiner (XV, 107–8). We do not know how to assess them, but they are in the same quandary as far as we are concerned and sometimes misinterpret the rôle we are playing (VIII, 142). You cannot always judge a bird by its plumage (IX, 335–36) or a person by his expression of the moment:

> Nous ne sommes pas un tout matériellement constitué, identique pour tout le monde et dont chacun n'a qu'à aller prendre connaissance comme d'un cahier des charges ou d'un testament (I, 31).

Proust likes to compare the difficulty of reading faces to that of deciphering manuscripts in foreign languages (V, 44, 144; IX, 23, 225; XI, 107).[1] People are also like landscapes or buildings (XIII, 236) which change their appearance in perspective. Very often we alter our first impression only to return to it later.

The great difficulty, as far as Proust is concerned, is to penetrate into the real nature of other individuals. This is harder, he says, than the study of astronomy (XI, 235), chemistry, medicine or law (XII, 142–43). The elusiveness of others leads Proust to compare them to mere silhouettes (XIII, 250), shadows (VI, 81; X, 235–36, 270–71) or turbulent colours (XIII, 127). Their eyes alone reveal something of their feelings, but very often they are only like reflecting mirrors (XII, 228) or black glass (VIII, 57).

Thoughts cannot be transferred in their essence from individual to individual; they are diffused in the corolla of the face (XIII, 49) or

[1] Cf. also p. 82.

the halo we add to them ourselves (IV, 36). The thought we assimilate from another is no more his thought than is the reproduced
sound at one end of a telephone wire the *same sound* that entered it
(XIII, 189; V, 198).

Proust compares his method of trying to penetrate the real
nature of others to X-ray examination (III, 199; XIV, 33) or placing
images in an inner stereoscope (VIII, 201).

We make a mistake in assuming that the brains of others are,
unlike our own, inert receptacles incapable of chemical reaction (I,
142–43). We are deceived by appearances, like a dog chasing the
shadow of an insect or a man looking in a mirror (IV, 85).

Other people are no more real as our friends than the furniture a
madman lives with and talks to (XV, 18). Even the person we love
is like an actress, her stand-in, or a simple projection—we cannot
tell which (VII, 228). What we love is not her but the image of
her which we possess inside us. This image is a sort of double (XII,
63) or *poupée intérieure à notre cerveau* (VII, 240). It is not a unique
image, as we might think, but it has been, *en réalité refaite par nous
bien des fois* (IV, 37).

Memory. The unity of any one individual is provided by his
memory. Memory is like a thread that joins together the most
disparate manifestations of the evolving personality (V, 100). The
interconnecting links between various memories form a pattern and
a strong tissue of cross-references that make the memory appear as
a sort of weaver (XV, 140, 208; XIV, 186). Memory is also a chain
where one link leads to another (XV, 12; V. 223). This chain may
be a magnetic one (XIV, 50; VIII, 203; XV, 29), since one memory
attracts another. From this point of view, memory is also a road
(XIII, 175) with various side-roads (IV, 149; V, 100), or a work of
art with overall linked strokes (VII, 188). Because of its dimension
in time, memory appears to have roots (XI, 119; XIII, 62). It is
only the present moment which floats for the time being without
roots (XII, 192).

For Proust, memory is a real storehouse. He compares it most
frequently to a book or manuscript (XI, 105–6; VI, 82; XIII, 116;
XV, 15; IV, 146–47) or a library (IV, 55; XIII, 158), but he also
compares it to a drug store (XII, 235–36) or a photographer's salon
(V, 153). Memory is like a quarry where our minds chisel countless
statues from the numberless blocks of stone to be found there (XV,

31; XII, 102). This solid quality of memory is emphasized particularly by Proust. Memories, for him, are like statues (XI, 245; VIII 25), furniture in a room (XIII, 157), natural objects under the water (XV, 23) or buildings restored stone by stone (I, 224, 251).

In the introduction to this study, we have already had occasion to comment on the predominantly visual quality of Proust's imagery. In analyzing images connected with memory, one cannot help being struck by the same thing. Proust's voluntary memory, at any rate, is essentially a visual memory. The passing days are like the pages of a book which can be turned back at will (XV, 15, 16; XIII, 104). Our memories are like works of art (XI, 31; V, 134; VI, 12; XV, 93; I, 33; VII, 210) or photographs (XI, 184; XIII, 96; XIV, 209; XV, 8; V, 135–36, 153). They resemble illustrations in books (XV, 157) or the little bits of paper which, when put in water by the Japanese, turn into flowers, houses and people (II, 69). Sometimes they are just spoken of as images (XV, 87–88; III, 79) or doubles (VI, 43). Backgrounds are like stage-settings for the drama of life (I, 68–69). They too are visual, and one can confront them with reality for verification, just as a musician refers to a score to check his memory (XI, 32).

Even though memory is like a store-house or a library, there are many items deposited in it which may never be referred to again. One impression succeeds another like images in a magic lantern, and they are forgotten just as quickly (V, 69). Memory, like personality development, is a cumulative process and we build on top of what has preceded *et que nous ne retrouvons qu'au hasard d'une fouille* (VIII, 182). People we no longer see are as good as dead for us (IX, 147), and our mind is like a cemetery where their memory is buried (XIII, 83; XV, 110). Forgetting is an obliterating force, like fog over the sea (XIII, 219). It is like a devouring python (XIII, 42) or a progressing malady (XIII, 179), but it is also a beneficial force:

> S'il est vrai que la mer ait été autrefois notre milieu vital où il faille replonger notre sang pour retrouver nos forces, il en est de même de l'oubli, du néant mental (V, 70–71).

Despite the fact that Proust's memory is predominantly visual, he attaches greatest importance to the organic memories of smell, taste and kinaesthetic sensation. Even though these memories are not an intellectual thing, they preserve impressions of the past long after the mind has consigned them to oblivion, just as certain plants or animals continue to live after man himself has died (XIV, 8). We find this phenomenon in kinetic sensations (I, 15) and in the sense of taste and smell (I, 68). It may also be a complex impression involving several sensory areas such as response to a calm fresh atmosphere (VIII, 24–25; XI, 36).

In any case, whenever an organic memory operates, it does so without the intervention of the intelligence. Proust calls it involuntary memory. The effect of this sort of memory is twofold. In the first place, it serves to recall a flood of visual memories that have long since sunk below the level of the conscious memory of recall. The experience is similar to that of being magically transported to other climes by a genie from the Arabian Nights (XV, 10). There is no effort involved, but only a feeling of ease and freedom, like a plane taking off or a carriage rolling on smooth grass (XIV, 200). The second important result is that involuntary memories serve to recall emotions as well as impressions. These emotions may be pleasurable, like the effects of love (I, 65), or painful, like a funeral service for one's father (XV, 28). They resemble the impressions one has of seasons—warm summer (XV, 35) or cold winter (XI, 31).

Time. The important thing about man is his memory, for it alone permits him to exist both in the present and the past. It alone allows him to be conscious of the passage of time and to evaluate it.

Man is *un de ces êtres amphibies qui sont simultanément plongés dans le passé et dans la réalité actuelle* (XIII, 145). Sometimes the past can be rejected, as it is by drunks or heroes or bees stupefied by smoke (V, 63–64). Then other people and ulterior considerations are no more important than soap bubbles or froth on a wave (V, 65). More often, however, our past is an ominous shadow for us casting its gloom over the future (V, 64), or a great mountainous weight on whose summit we are perilously perched and without which we cannot move (XV, 229).

There are two kinds of time—chronological time (which is the same for everybody) and *le calendrier . . . des sentiments* (IX, 201) which differs from individual to individual and within the individual from year to year, day to day, or even hour to hour.

We all have within us time-pieces or *cadrans intérieurs* (XV, 155), but they are regulated differently for each individual. This results in the fact that our daily habits of sleep and working, action and conscience, differ. We each follow a parallel path or a different train track, and the result is that our actions (like ornamental flower pots along alternate sides of the path) never coincide with those of others (XV, 142), and our speeds differ, so that some people arrive at premature old age long before others, just like an express train at destination (XV, 105).

To complicate matters, the speed at which time moves for one individual varies. It is as though we were automobiles with different gears. Some days are like steep slopes that require a long time to mount, and others are easy down grades that one rushes along (II, 233). An afternoon can seem a vast stretch of time with every second an individually noticed point (II, 253). A day can seem as long as those at the north pole in summer (V, 52–53) and a space of three days like the endless history of the Papacy (VIII, 7). A year can seem like a century (XIII, 86). The intervention of sleep in particular confuses the impression of time since sleep has its own clock (X, 150)

In theory, we know that time passes, but we are no more aware of it than of the revolving of the earth (III, 70). The world itself is like a great sun-dial where only the present is lit, permitting us to tell what time it is (XIII, 255–56). We are not conscious of change until we suddenly realize, like a day-time traveller, that the sun, instead of being ahead of us, is now behind us, and evening approaching (IV, 83).

What helps us to become conscious of time is our relations with others. They are associated with us in this fourth dimension which makes them seem like giants bestriding the years (XV, 230), and from the change in them and our associations with them, we can be made aware of the continuing evolution of life. For the narrator, the one person above all who performs this special function is Albertine. She occupies such a large space in his life and his thoughts that she becomes, as it were, a goddess of time (XII, 230) or a miraculous mirror which reflects time, both past (VII, 216; VI, 176), and, in the past, what was then the unknown future (XII, 182).

III

SOURCES OF IMAGERY

En moi, quand la maladie aura fini de les jeter l'un après l'autre par terre, il en restera encore deux ou trois qui auront la vie plus dure que les autres, notamment un certain philosophe qui n'est heureux que quand il a découvert, entre deux œuvres, entre deux sensations, une partie commune.

—A LA RECHERCHE DU TEMPS PERDU (XI, 13.)

THE title of this chapter is perhaps a little misleading, since to investigate the ultimate sources of all of Proust's images would be a task of incredible complexity. It is meant only in the purely literal sense that some images are derived from nature, some from science, literature or the arts, and others from personal experience.

In the preceding chapter, we have analyzed at some length the images associated with various themes in *A la recherche du temps perdu* and it is not the intention to provide here a cross index to that material. At the same time, it is most important to consider collectively all the images drawn from a given source without reference to themes. For example, Proust draws on flower imagery primarily in connection with the young girls, but it is also used by him in descriptions of eyes and clothing, and it is especially important in his analysis of the effects of sunlight and the sensations of sleep. Different aspects of the nature of flowers are stressed in the different cases, but the same essential source is used.

This appraisal of Proust's images is most significant from sheer weight of statistics (See Appendix 6). It reveals immediately, for instance, that by far the most important source of imagery in *A la recherche du temps perdu* is nature and not, as Mouton would lead us to believe, the arts.[1] Proust is very sensitive to flowers, fruit, trees, birds, animals and all aspects of landscape and rural life. He draws especially on water imagery—brooks, ponds, and the sea. One might relate these two fields of interest to his youthful visits to the country and his trips to the sea-coast, but whatever the cause for their utilization, they run as the principal *leit-motif* through the whole of Proust's long work.

[1] See p. 2 above.

NATURE

A distinction must be made between those images drawn from nature which are unlearnèd in quality and those which are more closely related to the special fields of botany, zoology, geology, and so forth. These latter will be considered separately under the sciences, but if the division seems an unnatural one to the reader, all he has to do is turn over a few pages and compare what is said here with what is said there under the above special headings.

Flowers. For Proust, blossoms symbolize the ultimate in beauty. Taken at the peak of their development, they represent in a tangible way the intangible and the transitory. Their perfume, their colour and their form seize our attention involuntarily and we perceive in their exquisite perfection a recurring symbol of our desire for the truly beautiful.

Proust compares perfection of literary style to the blossoming of a spring hedge, and the young girls who arouse in Marcel feelings of love and desire are said to be like flowers.[1] He also compares to flowers the older women he admired so much—Odette (IV, 47; XV, 112), Madame de Guermantes (XI, 45). The material of Odette's beautiful costumes is like flowers (III, 208; IV, 48), and the ravishing eyes of the Duchess are like periwinkles (I, 240; VI, 13) or myosotis (XII, 93). Her mouth is also like a flower (II, 155).

Proust invariably associates flowers with love. Love letters are like fresh flowers (IX, 304), kisses like spring blossoms (II, 33), and Marcel himself in love like a flower (XIII, 185). Mental images which he builds up about places or people he desires intensely to see are also like flowers (II, 263–64, 230).

Friendship is like a flower (VI, 127) and birds in their intangible but exquisite beauty are said to be similar to flowers (IX, 265, 269; II, 255). One is constantly running into curious cross-references in the imagery Proust selects. This comparison of birds to flowers is such a case, for we have already noticed that flowers are used to stand for the young girls Marcel loves; birds are used extensively for the same purpose, and the comparison of birds to flowers joins the third side of this interesting triangle of inter-related images.

---

[1] These flowers are very often roses. See Charles N. Clark, 'Love and Time: The Erotic Imagery of Marcel Proust,' *Yale French Studies*, no. 11 (1953), p. 84.

It is also pertinent to note that the love of Odette and Swann is symbolized by a flower (the Cattleya) as well as a piece of music. When Marcel first sees Gilberte, it is against a background of flowers, and the encounter of Charlus and Jupien is associated with the orchid of the Duchesse de Guermantes.

We have already noted how important a rôle sunlight plays in Proust's life.[1] It is no accident that he so often compares the effects of sunlight in the blue sky (VI, 173) or in the sunset (I, 178; V, 50) to beautiful flowers.

Virtues like goodness are similar to a red poppy blooming in a lonely valley (IV, 174), and the social intercourse of conversation, promenades and compliments are bouquets of a less noble order.[2]

Gardens. It is only natural when Proust has such a high regard for flowers that he should consider a garden, particularly in the calm hush just before the break of day, as a composite symbol of the acme in beauty. The young girls in a group are compared to a lovely rose garden (V, 170), and the city of Venice which is unique, as far as Marcel is concerned, in living up to the wonderful imaginary picture he had made of it is like a fabulous garden in coloured stone (XII, 261).

For Proust himself, sleep was something elusive and precious. Because of his asthma, he had great difficulty in finding normal sleep, and what is just an ordinary experience for most people became for him something unattainable and much to be sought after. Perhaps this is why he compares varieties of sleep to flowers in a garden (VI, 105; XI, 153). Albertine waking has the freshness of a garden in the early morning (XI, 143).

The mind of Elstir, filled with the wonderful things which he alone sees, is like an inner garden (X, 103).

Plants, Bushes, Trees. Proust is especially fond of comparing human life to plant life. The unvarying pattern of evolution in plants is considered by him to be analogous to the development of humans, which sometimes appears to us so fortuitous simply because it is spread over a much longer period of time. A human being is

---

[1] See p. 20 above.

[2] Actual flowers referred to by Proust in comparisons include the lily-of-the-valley and carnations (V, 103, 104); roses (II, 252, IX, 272 etc.); poppies (IV, 174; XI, 216); myosotis (I, 87; XII, 93); iris and buttercup (VII, 115); hyacinth (VI, 173); periwinkle (VI, 13); violet (IV, 48); magnolia (I, 28); camelia (V, 219); geranium (V, 33); nymphea (IV, 110–11); nenuphar (I, 227); lilac (I, 185); hawthorn (I, 155); cattleya (II, 28, etc.); orchid (IX, 12, etc.); *primula veris* (IX, 42); *lythrum salicoria* (IX, 41); colæus (IX, 304).

just like a plant or a bush or a tree; heredity here plays the same important rôle, even though environment may wield a modifying influence, as it does, for instance, when a tree grows on the edge of a cliff (II, 151–52).

Hair and skin are like distinguishing types of foliage (V, 149; I, 98; IV, 131), and individuals are indigenous to their district just like the plants that grow there (I, 213). The resemblance between people and plants is most striking when the former are immobile like the attendants around a hotel (IV, 132, 152–53; IX, 222) or like Albertine asleep (XI, 84).

The effect of light on a steeple or a balcony is sometimes to make such architectural elements appear like living plants or bushes (II, 240; X, 191). The reality or truth which Marcel seeks behind outer forms seems to be separated from him by a sort of bark which he has to tear aside or penetrate (IV, 149; I, 243; XIV, 61).

Within the individual, habit is like a plant or, better, a weed (XV, 56). It grows roots which penetrate deeper and deeper. Memory also is like a rooted plant but current events float for the moment unattached (XII, 192).

Fruit, Seeds. Just as he compares young girls to flowers, Proust compares older women to fruits or seeds. Young girls have delicate complexions like roses, magnolias or camelias, but older women or less attractive young ones resemble in their colouring raspberries (XI, 126), tomatoes (IX, 323), apples (X, 65), hedgeberries (X, 23) or overripe fruit (IX, 119).

Juicy fruits such as pears and oranges must undoubtedly have been among Proust's favourite foods (VIII, 256). He uses the visual similarity between the moon and an orange to form at least four separate images, and the refreshing juice which can be squeezed from an orange is used as a basis for comparing the satisfactions to be derived from love (XII, 232; XIII, 99; XIV, 172). The young girls are like sun-ripened fruit (V, 73–74, 224) and Albertine is the opulent fruit to which Marcel devotes all his energies (XI, 204). Her breasts are like fruit (XI, 96). When Gilberte uses Marcel's first name, he has the impression of being like the pulp of a ripe fruit held in her mouth (II, 250).

A surprise or anything intensely coveted is compared by Proust to a fruit ready to squeeze—the room where Marcel's family are entertaining Swann and from which his mother refuses to come (I,

48), the room where Swann thinks Odette is betraying him (II, 78). The sunset is sometimes like a rosy and appetizing fruit (IV, 74).

Seasons, Weather. From this source alone, Proust draws no less than 180 separate images. He makes reference to all the seasons of the year, to rain, snow, hail, sleet, thunder and lightning, wind and calm. He also utilizes the rainbow, northern lights, cloud effects and sunshine in different comparisons.

We have already noted that for the narrator, perfect weather is to be found on bright, clear days in spring.[1] He uses this as an ideal comparison (II, 232; XIII, 157). Once he compares beautiful fruit to a warm autumn day (IV, 122), and glistening snow is in itself an object of beauty to which he compares furs (IV, 45), cloth (III, 208) and moonlight (X, 141). Apart from these few favourable references, however, all the seasons of the year apart from spring are merely steps along the road to the death that is symbolized by winter.[2]

Sadness, disillusionment and despair are compared by Proust to cold and winter. Old age with its brittle rigidity and its snowy hair is also like this most unpleasant season of the year. Fog is associated by Proust with winter except for two instances, once when it is used to describe a dress worn by the Duchesse de Guermantes (XI, 39), and in the case of Mademoiselle de Stermaria where it becomes a symbol of her mysterious Breton origins and something that fascinates his imagination (VIII, 10–11).

When we come to wind, we find that Proust compares the faint sounds which reach the plugged ears of an invalid to the soft whispering of spring breezes (VI, 91). Except for that one favourable reference, again to Proust's preferred season of the year, wind is used in comparisons to indicate unpleasant contrary influences, emotional upsets and quarrels (XII, 249; VII, 206; VI, 76; IX, 221).

Quarrels are also symbolized by electric storms (X, 91, 94; XII, 29; XI, 53), though thunder is itself used separately to describe the noise of a bus (II, 210) or laughter (VIII, 130–31), and lightning to characterize glances between individuals (IV, 189; VI, 75) or sudden intuitions (IX, 333; XIII, 156). About all that can be said in favour of storms is the relief one feels after they are over (XI, 238; X, 200). This comparison serves to describe a feeling of relaxation or abandon.

[1] See p. 23 above.
[2] Note, for example, the references to summer at V, 171; XV, 81.

For Proust, clouds are usually a sign of an approaching quarrel (XI, 127), but they also symbolize other sorts of presages such as the influence of heredity (IX, 123). In the sunset, clouds are objects of beauty (II, 251; VI, 42). The rainbow and northern lights are also signs of beauty (V, 97–98; X, 243).

Proust uses the dawn to describe spiritual rejuvenation (XIII, 190) as well as youth (V, 171, 201; XIII, 279). Old age is like the sunset, and the disappearing beauty of ageing women resembles the fading rays of the sinking sun (X, 335–36; XV, 107). Bright sunlight is used synonymously with fire, and tapestries, flowers and masonry are said to be on fire when they are brilliantly illuminated (XIV, 8; III, 209, 210; I, 92). Other bright objects such as eyes, faces and even noses are said to seem to be on fire (IX, 50; IV, 72; X, 66).[1]

Since sunlight represents peace, joy, beauty and pleasure (XI, 69–70, 195; IV, 59), shadow quite naturally stands for such opposites as confusion, uncertainty, sadness and despair (XV, 46; III, 114; XIII, 146; I, 246). It is also used, however, to symbolize something that is attached to our personalities and from which we cannot flee —our past or our future (V, 64). It is further employed to stand for that which is mysterious or impenetrable, such as the personality of another individual (VI, 81; X, 270–71).

The sky is used by Proust to describe umbrellas and eyes, because of their roundness (IV, 49; VII, 33, 60), and the latter also because of their blue colour (V, 149; X, 65; I, 239).[2]

General atmospheric conditions are used especially in describing moral atmosphere and truth. Self-evident facts make their influence felt like temperature or air-pressure (VI, 79–80; XI, 184), and Marcel's own mind and memory are subject in their reactions to the same sort of all-pervasive influences (VIII, 25; XI, 67; XIII, 43, 90; XII, 201).

Landscape, Perspective. Proust uses landscape and perspective in a variety of ways. He compares the physiognomy of individuals like Albertine to a landscape (XI, 84, 96; XII, 226) and he also considers their moral nature to be three-dimensional in perspective (V, 133). He regards his memory as a sort of landscape in panorama, and

---

[1] For images relating to the moon and stars, see below under Astronomy.

[2] It is interesting to note that the only eyes Marcel finds beautiful are blue eyes. Albertine has blue eyes (V, 220; XI, 21) and so do the members of the aristocratic Guermantes clan: Mme de Guermantes (see pp. 73–74), Robert de Saint-Loup (XIV, 185), the Duc de Guermantes (X, 55).

different episodes stand out against it in relief (XI, 131; XII, 230; XIII, 167–68). Sleep presents us with a different sort of landscape (XI, 153).

The world of society is also like landscape and the human vegetation in it changes with the seasons just like trees and plants (X, 285; XV, 81; IV, 129; XII, 36). The changing world of the theatre is another realm in which landscape and perspective affect the view (III, 131; VI, 53–54).

People, because of their associations with the geographical area from which they come, are often spoken of by Proust as being like the landscape of their native habitat (VI, 16; VII, 97).

Birds. It is only natural that along with flowers and plants, Proust should compare people to various orders of living creatures such as animals and birds. For this purpose, he also actually utilizes such sources of imagery as insects and fish, but all of these different categories merely serve to emphasize particular qualities of man's nature as well as to relate him to the other orders of life around him.

Proust occasionally uses bird imagery casually. He compares children at play to black martins wheeling and circling (VI, 115) and servants with their apparently undirected motions to macaws at a zoo (V, 58). Stupid people are parrots (XV, 49) and turbanned women following the new style a sort of noisy kind of bird (XIV, 45). Madame Verdurin is also like an unpleasant sort of caged bird, possibly a parrot (I, 278), and Monsieur de Norpois is, according to Bergotte, a cranky old canary (III, 168). Inept repartee is compared to birds flitting from perch to perch (IV, 9; VIII, 157).

Apart from these few derogatory comparisons, Proust generally uses bird imagery, like flower imagery, in connection with what he admires or desires or what he considers beautiful. A lovely sound is like a bird's song (I, 12; VI, 55; V, 62–63), and the music of Vinteuil itself reminds Marcel of birds' calls (II, 180; XII, 60). Beautiful costumes are like bird plumage (II, 110; VI, 69); stained glass throws light like a peacock's tail (I, 87), and an exquisite sunset (which we know to be much admired by Proust) is compared to the tints in a bird's wing (IV, 69).

The Guermantes family are said to have something ornithological about their appearance (XV, 143; VI, 97).[1] This shows up

[1] Cf. pp. 71–72.

especially in Madame de Guermantes (VI, 34–35, 74–75, 97) and
Saint-Loup (XIV, 15), but is even evident in the young daughter of
Saint-Loup and Gilberte (XV, 210). Madame de Marsantes is like
a mother bird whose favourite young one is her son Saint-Loup
(VII, 94, 126; XIII, 309).

Proust associates birds with Gilberte and her friends (II, 244;
XIII, 210; XV, 23), with the young girls at Balbec (V, 31, 36, 37,
174, 225; X, 331), with Albertine especially, and by extension with
love in general. He compares the narrator in love to a captive bird
(XII, 247)[1] and uses bird imagery in describing the relations between
Mlle Vinteuil and her friend (I, 219) as well as Charlus and Jupien
(IX, 13) and Charlus and Morel (X, 248–49; XI, 65; XII, 143).

The most consistent use of bird imagery in this connection is, of
course, that associated with Albertine. She is herself like a bird
(XIV, 186; XI, 214) or an elusive winged creature (XI, 113, 213,
214); her eyes are like a bird's nest (XI, 86), her hair like a bird's
wing (XI, 94; XII, 226), and her voice like that of a bird (XI, 142;
VII, 223). Her leg is like a swan's neck (XI, 96; XIII, 138) and her
dressing-gown is adorned with birds (XII, 245). Even the window
she opens in defiance just before she goes away makes a sound like
the cry of a screech owl (XII, 248). The rings she leaves behind her
are carved with an eagle's head (XIII, 63). Marcel in his worry over
Albertine is like a caged bird (XII, 247), and after she leaves him he
is like the enchanted bird which could only repeat the name of the
beloved (XIII, 23).[2]

Albertine is associated by the narrator with the seabirds at
Balbec because she and her friends first used to appear on the beach.
Later, when she becomes his captive, she is like a caged bird whose
natural habitat is elsewhere and who is unwilling to be confined in
restricted surroundings. Representing as she does an object of love,
it is logically fitting that she should be compared to transient and
elusive things like birds or flowers.

Animals. Proust regards men from one point of view as merely
an order of living animals—likeable in certain respects if you wish,
just as pet dogs or cats are likeable, but more often unattractive as

[1] The narrator is also compared (though not in connection with love) to an owl (X,
152) and a jay (IX, 313), and when he goes to bed as a child, it is as though he were
making himself a nest (I, 16–17).

[2] Specific birds associated with Albertine are the gull (XIV, 186), the swan (II, 96),
the kingfisher (XI, 86), the gold finch (VII, 223; V, 220) and the screech owl (XII, 248).

symbols of baseness and stupidity. Intelligence alone sets men apart from animals, and when it is inoperative, as for instance when men sleep or feel the approach of death, then the animal side is predominant (VII, 195; I, 14; VIII, 241; IX, 240–41). Homosexuals in particular are like cornered or caged animals (IX, 60, 61; IV, 197).

Proust uses animal imagery most often in describing the world of society. Here one might say the intelligence is least in evidence, and Proust delights in comparing all sorts of different ranks to animals of one kind and another. Servants are like the animals one catches to domesticate for labour (II, 144; I, 162). Jews are like hyenas (VII, 15; XV, 132). The so-called élite of society are like rabbits (VIII, 99; VI, 50), sheep (X, 8), donkeys (VII, 141) or bats (XI, 48), and even the exalted rank of *altesses* are just a type of animal (VIII, 57). The Princesse de Luxembourg is condemned particularly because she tends to regard Marcel and his grandmother as animals in a zoo (IV, 124; VIII, 57). Relations between the Duc and Duchesse de Guermantes are like those of a wild beast and its intrepid trainer (VIII, 152; IX, 97; XV, 195). Madame de Cambremer, in talking about music, is like a disgusting sort of animal that slobbers all over the place (IX, 266, 277–78).

The two kinds of animals Proust refers to most often are cats and dogs, which is prosaic enough. Servants or lower classes are like humble dogs (XIV, 67; IV, 63; XIII, 23; II, 143). Well-trained, dogs are used in describing an orderly fire (VI, 90) or Andrée's docile hands (V, 187); impetuous and energetic, they serve to picture the animal spirits of the youthful Albertine (X, 199; XV, 60). Albertine is also often compared to a cat (XI, 16, 93; V, 220; IX, 294; X, 243, 336), and both these comparisons to animals which are virtual household prisoners are logically appropriate to the situation in which Albertine finds herself in Marcel's home. Before she is captured and trained, she is a wild beast (XII, 225; XIII, 237).

By and large, Proust's animal images are logical and can be explained satisfactorily. There are two special cases, however, which ought to be mentioned even though they are not explained. Their final source lies perhaps in the realm of the psychological and we shall have to wait for others to offer it. The first concerns Swann. Thinking of Odette, it is said that he felt that . . . *cette pensée y avait sauté en même temps et s'installait sur ses genoux comme une bête aimée qu'on emmène partout et qu'il garderait avec lui à table à l'insu des convives* (II, 74).

I

The second concerns the narrator waking up and trying to decide whether he had called Françoise or whether she had just come on her own accord. He asks himself if she does not just exist in his chest:

> La distinction des personnes et leur interaction existant à peine dans cette brune obscurité où la réalité est aussi peu translucide que dans le corps d'un porc-épic et où la perception quasi nulle peut peut-être donner l'idée de celle de certains animaux (XI, 151).

Rural Life. It is always somewhat artificial to divide sources of images into various classes, but there seems to be no way out of it. Under this heading, for instance, it seems expeditious to include references to cultivation of the land, rural scenery, farm creatures like fowl, cows and horses, and general references to peasant life. The living creatures could perhaps have been considered above among animals and birds, and one might argue that peasant life does not really belong under the general heading of Nature. There is some justice in these arguments, and if the reader feels that the statistics in Appendix 6 are erroneous on that account, he can readjust them accordingly.

Proust makes many references to ploughing and ploughed fields. The church steeple ploughs the furrows of the sky (I, 90) or its impression ploughs a furrow in our minds (XV, 38–39). The sea, on occasion, looks like a white and dusty ploughed field (IX, 235–36). The narrator's grandmother has cheeks brown and furrowed like autumn fields in fallow (I, 198), and a woman who attains a new sort of beauty in middle age is like a field which could not produce grapes but is ideally suited to the cultivation of beets (XV, 101).

The references to chickens in Proust are mostly associated with the laying or hatching of eggs. The narrator compares his impression of joy after writing the piece about the three steeples to that of a chicken crowing after it has laid an egg (I, 245). The chick which comes from an egg or the egg in which one hears sounds of the young bird about to emerge are so disparate and bear so little relation to each other that Proust uses the phenomenon to illustrate social change (XIV, 48) and the feeling of excited anticipation one has before the curtain goes up at the theatre (III, 26).

Apart from the above references, chickens as well as cows and horses are used in describing the stupidity, vulgarity or actual physical repulsiveness of human types (XI, 48; VII, 66; X, 278; XIV, 72; IX, 87; V, 89).

It cannot be denied that Proust reveals in his general references to rural life a detailed knowledge of peasant customs and a keen interest in their traditions, which is perhaps no more than one might expect from his many visits to Illiers.

The fields at Méséglise are said to be continually criss-crossed by the wind which is likened to a vagrant tramp (I, 197). Françoise in the home of Marcel's parents in Paris brings with her *l'air de la campagne et la vie sociale dans une ferme* (VI, 77).

Proust delights in comparing the Guermantes family who are at the very top of the social ladder to peasants who are so close to the land and nature. Both the Duc and the Duchesse de Guermantes illustrate this feature in their pronunciation (VIII, 47, 127; XI, 41–42), and Madame de Villeparisis in her dress (VII, 25), even though in their conduct they are so far removed from attachment to the traditions of the soil (VIII, 72–73; IX, 110–11).

The Sea, Water. If the examination of the sources of Proust's imagery undertaken in this chapter revealed nothing else, it would be significant in drawing attention to the extent to which Proust draws on water imagery. We have already mentioned that images drawn from nature provide the largest class of images in *A la recherche du temps perdu*, and within it, those drawn from fresh water and the sea constitute the most important single source of imagery in the whole of Proust's long work. These images occur in profusion from the very first volume right through to the end of the last volume. They are particularly common in the parts dealing with Balbec, but they are by no means restricted to the consideration of any one or two main themes. They total no less than 326 separate images in all.[1]

Without going into any possible psychoanalytic reasons there might be for Proust to concentrate to such an extent on water imagery,[2] one can say at the outset that this particular source of metaphor is logically well-suited to his conception of the nature of the universe. He constantly emphasizes the process of continuous

---

[1] For the distribution of water images throughout the 15 volumes, see Appendix 7.

[2] The sea is a common maternal symbol. Proust associates it with milk (X, 46), and nearby cliffs with breasts (IX, 235; V, 204). See Gaston Bachelard, *L'Eau et les rêves,* Paris (1942), pp. 20, 156, 158, 161, and C. J. Jung, *Psychology of the Unconscious,* translated by B. M. Hinkle, New York (1947), p. 244.

change that is going on around us in other people, in society, in nature and even in those apparently permanent things like buildings and institutions. Water, as fluid, best represents this state of constant change. The sea is continuously fed by streams of all sizes and its surface may vary as the weather varies, but essentially, despite its movement, it remains a mysterious, impenetrable constant (XII, 230; XV, 117).

Broadly speaking, any recurrent metaphor tends to become a symbol. Flowers symbolize young girls and storms symbolize quarrels. When this convention is accepted by the reader, the author can refer to flowers or storms without the intermediary of the metaphor or the simile and know that his reader will understand what he means. These become public or common symbols.

Private symbols are another matter. Here the author may use a repeated metaphor without ever indicating to the reader what he means by it. The reader may form his own conclusions, but he has no way of verifying them except by weight of evidence and laws of probability. It does not always matter whether the reader understands the author's symbol or not.

Proust belongs to the Symbolist tradition in French literature, but he differs from the other members of the group in his desire to express clearly in words the most elusive sensations and thought processes.[1] By the particular use he makes of imagery, he renders in concrete, visual terms the most elusive mental conceptions. At the same time, he remains faithful to the leadership of Mallarmé in retaining for his own personal delectation certain private symbols that do not in any way obscure the meaning of his work but which add to it, once they are understood by the reader.

The private symbols employed by Proust are based on the etymologies of proper names. Among the proper names in *A la recherche du temps perdu* some are entirely invented, others modified in form and still others ordinary names of common currency. It would be a mistake to assume that every single name had some special significance for Proust, but in view of his profound interest in philology, it would be equally wrong to suggest that he was unaware of the etymology of the very important proper names which recur again and again throughout his long work. Guermantes is such a name, and we have already indicated our theory concerning

[1] See, for example, the following: Emeric Fiser, *La Théorie du symbole littéraire et Marcel Proust*, Paris (1941), Intro.: pp. 9–11; Irma Tiedtke, op. cit., p. 21.

the etymology of that name.[1] Combray is another, and it is intimately tied up with water imagery.

The etymology of Combray (Combres, etc.) is well-known to all philologists. It means a confluence or the meeting or junction of rivers. Combray is Proust's private symbol for the meeting or junction of his past and the present and of the lives of so many people who seemed to him far removed from each other and from him—those like the Swanns, the Guermantes, Legrandin and the Vinteuils.[2]

The special significance of the name Combray is clearly indicated by Proust in the final volume of his work where he gives keys to so many of the enigmas of the earlier sections. In speaking of the successive changes in social position which any one individual experiences, he says:

> Je voyais que ce phénomène social n'était pas aussi isolé qu'il m'avait paru d'abord et que du *bassin* de Combray où j'étais né, assez nombreux, en somme, étaient les *jets d'eau* qui symétriquement à moi s'étaient élevés au-dessus de la même *masse liquide* qui les avaient alimentés (XV, 134).[3]

On the next page, in referring to the career and life of Legrandin in relation to his own, he goes on to say that

> . . . celle de Legrandin me semblait n'avoir aucun rapport et avoir suivi un chemin opposé, de même que celui qui suit le cours d'une rivière dans sa vallée profonde ne voit pas qu'une rivière divergente, malgré les écarts de son cours, se jette dans le même fleuve (XV, 135).

Surely here Proust provides us with a very obvious key to this particular private symbol! Added weight is given to this interpretation when we consider the number of water images associated with Combray. The narrator's room is as fresh as water (I, 117). The people sitting at their doors are like seaweed or shells festooning a river bank (I, 125) and soldiers passing through the streets are like a furious current scarcely contained by its channel (I, 124).

The two principal ways which diverge from Combray and finally meet there again are those of Swann and the Guermantes. Their union is symbolized in the person of Mlle de Saint-Loup,

[1] See p. 70 above.
[2] The importance of Combray as the very centre of the novel has been emphasized by Benjamin Crémieux. See Curtius, *Marcel Proust*, p. 109.
[3] The italics are mine.

grand-daughter of Swann and daughter of Robert de Saint-Loup. The proper name Swann would appear to be a rather obvious water image (see especially XV, 173) and even though Proust associates fire imagery with the Guermantes, he also associates water imagery with them. It seems incredible that Swann's way and the Guermantes way should eventually come out at the same place, just as water and fire symbolize incompatibles, but in the long run they are shown not to be irreconcilable. The burning golden sun sinks at length into the blue ocean and all men are shown to partake of the same essential qualities.[1]

The ocean quite logically stands for the world of society (XV, 135). Compared to it, the social life at Combray for a person like Swann is a mere lagoon (III, 179–80). In the vast ocean of society, certain characteristic features contribute an impression of permanence, despite the fact that the details may change (VII, 113). There is always a Princesse de Guermantes, even though the title is held consecutively by different individuals (XV, 117), and there is always love, even though the individual we love may differ (XIV, 176). To this extent, both these phenomena may be compared to the sea. The eternal variety of the presence of young girls is like contemplating the sea (V, 172), and Albertine herself summarizes the mystery and the infinity of the sea (XII, 230).

Proust is consistent in his association of water imagery with Albertine despite certain other obvious related image-patterns such as flowers, birds, captive animals, etc. Even in these latter cases, however, there is often a connection with the sea. Albertine is a *jeune fille en fleurs*, but the flower is *la rose carnation d'une fleur de plage* (IX, 171) or *un géranium au bord de la mer ensoleillée* (V, 219). Referring to Albertine and her companions, the narrator says: *Ces jeunes filles, tiges de roses dont le principal charme était de se détacher sur la mer* (V, 217). In a group, they sometimes remind him of marine specimens— zoophytes, madrepores, polyps and minnows (V, 73, 75). In addition, he often compares them to seabirds such as gulls (V, 31; IX, 214; XI, 86; XIV, 186) or migratory birds assembling on the shore before they fly south (V, 36, 225; X, 331).

Albertine's personal appearance is constantly related to the sea (V, 81, 221; XI, 83). For the narrator, her nose is like a little wave

---

[1] Let us remember here the golden hair and the blue eyes of the Guermantes clan as well as the blue eyes of Albertine. It would appear to be significant that when we are finally told the 'true' surname of Françoise, the epitome of the French peasant and of Combray, it should turn out to be *Larivière* (XIV, 184).

(V, 154) and her hair seems to be transposed into waves (XI, 21). Her breath is like a sea-breeze (XI, 84–85). Her eyes are fluid like the sea (V, 220; XI, 21), and even her cheeks, when flushed with joy, are bathed in . . . *une clarté si mobile que la peau [devient] fluide et vague* (V, 220). Her *peignoir* reminds him of Venice and its canals (XII, 209–11, 240–41), and when she leaves him, it is as though he had lost a sea-shell which he never valued at its true worth until it was no longer his (XIII, 49). In the famous description of her sleep (XI, 84–89), Proust extends the metaphor; her breath is a sea-breeze or the sound of waves, her pearls like the chain holding a boat at anchor, her legs are like a swan's neck (XI, 96, but also XIII, 138) and Marcel's leg against hers like an oar dragging in the water. She herself is the vast and complex ocean (XI, 83, 129).

Even after Albertine has left Marcel, she continues to be associated with water imagery. He imagines her bathing with other young girls (XIII, 138), and conflicting ideas about her beat back and forth in his mind like ocean waves (XIII, 145). When he receives letters from her posthumously, it is as though he saw . . . *la même place de sa chambre occupée par un canapé et par une grotte* (XIII, 77).

Albertine is always associated by the narrator with Balbec, and this constantly recurring proper name runs through the novel as a *leit-motif* representing Marcel's love affair with Albertine.

> Je ne sais trop si c'était le désir de Balbec ou d'elle qui s'emparait de moi alors, peut-être le désir d'elle étant lui-même une forme paresseuse, lâche et incomplète de posséder Balbec (VII, 217).

Albertine and Balbec are practically synonymous (VII, 230; IX, 231).

In the novel, the etymology of the name Balbec is discussed at length by Brichot (X, 95–96). The first syllable is said to be a corruption and it is not fully explained, but the termination *-bec* clearly means 'a stream' in Norman dialect. Various other occurrences are cited. For the narrator, then, Balbec represents his love for Albertine, the stream which opens into the sea of love and by its special qualities acquaints him with that vast, fundamental and enduring experience known to all men in all generations.

People are often compared by Proust to fish. The glassed-in dining-room at Balbec is like an aquarium (XIII, 130) and its occupants like exotic specimens of all sorts (IV, 101–2). Other restaurants are also compared to fish pools (V, 61, 62) and various individuals in higher society are compared specifically to fish: Madame de Guermantes (XV, 82), Monsieur de Guermantes (VII, 56–57), Charlus (X, 235–36; XI, 253), Monsieur de Palancy (II, 149), etc. In love, Proust uses the old metaphor of being 'caught on the hook' (XIII, 54), but he also compares the girls who attract one's fancy to fish to be angled for (V, 41).

The extension of sea imagery to social relationships is very elaborately developed by Proust. An individual in society is like a swimmer in the ocean. New surroundings or new experiences are as hard to take as a header into cold water (IV, 98; I, 288), and trying to go against social prejudice is like swimming against the waves (VII, 254). The Princesse de Parme, exposed to the daring unorthodoxy of Madame de Guermantes, is like a bather prudently trying to enter the stinging but refreshing waves of the ocean (VIII, 95, 109–10, 120, 140).

Besides being like a swimmer, the individual in society is like a passenger on a boat. Social upsets are compared to shipwrecks (VII, 68; IV, 108), and great controversies like the Dreyfus Case or international war are compared to violent storms at sea (VII, 15; XIV, 95; IX, 105). The movement of people or the dissemination of ideas or customs is much like the irresistible force of sea waves or the power of the tide (III, 119; VII, 146; XV, 100; VII, 41). The bourgeois Madame Verdurin launching herself in higher society is similar to a voyager trying brief crossings but unable yet to overcome sea-sickness on the high seas (X, 138).

People are sometimes compared by Marcel to ships (XIII, 326), and when he hears the double news of the strangely assorted marriage of Saint-Loup with Gilberte and Jupien's niece with the young Cambremer, it is as though two ships attached to his past were raising anchor and sailing away (XIII, 299). Social position is similar at any given moment to a ship riding at anchor (XIII, 291).

Social relationships generally, with their appearance of unity in the midst of continual change, are quite vividly epitomized by Proust by comparing the social hierarchy to the open sea (III, 179–80; XV, 135). Each wave in the ocean might be said to represent a social group as it comes to the surface and rises or falls. Its sense of perspective is derived only from those entities immediately above or below it, while those which are more remote might just as well be lost in the sky (III, 55; XII, 36) or across a bay on the opposite shore (IV, 129). Ideas in a group are propagated by the same irresistible force as the tide or great waves (X, 8; XV, 100).

Proust uses sea and water imagery very extensively in his analysis of the intellectual workings of the narrator. This overall pattern relates to the mental cycle of memory and intelligence which finds its beginning and its end in Combray. Our very minds are fluid, and any impression, whether it be factual memories or emotions such as sorrow or love, is like a construction in sand and water; it is bound to disappear eventually (I, 283; IX, 233). Forgetting is like an obliterating fog over the ocean (XIII, 219).

The narrator speaks of his memory and of the rôle other people play in it in terms of depth. Sometimes our disparate memories of other people are like drawing a pail up a well so that the container swings from side to side touching opposite walls of the shaft (XV, 140). More often memory is like something stirring at great depth which releases, as it were, a bubble that surges to the surface where it bursts (IV, 78; IX, 149; I, 67; VI, 45). Individuals, because of their transient importance in our lives, are like soap bubbles (V, 65).

Proust constantly speaks of the narrator in terms of marine imagery. Life is like a sea or a beach, and jealousy or separation have the effect of isolating Marcel amid the bleak surroundings of a desolate seascape (XIII, 129, 147). Tears of sorrow or disappointment flow in their own particular channel (IV, 20), and love itself merely opens a lock in the reservoir which supplies us with fresh streams (XIII, 46). Misunderstandings seem to introduce a waterfall between Marcel and Gilberte (IV, 18). Waiting for love from a woman who, it is clear, will never give it, makes the narrator like those bereaved mothers who continually wait for news of their sons lost at sea when it is quite evident that they are never going to come back (III, 203).

In the realm of nature, the narrator is always seeing marine effects even in those aspects of landscape that are far removed from the sea. This is a part of the technique of reciprocal images about which we have already spoken, but in this case the explanation of it goes deeper. It is obviously directly related to Proust's conception of the sea as a symbol of the eternal constantly changing.

Spring blossoms are compared by the narrator to sea foam (IV, 133; I, 185) or boats (I, 189). They are as fresh as water drops (I, 193), and the breeze bearing their perfume is like sea breakers crashing at his feet (I, 198). Lighted houses at night are like little boats floating on the dark water (I, 206). Fresh air and fine days are like cool water (VII, 160; V, 195), and the effect of sunlight is often to make things look wet or as though they were at a great depth under sparkling water (II, 276; VIII, 14; VII, 241). The sky with its clouds is like the sea with its sportive sharks or dog-fish (I, 223).[1]

Proust compares many common things to marine objects. Churches are like cliffs (II, 227; V, 165–66), sea-shells (I, 94) or fish (X, 193) and cherries are like coral (X, 175). Silks and muslins are fluid in their grace (IV, 23), and hair arrangements especially remind the narrator of waves or seaweed (V, 218; II, 145). It is specially significant that the little *madeleine* cake which, when dipped in tea and tasted by the narrator, calls up the whole train of reminiscences about Combray, is shaped like a shell (I, 65), and lest it be thought that attaching any importance to this is altogether ridiculous, we should note that in the sketch of this episode in Proust's early work, *Contre Sainte-Beuve*, it is not a *madeleine* at all which evokes the experience, but a bit of toast.[2]

The most elaborately developed sea or water image—and, indeed, the most complicated single image-pattern in the whole of *A la recherche du temps perdu*—is the comparison drawn between members of the *Faubourg St.-Germain* in their boxes at the theatre and marine deities in their grottoes (VI, 42–69 but especially VI, 47–49). This image draws upon Proust's knowledge of the classics, and we shall consider it again under that particular heading, but it also is fundamentally a water-image which relates members of the Guermantes clan to the *bassin de Combray*. Madame de Guermantes, like the *madeleine*, symbolizes for the narrator *tous les plaisirs du faubourg Saint-Germain . . . sous ce petit volume, comme dans une coquille entre ces valves glacées de nacre rose* (VI, 42).

From one point of view, *A la recherche du temps perdu* is the story of how Proust came to write his great work. His desire to express himself by means of the written word dates from Combray, and it is in memories of Combray that he finally experiences the activating stimulus which sets him to writing. Proust regards the mind and memory as fluid and uses water imagery in connection with both. It is not surprising then that he speaks of literary composition in the same terms. The charm of certain aspects of Bergotte's works is *pur comme celui d'une source* (III, 162), and a real masterpiece is like an

[1] It should be noted that five of these examples (I, 185, 193, 198, 206, 223) are drawn from the scenery on the walk to Méséglise—*Swann's* Way.

[2] Op. cit., p. 54.

artesian well; the deeper the human heart is penetrated through suffering, the higher it will mount (XV, 59). Any work of art is like a ship and it must be launched well into the future where there is depth enough for it to float (III, 131). Genius is a rising tide that engulfs life and transforms that which it portrays (V, 107).

In describing the effects of music, Proust uses many marine images. Certain devices employed by Wagner resemble great storms at sea (XII, 60; XI, 208-9), and the music of Vinteuil reminds both the narrator and Swann of water. The accompaniment in a certain passage is like the lapping of waves in the moonlight (I, 282) or the enveloping spray of sea billows (V, 229), and the little phrase when it appears, is like a climber in the mountains seen at a great distance through the veil of a falling cataract (II, 67). The overall effect of the music is like the eternal variety and satisfaction to be found in the waves of the sea (XI, 197; XII, 68).

In the theatre too, applause is likened by Proust to the sound of mounting waves in a storm (III, 31). The gestures of La Berma are reminiscent of leaves and vegetation displaced by water as it escapes (VI, 57), and both the stage and the actress are compared by Bergotte to submarine effects (III, 167).

In all these fields, water imagery implies, we believe, the quality of eternal presence and change. Music, literature and drama, as well as painting, provide the deep satisfactions which are comparable to the feeling which comes from the contemplation of the sea.

One might go on almost indefinitely pointing out the very many different ways in which Proust uses water images. Sleep, because of its rhythm and its immobility, is often compared to the sea (V, 71; VII, 195; VI, 103; II, 217). The conversation of Madame de Guermantes is like the sea (VIII, 138), and street criers remind Marcel of the sound of waves (VI, 158). Charlus in his manner of speaking throws out words as the tide does little waves (XIV, 204-5; X, 134). Madame de Guermantes and the Guermantes name remind the narrator especially of water (VI, 11, 14, 16, 42), but the same is true of Marie Gineste and Céleste Albaret (IX, 312, 316, 317, 331). Death is comparable to the tide which carries off some men and leaves others (X, 8). Waves are also used to describe the effects or the attractions of love (XIII, 109; V, 177, 186, 199; VII, 232). They describe the effects of heredity, particularly as it operates in the case of the *jeunes filles*, Gilberte Swann and the Guermantes (V, 154; VIII, 73; III, 171).

Time itself is like water, and the days are crests of waves in the eternally moving sea (IV, 71). Man is guided in his orientation by a sort of inner compass (IX, 177–78; III, 196), and, in his ability to live both in the present and, through memory, in the past, he is a kind of amphibious creature (XIII, 145). He is as it were a swimmer in time (XV, 95), and by means of his memory he can alter the level of the basin in which he floats so that he is now able to recall one part of his life, now another (XIII, 241–42).

Images drawn from water and the sea play a vital rôle in *A la recherche du temps perdu*. They are the images best suited to Proust's conception of the universe, and he utilizes them for that reason in describing the social hierarchy and the relation of the individual to it. He also uses them in describing the individual's relation to love and to time, and the result is to make of this one source of imagery the most important underlying pattern of imagery in the whole work.

COMMON OBJECTS

Before proceeding to a consideration of the images in Proust drawn from literary and artistic sources, it would seem reasonable to consider here those comparisons which employ as their second term some common object from everyday life. Grouped together will be found such disparate things as gold, silver, jewels, mirrors, leather, doors and keys. It would seem artificial to classify these objects under such sub-headings as mineralogy, handicrafts, carpentry and applied physics, and for that reason they will each be considered separately here. If the reader wishes to alter statistics, he may easily do so on the basis of Appendix 6.

It is self-evident that when an author uses a familiar object or material in a comparison, he must utilize those particular character-istics which are universally recognized and accepted as distinguishing that object from other objects. Lead is heavy, steel is hard, and gold is precious. To this extent, any author's use of common objects in figures of speech is bound to be unoriginal, and this is just as true of Proust as of any author. The only way a writer can introduce new perceptions is in pointing out features of common objects not ordinarily noticed or in building up consistent patterns based on the ordinarily accepted connotations. Both these devices are used by Proust in order to avoid the platitudinous, which he hates so much.

Metals, Jewels and Enamel. Lead is twice used by Proust in describing the effects of old age where the soles of the shoes seem to be weighted with that metal (XV, 74, 92). Silver is used to describe the hair in old age (XV, 103) and it is also used to characterize the class of society between the *Faubourg St.-Germain* (which is pure gold) and the lower *bourgeoisie* (IV, 51).

In *A la recherche du temps perdu* one can isolate various quests which the narrator pursues consciously or not in his search for a meaning to life. These are all closely associated with imagery drawn from gold. Marcel's first love is nature, and on the walks at Combray he seeks truth in nature. Through the many elaborate descriptions of trees, flowers, birds, and fish in *Du Côté de chez Swann* runs the elusive glint of the gold which represents the ideal being sought. Light is gold (II, 78), and the effect of the sun on rocks (I, 240) or wet surfaces (VI, 71; XI, 11, 13; XV, 159), a wall (V, 229), leaves (I, 198; XI, 11) or snow (II, 241), is to transform them into gold. Fine days are like precious gold (II, 240, 241, 244, 251, 275; V, 229–30; VI, 107), and when the curtains in his room are drawn back to reveal outside a hot, midsummer day, the narrator is reminded of a precious golden mummy (V, 230). The narrator tells us, significantly, that if he were on his deathbed and a warm ray of sunshine penetrated the room, a part of his personality would respond to it and rejoice (XI, 13). The golden sun has the power to rejuvenate him (IX, 11), and in the significant aesthetic experience of the three steeples, the towers themselves are said to be gold (I, 245) along with the notes of the striking bells (I, 122, 225; XI, 101). Behind the golden sun on the rock (I, 240) and the three steeples (I, 242–43), there is some message which the narrator cannot quite seize.

Gilberte was the narrator's first innocent love, and again a gleam of gold runs through the references to her. Her hair and skin are golden (III, 170) and her eyes are like gold or fire (II, 247–48). Her team in the Champs-Élysées is also gold (II, 244) and Marcel eagerly covets a place on it. The Swann home where he has his first experiences in the world of society is like gold (III, 125, 141, 209).

Through the years the narrator is constantly attracted to strange girls. They may be milk-maids, waitresses, passers-by whom he never meets, but the sight of them fills him for the moment with urgent desire. These girls are often compared to gold, flame or the sun (II, 279; IV, 71–72; V, 138, 184; XI, 172, 206; XIII, 86, 181, 332). One in particular whom he sees from a railway carriage is especially remarkable:

> Au-dessus de son corps très grand, le teint de sa figure était si doré et si rose qu'elle avait l'air d'être vue à travers un vitrail illuminé. Elle revint sur ses pas, je ne pouvais détacher mes yeux de son visage de plus en plus large, pareil à un soleil qu'on pourrait fixer et qui s'approcherait jusqu'à venir tout près de vous, se laissant regarder de près, vous éblouissant d'or et de rouge (IV, 72).

In another comparison, water and fire are symbolically linked with a specific reference to alchemy which makes the image particularly significant:

> Et cependant, la supposition que je pourrais un jour être l'ami de telle ou telle de ces jeunes filles, que ces yeux dont les regards inconnus me frappaient parfois en jouant sur moi sans le savoir comme un effet de soleil sur un mur, pourraient jamais par une alchimie miraculeuse laisser transpénétrer entre leurs parcelles ineffables l'idée de mon existence, quelque amitié pour ma personne, que moi-même je pourrais un jour prendre place entre elles, dans la théorie qu'elles déroulaient le long de la mer—cetter supposition me paraissait enfermer en elle une contradiction (V, 40).

This refers of course to the band of young girls whom the narrator met at Balbec. As a group, these girls are shining rays of light or *gouttes d'or toujours dissemblables et qui dépassent toujours notre attente* (XI, 77). One of them, Andrée, has hands as gold as autumn leaves (V, 187); another, Gisèle, is all gold (V, 149), but most especially, Albertine, the great love of his life, is associated with gold (XII, 159). The light on the stairs signalling her arrival (IX, 166) and the light in her room (XII, 159) are gold. In the curious symbolic passage where the narrator falls desperately in love with her just after convincing himself that the attraction was transitory, we find this description:

> Je ne pus retenir un sanglot quand, dans un geste d'offertoire mécaniquement accompli et qui me parut symboliser le sanglant sacrifice que j'allais avoir à faire de toute joie, chaque matin, jusqu'à la fin de ma vie, renouvellement, solennellement célébré à chaque aurore, de mon chagrin quotidien et du sang de ma plaie, l'œuf d'or du soleil, comme propulsé par la rupture d'équilibre qu'amènerait au moment de la coagulation un changement de densité, barbelé de flammes comme dans les tableaux, creva d'un bond le rideau . . . dont il effaça sous des flots de lumière la pourpre mystérieuse et figée (X, 334–35).

At Balbec, which is also said to be gold (IV, 93; VI, 98), the narrator first met Saint-Loup who was to become his great friend and the Open Sesame to the Guermantes clan. Saint-Loup like all the rest of the family (VII, 42; VIII, 72; XV, 143) has hair and skin of gold (IV, 159; VI, 73, 74; XIV, 82), but he is the most notable:

> La couleur qui était la sienne plus que de tous les Guermantes, d'être seulement de l'ensoleillement d'une ournée d'or devenue solide (XIV, 15).

Madame de Guermantes has the same colouring and even the hair on her arms, impalpable as that of a Duchess should be, is *comme une vapeur dorée* (VII, 244). In her voice *traînait . . . l'or paresseux et gras d'un soleil de province* (VII, 33. Cf. XII, 211). Knowing Proust's interest in names, one can be certain that the choice of her Christian name—which is O*r*iane (cf. VIII, 119)—was no accident.

The narrator does not find the truth he was seeking in social relations with Mme de Guermantes any more than he did in love or friendship. He does not find it in travel either. He had always wanted to visit Italy and especially Florence and Venice, cities of gold (II, 227, 235; XII, 240–41, 245). When he finally does see Venice it charms him but, like everything else, it does not bring him the complete satisfaction which he sought. It is only after the narrator has finally renounced all desire to write and reconciled himself to mediocrity that he accidentally discovers the touchstone he had been seeking.

Throughout his life, the narrator had been interested in the expression of beauty through art (Cf. I, 118). The great actress, La Berma, whose soul he described as a central ray or flame (VI, 58), used her golden voice to recreate dramatic masterpieces (III, 19) which, like other aesthetic experiences, the narrator in his youth completely failed to understand. The painter, Elstir, and the writer, Bergotte (who himself is gold (I, 138)), transmute reality as it reaches their senses into a strange form which is representative of their inner worlds (V, 87–88, 90–92; XIV, 93). Their genius operates at high temperatures which have the power to dissociate and re-group atoms in completely new ways (V, 118). It is the catalyst or transforming power. Bergotte is even spoken of as an alchemist, since he transforms into the gold of his art the cheap gold he uses to pay girls who provide the experiences which activate his artistic powers (XI, 227). For Bergotte, art is more important than life, or perhaps we should say Art *is* life. When he is very ill, he goes to see a painting by Vermeer, despite the fact that it may be the death of him. This is actually the case, but Bergotte dies revelling in the truth presented to him by the contemplation of an exquisitely painted bit of yellow-gold wall in the picture he has gone to see (XI, 231–32). This truth is like the narrator's golden sun on the rock (I, 240) or the three gold steeples (I, 242–43), but it is presented to us through art, the only transmutation which we are able to assimilate.

Jewels also stand for anything precious or beautiful in Proust's mind; the dead grandmother's handbag (IX, 218), a lovely woman (II, 108), an exquisite dress (XI, 45)—all these are compared to gems.

In particular, Proust uses onyx, diamonds, opals, pearls and agates in comparisons with eyes, which he loves to compare to jewels (IX, 51; VI, 52; V, 220; XII, 226; XV, 148; XI, 212; VII, 87). The changing expression in eyes is our only clue to the thoughts that are going on in the minds of others, and this elusive change is compared by Proust to flaws in jewels (IX, 149; XIII, 163).

Images referring to opals or agates with flaws or distinguishing veins or markings are frequently employed by Proust. Such gems are used to particularize outstanding family traits such as are found in the different members of the Guermantes clan (IV, 160; VIII, 72). They are also used in more invidious comparisons where Jews are individualized (VII, 138). The effect of moonlight in woods (XIII, 81) or sunset (V, 55) is compared to agate or onyx. Synaesthetically, Proust compares such disparate phenomena as the conglomerate odours of spring (XII, 258–59), a heterogeneous vocabulary such as that of Françoise (VI, 26), and musical effects to veined agates and opals (XII, 71).

Proust often uses jewels in his descriptions of nature. Water in the sunlight is sapphire (XIII, 256) and ocean waves are emerald (IV, 91), topaz (IV, 93) or agate (V, 80). Snow under moonlight is jade (XIV, 57), and the darkness of night encrusts buildings with an opalescent mother-of-pearl (IV, 69). A grey day does the same sort of thing (VII, 215). Sunlight through stained-glass windows is sapphire (I, 87) and the red-tiled floor at Combray is porphyry (I, 102).

In an isolated comparison, potatoes are compared by Proust to ivory (XIV, 25). Another substance which is used more frequently by him is crystal. It is used to describe the quality of voices (X, 131) or music (II, 154), and Norpois employs it conversationally to indicate that Vaugoubert's motives and character are too transparent (III, 144). Most often, however, like gold and jewels, it is used to describe the effects of illumination, either of the sun (V, 92; XI, 32) or a glowing fire (III, 125).

Enamel is used in two sorts of images by Proust.

First of all, because of its use in works of art, it is employed to describe static beauty. A fish (VI, 143–44), mistletoe berries (II, 276), the sea (X, 46), and sunlight on buildings (V, 230) or grass (VI, 112) are all compared for their effect to products of the enamel worker's trade.

Then, because of the hardness of enamel, Proust uses this figure to describe Gilberte's attitude toward her new name of Saint-Loup, which she thinks has been *incorporé à elle comme un émail mordoré* (XIII, 307). A fixed stare is also *aussi indestructible qu'un émail cuit* (X, 203).

Mirrors. In mirrors, Proust finds a very fertile and stimulating source of imagery. The fact that mirrors reflect, that they reflect in reverse and that they reflect accurately in every detail provides him with several incidental features which he fully exploits in widely different fields of analysis.

There is a common French proverb to the effect that: *Les yeux sont le miroir de l'âme.* Proust concurs that eyes are like mirrors (IV, 144; V, 220), but he says that they merely give us the illusion of being admitted to the soul (VII, 129). More often than not, what we see in eyes is our own reflection (V, 132), and we can never penetrate past the unique brittle surface which any given individual presents to us and to us alone (VII, 129).

On the other hand, mirrors do reflect accurately, and mutual attraction between lovers or friends may be said to compare to faithful reflection. Those we like are those who mirror our own tastes and habits (IV, 152). The only way we can ever see change in ourselves is to see that change reflected in others who have altered in a way paralleling our own evolution (VI, 126; XV, 86).

Mirrors present us with reflections which are the reverse of reality. Memory is like that, since it usually begins with the present and moves back into the past where beginnings logically lie (III, 187). For this reason, appearances can deceive us, and reality may be just the reverse of what we believe it to be (IV, 85). Any loved one is, as it were, a mirror of the past, since through this person we can retrace in inverse direction the change which has occurred in our own personality (VII, 216; VI, 171).

K

For Proust, mirrors and their images symbolize the identical or the inseparable (V, 66; IX, 234). Looking into the past, one can see in individuals reflections of what they later became, even though, at the time, it would have been impossible to forecast those very developments (XII, 182). Creative artists must identify themselves with what they are portraying, just as a mirror does (XIV, 37). The result of this is that their works, whether in painting or literature, also may be said to be mirrors of the world or mirrors of truth (VI, 153; I, 134).

Household Utensils, Furnishings, Etc. Proust uses many common household objects in his images, very often no doubt without consciously considering their actual source. No arguments are being advanced as to the significance of the choice of particular images and for that reason a division of this sort ought not to be controversial. Its only aim is to be logical.

Proust compares specific events to moulds of unique form (XIII, 115), and memory is said to be a mould which determines our attitude toward situations or people we have previously encountered (IX, 283).

Baskets are used by Proust to describe the distended abdomen of the pregnant kitchen-maid (I, 113), the bay of Balbec (IV, 95), and the upper balconies in a theatre which seem suspended there like the containers in which flower pedlars carry their wares (VI, 165).

Containers referred to as *enveloppes, vases clos, boîtes* or simply something with a cover are used by Proust in a variety of ways. People, houses, flowers, *Le Côté de chez Swann, Le Côté de Guermantes,* —all of these things are regarded by Proust as external manifestations which cover an inner truth to which one must penetrate (I, 32, 184, 241; IV, 12; XIII, 84). He even regards his own body as a container in which spirituality is enclosed (IX, 201). The dimensions of this container seem to change depending on our attitude and the attitude of others (III, 61), and the memory of others is enclosed within us until something occurs to bring it out into the open (XIII, 273). Even such intangible things as a space of time or a spoken sentence are regarded as containers, the one holding smells, sounds, emotional and bodily sensations (XV, 30) and the other holding (or refusing to hold) truth or a hidden meaning (II, 185; X, 70).

Walls or barriers are used in quite ordinary ways by Proust. They stand for obstacles in love (IV, 19), protective interest in others (VIII, 94) and the exclusive quality of conversation in a foreign tongue (III, 193). Habit builds walls (XV, 55), and reality in its solid undeniable firmness is also a wall (XI, 112).

Windows quite logically represent openings in walls or barriers of one kind or another. Eyes are like windows since they reveal to us the little we can perceive of the souls of others (I, 192; II, 267; III, 95). A great interpretative artist is like a window opening on a masterpiece (VI, 56–57). Windows also let in fresh air and the sight of beauty out-of-doors. Women in a salon, for that reason, are like windows (VII, 34), and Odette promenading, surrounded by men, is like a window framed by *les mouvements presque mécaniques d'un cadre inerte* (IV, 47).[1]

Locked doors are barriers or obstacles just like walls. A dialect is such an obstruction (XI, 191), and the only key which will open this particular door is the learning of the *patois* (XI, 192). In our relations with others, we are separated from truth or reality by locked doors, and the only way we can penetrate beyond these barriers is by using the keys provided in subtle comments or changing attitudes (IV, 140; VII, 103, 104; XIII, 232). Experience is a lowly and humble door, but imagination is a golden one (IV, 122).

Stairs are only once used by Proust when he speaks of climbing the stairway of dreams back to consciousness (XI, 90). A cloth material and the evening sky are compared to wall-paper (II, 277; VI, 116). The rosy sky at sunset is also compared to kitchen fires (XIII, 187). A church steeple is said to be like a brown velvet cushion resting on the pale sky (I, 93). Memories are like furniture in our minds and we are careful to avoid bumping into objects that will hurt us (II, 141; XIII, 157).

Knives are used by Proust in two sorts of comparisons. Because of their metallic colour and the sinister cutting edge which is associated with it, they are employed in a description of the first light of dawn in the sky (XIII, 83; II, 276). The hostile blue eyes of the Duc de Guermantes partake of the same quality (VII, 43), and a certain dark-haired editor is like *un couteau à papier en ébène* (X, 55). Because of the sound knives make when they are sharpened or struck against a plate or a glass, they are used by Proust in descriptions of auditory impressions such as the noises a car or street-car makes (X, 171; XI, 29), or unpleasant voices (XI, 51; IX, 74).

---

[1] The significance of windows in the sexual experiences described by Proust is pointed out by Howard Moss, op. cit., pp. 44, 46, 54–55.

Saint-Loup's glance is like a drill rather than a knife (VI, 145), and the Prince de Foix makes you feel that your hand is in a vice when you shake hands with him (VIII, 64). The balance scale is used by Proust in figures involving the basis of judgment in personal affairs (IV, 179; III, 196–97; III, 23), politics (VII, 101) and aesthetics (XI, 232).

Divisions, Pieces, Fragments. Certain divisions which Proust uses in metaphorical expressions are closely related to walls but they are referred to by Proust by the vague term *cloison* rather than *mur* or *muraille*. Many abstract things are seemingly isolated by a *cloison*— the life of a strange girl (IV, 72), the seasons of the year (IV, 46), different parts of our existence (VII, 107), our habits (IV, 99).

But any of the above and many things which we consider indestructible can be broken up into fragments. Our idea of a strange girl (V, 119), our pride (XIII, 135), a long isolation (V, 167) —these can be crumbled into bits either actively or retrospectively.

Individual facts or words are like hard little pebbles which we push into our heads or let fall into a bottomless abyss (XV, 142; V, 142–43). They, as well as our faults or virtues and our more grandiose ideas, will fall into dust in a few years. Fading memories as well as those who are lost to us through death or separation are nothing but dust (XI, 217; V, 200). Reality itself is mere dust and of interest only when golden sand in the form of some ordinary incident which becomes *un ressort romanesque* is mixed with it (V, 123).

Chains, Links, Networks. Any continuing relationship or routine is likened by Proust to a chain because of the repeated identical units which constitute it. This is true of the passing days (V, 223) and of habit which is said to be like a chain or an elaborately woven network (II, 172; X, 152). Memory, which links us with the past, is a kind of chain (X, 19; XV, 12) and so are our linked words which are directed toward a particular aim (VII, 223).

In love especially, we are joined to the loved one by a chain which may be a comforting link (XI, 216, 240; IX, 294) or a restricting bond (IV, 34; XI, 33, 220, 225). This chain may elaborate itself into a complicated network (II, 18, 242, 255).

Thermometers, Barometers, Clocks. Fine weather is compared to a mounting thermometer by Proust (XII, 258), and the narrator com-

pares himself, in his reaction to it, to a barometer (XI, 95) or to one of
those little figures in barometric devices which come out of a miniature house and take their hats off when the weather is fair (XI, 12).

The fixed, complicated movements of certain mechanical clocks
are used to describe routine gestures such as salutation, the movement of servants, or fixed mannerisms (IV, 52; VIII, 68; XI, 254).
Clocks also stand for punctuality even for such elusive things as
odours (I, 73), and their regular movement is used, along with the
sound of ocean waves, to describe sleep (XI, 140). The moon has a
face like a clock (XI, 217), and the world itself is like a giant sun-dial
on which we can perceive the time only by the lighted portion (XIII,
255–56).

Proust compares the face of the Princesse de Nassau to a sort of
horloge astronomique (XV, 148) and, metaphorically, he says that every
individual goes his way regulated by an inner clock which is unique
for him and which never coincides with the clocks regulating any
other individuals (XV, 155).

Materials and Trades. Proust frequently uses materials in a
graphic and interesting way. Of necessity, such images are visual
and some of them are among the most vivid employed by him.

Important people are said to be surrounded by *cet empesé des
grands emplois* (VIII, 116). Swann's hair is rather like ratty fur (IX,
119), and leather is used to describe tree trunks (II, 241), the skin of
a lemon (IV, 92) and the calyx of sweet-scented stocks (I, 191). Wax
characterizes the cheeks of young girls (XI, 93; V, 205, 220).

Veils are used by Proust probably without complete consciousness of their metaphorical quality. Along with walls or barriers,
they stand for a separation of any sort. An exclusive society (IV,
102; VI, 127), habit (XIII, 157), silence (XI, 141)—all these are
represented as veils. Veils also prevent us from penetrating to the
true nature of others (IV, 112), and sometimes this is a blessing, for
when the veil is lifted at the corner, what we see may be hell (XIII,
14). For Proust, there are two very different sides to the cloth of
reality (X, 234; XIII, 250). Memory may interpose a veil between
our eyes and what they actually see if the scene is reminiscent of
something else (X, 236).

Proust uses cloth to describe the effects of light. The sun adds
yellow velvet (V, 128) or gold silk (I, 198) to scenes. It interweaves
golden threads in snow (II, 241) or makes it look like a rich brocade

with metallic fringes and rosy and gold patterns over white (II, 244). Flowers make a field look like tapestry (I, 189), and moss is velvet (XV, 140). The slanting rays of sunlight are like a curtain (II, 232) or fine muslin (VII, 159), and sometimes they seem to put furniture covers on the chairs (XII, 237). The evening sky is purple velvet (I, 91).

The little phrase of music by Vinteuil is said to be dressed differently in its different harmonizations (XII, 59), and this idea of clothing is also applied metaphorically to La Berma for whom her face, the theatre and the audience are said to be extensions of what she wears (III, 26, 75). The conversation of Madame de Guermantes is a sort of medieval tapestry (VII, 38).

One of Proust's favourite images of this sort is that of weaving. He speaks of our memories and our past experiences as threads (XV, 129). The mind continues to interweave them like a busy worker (V, 100; XV, 139, 208), not always with the conscious intervention of the will (XV, 140; XIV, 186) or even with the desire to please the ego (II, 259). Our appearances, to others, are a tissue of lies woven with the express purpose of hiding our true nature (XII, 233). Habit is itself a sort of patient weaver (V, 56).

Proust also speaks of light as a weaver, and this conception harmonizes with the idea he so often expresses that patches of light look like cloth of one kind or another (VII, 211; X, 294). Nature, in recurring manifestations of the influence of heredity, is like a weaver in tapestry (IX, 333) and when she produces twins, it is as though, for a moment, she were industrialized (IX, 323).

Comparisons drawn from the wood carver's trade are utilized in describing the effect of heredity in nature (III, 170) and the method of a creative artist in such a medium as music (XI, 198). This latter figure is synaesthetic and rather startling, but it is an example of another set of reciprocal images. We have already seen how Proust compares common artisans to artists,[1] and here he compares artists to workmen.

Marcel regards his own memory or conscious will as a kind of artisan (IV, 16; XIII, 129), and the morning is personified as a roof-worker getting quietly at his job before the rest of the city is awake (IV, 87).

[1] See p. 51 above.

SCIENCE

Under the general heading of science in its very broadest sense are included all images which might be classified as displaying some technical knowledge of such widely varied subjects as biology, physics, mathematics, astronomy, chemistry and inventions of one kind and another. It may be that certain images under biology or astronomy could be included under nature images but, as far as possible, images dealing with one subject have been grouped together rather than split under two headings.[1]

Proust displays a considerable interest in science and most images from that source could no doubt be traced eventually to his school studies in scientific subjects. For interest, the reader may wish to compare this section with the later one which deals with images referring to childhood and school.

Biology. Under this heading, we have one of the most important single sources of imagery in the whole of *A la recherche du temps perdu*. Fundamentally, Proust is here still choosing figures from nature, and if one combines them with those already examined in the first section of this chapter, one merely adds to the overwhelming preponderance of images drawn from this particular source. Proust really displays quite an amazing interest in natural history and a more detailed and technical knowledge of it than of any other of the sciences.

Proust confesses his delight in regarding people as specimens of natural history—a word he uses numerous times (V, 54, 55; VII, 129; XV, 79).[2] Certain memories of people and certain well-

[1] See Reino Virtanen, 'Proust's Metaphors from the Natural and the Exact Sciences', *PMLA*, LXIX (1954), pp. 1038–59. This article deals with images from geology (12), botany (10), chemistry (with special emphasis on crystallization) (30), physics (including electricity, optics, atmospheric pressure) (100), mathematics (no figure given) and astronomy (100+). Professor Virtanen includes some images classified in a different way in the present study and he also calculates statistics differently. The high figure for astronomy, for example, results from his multiple count of the elaborately extended comparison of the restaurant at Rivebelle to a solar system (V, 58).

[2] Statements regarding Proust's preferences in this respect are numerous and contradictory. Pommier declares that 'Ordinairement, c'est aux animaux que Proust assimile les hommes' (op. cit., p. 38). Curtius states that the vegetable conception of man predominates (op. cit., pp. 110, 111, 112), and Beckett goes so far as to say that Proust 'is conscious of humanity as flora, never as fauna'. Tiedtke quite erroneously states: . . . 'Eine Art mystischen Kults hat Proust den Blumen geweiht, in denen er die höchste Entfaltung des natürlichen Lebens sieht und zugleich Analogien mit dem menschlichen Wesen und Dasein entdeckt' (op. cit., p. 103). One of the few well-considered judgments in this connection is that of Pierre-Quint in his principal study on Proust, pp. 28–29.

preserved individuals are like paraffin-injected specimens (XV, 108; V, 44). Monsieur de Bréauté has a monocle through which he looks as he would through a microscope (II, 148).

Some people are vegetal in their distinguishing characteristics. The hair of the Guermantes family (VIII, 72), a valet (XV, 92), the Duchess herself (VIII, 182)—these are all plant-like in appearance. Certain hereditary traits are similar in form to the common features of *Ranunculaceæ* or *Papilionaceæ* (IX, 281; V, 155). Young girls are like flowers or pellitory foliage (I, 206), and Gilberte beside Madame Swann is like a white lilac beside a purple one (III, 170–71).

Other humans are like birds (IX, 335–36) or ugly whales (XV, 102). Proust compares the indistinguishable individuals of a group like the band of young girls to zoophytes or madrepores (V, 73, 75, 111, 183). Here hereditary traits are compared to distinguishing zoological features (X, 142; II, 247).

People are also like insects, and the different stages they go through in development are similar to the metamorphoses of butterflies or moths (XV, 76–77, 92; I, 195; II, 103). Sorrow or illness have the effect of speeding up such evolution (IX, 217; XIII, 32). Within the individual, sleep and waking are like two separate states, and the progress from one to the other is similar to a sort of metamorphosis (V, 107).

Proust is familiar with many common biological conceptions and he uses them freely in figures of speech. A nation of individuals is said to be similar to one individual with its multi-cellular system, except that the units are relatively very large instead of being the size of infusoria (XIV, 94–95). Happiness and misfortune in life seem to counterbalance each other according to a process of 'natural selection' (XIII, 209), and our vices or virtues are just as much the result of Mendelian laws as the colour of our eyes (I, 201). Even the apparently spontaneous attractions of love are guided by 'the interest of the species' (IV, 157; III, 55).

It is to biology and natural history that Proust turns when he wishes to concretize the most complex and abstract of mental conceptions. The broadening of a personality or the multiplication of ideas in the mind of an individual are exactly similar, he says, to the reproduction of cells or cell-groups (II, 216; XI, 83). Memories of different individuals in our minds are like parasitic flora which disappear when we die (XIII, 220; XV, 160). The only immortality our ideas can attain is through their expression in works of art which influence others. By such creations we graft a bit of ourselves onto the living hearts of others where our thought can continue to exist (XIII, 133).

In the realm of society and our relations with others, Proust also draws extensively on images based on biology. Servants are said to live in symbiosis with their masters, they being plants and the latter animals (VI, 22). Individuals in society are microscopic—mere protozoa (XI, 45-46; VI, 70). They are all influenced by their environment, however, just like plants or other organisms (V, 143).

In society, as well as in physical nature, an incipient tendency is said to be in its embryonic state (V, 210; 111, 171). Circulating diners in a restaurant are like corpuscles moving by attraction from one group to another (V, 62). The different theories or schools that succeed one another in life are similar to microbes or globules which prey on each other, thus assuring the continuity of life (IX, 275).

In the realm of speech, orthography and literature, Proust again utilizes biological figures. Archaic tendencies in the first two are compared to vestigial features like tails or primitive ancestors of such animals as the whale or giraffe (XIII, 211; IX, 176). The artist in utilizing materials in life for his works is like an animal eating by instinct the very plants which are efficacious (XIII, 17). Early productions of an artist, in their primitive ineffectiveness, are like the prehistoric predecessors of contemporary living animals (XV, 39-40).

The narrator in *A la recherche du temps perdu* often speaks of himself in terms of natural history. His body, compared to his mind, is

> . . . une imperfection encore aussi rudimentaire qu'est l'existence commune des protozoaires en polypiers, que le corps de la baleine, etc. (XV, 214-15).

In his suspicions about Albertine, he is like a small animal hypnotized by the circling *oiseau fascinateur* (XIII, 162). Suspicions are antennae directed toward the truth (XII, 164). Joy or anticipation caresses the heart with antennae (VI, 44), and a feeling of exultation is similar to the sloughing of a heavy shell (II, 236). The involuntary memory, compared to the intellectual memory, is like certain animals or vegetables which live longer than man himself (XIV, 8).

In treating sex, Proust quite naturally draws heavily on images based on botany and zoology. The specific attraction of one individual for another is compared by him to the attraction of certain flowers for insects (IX, 63–64) or pollen for pistils (IV, 139). This attraction is as strong as that of a serpent for a bird it preys on (XII, 131), and its exclusive quality is illustrated by the example of lions which do not mate with tigers (XII, 19–20).

This exclusive quality of choice in love, with its highly fortuitous character, is developed to greatest lengths by Proust in his treatment of homosexuality. In the celebrated encounter of Jupien and Charlus, the stationary tailor is compared to a rare orchid which can be fertilized only by a particular bee (IX, 11–12, 14, 39, 43, 45). Jupien and Charlus are also like insects of the same species (IX, 39) or plants of the same rare type (IX, 41, 42, 43).

Insects are used by Proust in comparisons which draw on the sounds they make, as well as their appearance or other features. Airplanes in the sky look like insects (XIV, 54, 128) and they sound like them (XII, 252–53). Music sometimes sounds like insects (IX, 231) and flowers on branches resemble insects (I, 156–57; II, 268).

Bees are especially favoured by Proust because of their primary distinguishing characteristics. A woman of society visiting various salons is like a busy worker bee flitting from flower to flower (III, 111; IX, 94). The narrator preoccupied with the present is like a bee stupefied by smoke (V, 62). Thoughts continue to turn round in his head like bees buzzing in a hive (V, 185). The common people outside the dining room at Balbec are like a swarm of bees outside a hive (V, 53). Honey is used to describe the sound of the bells at Combray (XI, 101), the appearance of the worn yellow stones of the church (I, 85) and the faces of young girls (V, 156).[1]

People are like insects, particularly in their social relations. M. Verdurin is a crafty spider (XII, 35) and his wife a quick-moving may-fly (X, 118). Marcel's grandmother is attracted by the light from the salon at night like an insect (I, 22). Françoise in her studied cruelty toward the kitchen-maid is like the burrowing wasp which paralyzes by its sting prey which is later to be used as fresh food for its hatching larvae (I, 169).

Among the most interesting biological figures used by Proust

---

[1] Harold March in *The Two Worlds of Marcel Proust*, p. 20, exaggerates beyond reason the importance of honey images which, after all, play a very minor rôle in Proust's work.

are those which draw on butterflies. For him the butterfly symbolizes the ephemeral and the truly beautiful. An exquisite material (XI, 52), the effect of sunlight (I, 116), and lovely flowers (I, 229) are like butterflies. So is a ballet dancer (VI, 216) or the bit of yellow wall in Vermeer's painting so much admired by Bergotte (XI, 232). In his preoccupation with beauty, Marcel compares himself to a butterfly (X, 195), and an envied salon presents a butterfly image for him (IX, 192).

The eyes of Albertine are like mauve butterfly wings (V, 220; XII, 226), and this characterizes both their beauty and the shallow transitory character of her personality. The noses of Saint-Loup and Swann are compared to butterflies because of the shape and the name of the sides of the nostrils ('ailes') and because of the fact that, in love, the nose comes in contact with the flesh or flower which is the object of desire (IX, 140; VIII, 38). Saint-Loup's monocle is like a butterfly flitting ahead of him (IV, 160).

Sails on the sea are like butterflies (VI, 186; V, 92), and real steamers in the distance appear to move more slowly than a wayward butterfly hovering on a flower which is between the ship and the line of vision of the spectator (V, 43–44).

Physics. Proust's knowledge of physics, including the branch subjects dealing with optics, magnetism and electricity, is not nearly as technical as his knowledge of biology. At the same time, he reveals a background of accurate and interesting observations that contribute significantly to the scientific images he uses.

Reality and what one had imagined it would be are like two disks for Proust; in time they can be manoeuvred so as to coincide, but at first they often cannot be made to line up (I, 237; III, 137).

Our method of interpreting reality or our reaction to a given stimulus is like a particular optical instrument which we use at a given moment (III, 198). A writer's work is nothing more or less than such an instrument (XV, 62), and our interest in others or their interest in us is like a magnifying glass applied at that particular point to a train of acts otherwise indifferent (VII, 229; IV, 126; VIII, 201). Memory is another such magnifying glass (XIII, 295; XV, 102; II, 231).[1]

Consciousness is a sort of spectrum (I, 118), and those intangibles which elude our analysis may be said to belong to the world of

[1] Cf. Howard Moss, op. cit., p. 10; Harry Levin, op. cit., pp. 396 ff.

infra-red or ultra-violet light (II, 175, 266). They exist, nonetheless, and an artist like Vinteuil who builds in a musical idiom is exteriorizing *dans les couleurs du spectre la composition intime de ces mondes que nous appelons les individus* (XII, 69). His universe is one of colour (XII, 66), and that is why his septet can be called red and his sonata white (XII, 65, 216; XV, 21).

Colour is vibration, and Marcel is aware that the tension of his own nervous system can alter the tonality of what he sees. Thwarted desire or anticipation are like cords which suddenly regain their elasticity (II, 122; V, 112; IV, 72). The dissimilarity between what we perceive and reality as it exists may be compared to looking through smoked glass which conceals or distorts (III, 153; XV, 108; VIII, 57).

Our minds are also subject to the laws of atmospheric pressures and movements of currents. Our interests are a sort of centrifugal force (VI, 67), and the concepts with which we fill words are influenced both by pressure and vacuum (IV, 76). For different observers the personality of another individual is like a thin sheet of paper maintaining itself between the colossal pressures of two atmospheres (VI, 195). Our feelings of anticipation and the ideas we build up are maintained in an order and by laws comparable to those governing hydrostatics (V, 112).

Proust uses electricity to characterize memory and our relations with others. Events recalled to the mind are connected like a magnetic train (XV, 29; XIII, 144, 150; V, 82; VIII, 203; XIV, 50). Energy is electrical (XIII, 95; II, 72–73). Our minds are electrical piles (VI, 53; X, 333), and the truth is a pure current, invisible but very real (X, 295; XI, 29). It may sear and scar (XIII, 70, 138), but we can profit from its heat to examine the truth in the same way that electricity in lightning can be used to photograph (XV, 57). Glances exchanged with others or physical contacts are electrical in nature (VII, 140; VIII, 218–19; IX, 67; XI, 111).

The most technical image drawn from physics which Proust uses describes his inability completely to assimilate the truth contained in an outside object:

> Quand je voyais un objet extérieur, la conscience que je le voyais restait entre moi at lui, le bordait d'un mince liséré spirituel qui m'empêchait de jamais toucher directement sa matière; elle se volatilisait en quelque sorte avant que je prisse contact avec elle, comme un corps incandescent qu'on approche d'un objet mouillé ne touche

pas son humidité parce qu'il se fait toujours précéder d'une zone d'évaporation (I, 118).

Mathematics. Under the heading of mathematics may be included those images which deal with shapes such as the fan, sphere, triangle and those which utilize slope even though some of these are perhaps not thought of by Proust in a strictly mathematical sense. Indeed, Proust's references to mathematics are even less technical than his references to physics. The terms he uses are of the most general and vague.

The fan shape is used by Proust to describe connecting corridors in the hotel at Balbec (IV, 82), the sea glimpsed between foliage (IX, 266) and the pattern made by a lawn sprinkler (I, 191). Madame Verdurin's temples are said to be spheres (X, 127, 136), and the triangle is used to describe both the shape of a moving flock of sheep (XIII, 326) and the physiognomy of Charlus (VII, 113). Slope is used by Proust to describe the proclivity for vice of Charlus (X, 108; XII, 150), the relative ease of following imagination rather than introspection (XIII, 64) or the pattern of succeeding days (VI, 151).

Algebra stands for anything intangible or mysterious. The sexual aberrations of Morel (XI, 201) or Albertine (XIII, 138) are as insoluble for Charlus or the narrator as algebraic problems. For the narrator, desire and jealousy correspond to algebraic unknowns, and a change in mathematical sign can completely alter the value of the unknown quantity (XIII, 125).

In our social relations, we apply the principles of algebra and geometry. For Marcel, other people are like mathematical problems to be solved. Madame de Guermantes is a geometrical theorem to be studied (VI, 96); Albertine is a table of logarithms (XII, 197), and the real Bergotte is the solution to a problem for which anticipation and imagination were the original data (III, 150); one must make the two correspond. The conversation of any one individual or a letter written by him corresponds to his personality with the same logic as that of a theorem deduced from its premiss (VIII, 228; XIII, 49–50). Norpois has,

> . . . dans ses yeux ce regard vertical, étroit et oblique (comme, dans le dessin en perspective d'un solide, la ligne fuyante d'une de ses faces), regard qui s'adresse à cet interlocuteur invisible qu'on a en soi-même (III, 65).

The title of a person is like a mathematical sign altering value (VIII, 225), and Marcel observes society in general like a mathematician, *i.e.* he abstracts (XIV, 33). From a given fact, he can deduce the whole truth in the same way that the size of the circumference of a circle can be estimated from one tiny part of its arc (X, 80).

In observing nature, Proust likes to regard perspective from a mathematical point of view. A church steeple from an unfamiliar angle is like a solid seen at an unusual moment in its revolution (I, 95). The evening sunset is like a conical section taken in the sky which reveals the different contributing layers of colour (VIII, 14–15).

Astronomy. The two longest developed images in *A la recherche du temps perdu* are the one in the theatre where the society folk are compared to fish and marine deities and their boxes to grottoes or an aquarium, and the one in the restaurant at Rivebelle where the waiters circulating around tables and the various social groups at those tables are compared to an astronomical system (V, 58). This latter comparison fits very well into Proust's conception of the hierarchical nature of society with its continuous process of change and its complicated but well-ordered system of movement.

For Swann, Odette is a star moving in a particular orbit (I, 264), or the moon (II, 31). Marcel regards Mme de Guermantes in the same way (VII, 248), and for him, the band of young girls, because of its homogeneity and its brilliant but unpredictable appearances, is rather like a comet or a bright constellation (V, 35, 38, 73, 83, 224). Albertine is like the moon (V, 195) and a young girl desired like a star (V, 113). All of these objects of love are very fittingly compared to heavenly bodies which are aloof and remote and yet beautiful and coveted.

The social evolution of such disparate types as Vaugoubert (IX, 59), Charlus (XI, 253) and Odette (XV, 160) is compared to astral cycles. In observing others, Marcel applies the same sort of abstraction from the rules as we found in his mathematical approach. We can draw certain conclusions even though the observations cannot be made (XI, 180), and we can know truth in theory that we can never approach physically (XI, 235).

Astronomical comparisons are freely used in the world of society. The queens of the *Faubourg St.-Germain* are compared to stars of the first magnitude and pretenders are said to be false stars (VII, 249; IX, 81–82). Salons are like separate little universes, and the elements of them are in time lost or altered by attraction or repulsion (V, 130; XV, 118). Individual members of social sets have astronomical comparisons associated with them in a way that relates them to this one unified idea. Monsieur de Saint-Candé's monocle is like Saturn's ring, and the eyes of Madame de Nassau are like an astronomical clock (XV, 148). Swann's face in illness is like the waning moon (IX, 118).

The remote beauty of stars also leads Proust to use them in aesthetic comparisons. Bergotte (XI, 228) and La Berma (VI, 59) are compared to astronomical phenomena, and the theatre is said to be a world as exotic and unreal as that of another planet (III, 26). The actress Rachel is compared to the moon or a star (VI, 213, 214, 216). A composer in music is said to have at his disposal resources as varied and complex as if they came from different planets. Far from being limited to a single scale of notes, he is able to explore infinite possibilities (II, 177).

Airplanes are objects which stimulate the imagination because of their ability to transcend the humdrum world of everyday, and they resemble stars because of their formations and their lights (XIV, 78, 128, 129).

Glances between individuals or communicating smiles are said to be like astral signs or stars (IX, 107, 318, 319, 320). Memory is also like a comet with a long tail (VI, 72), and these two types of images employed in this way run exactly parallel to images used for the same purpose drawn from electricity.[1]

The narrator uses astronomical images in connection with himself. Monsieur de Norpois regards him as a star in an unusual position in its orbit (III, 32). His love is like a star (XIII, 180) as is his certainty that Albertine will come back (XI, 194). His action growing out of lethargy is like a comet appearing from nowhere (XIII, 286), and his observation of others, as an author, is said to be similar to those sensitive plates installed by astronomers when they wish to observe an eclipse or the passage of a rare comet (VI, 52).

Geology, Archaeology. Proust likes to regard the mind and the impressions made on it as phenomena of geology. Each day adds its layer of impressions or memories to what preceded (IV, 56).

[1] See p. 144 above.

These layers are not immovable but heave and reappear at the surface under the action of memory (XIII, 158). This memory has certain essential characteristics of an identifying geological pattern (I, 250–51; VI, 111), and the mind itself is a rich mineral basin which can be exploited only by the individual himself (I, 248; XV, 216).

The physiognomy is also affected in a geological way. The faces and appearance of others have changed and altered with the years just like terrain (XV, 199). Our ideas of them have built up like stalactites or stalagmites (III, 150), and this is especially true in love (XIII, 31).

Social change is comparable to geological periods (XIV, 47), and social attitudes are sometimes almost fossil-like in their rigidity (VIII, 229). They can be examined archaeologically and will permit logical deductions as to cause and origin (IX, 108).

Chemistry, Alchemy. Proust favours above all one particular category of images drawn from chemistry. This category has to do with reversible actions or actions in which a precipitate is formed only to volatilize again under different conditions. It is a very common chemical phenomenon and one with which any elementary student of the subject would be familiar.

Suffering or suspicion are said by Proust to crystallize in the heart, tearing it and paining it (II, 134; XIII, 8, 122). Love itself rests in the heart in a state of unstable equilibrium (XII, 28). Memory is fluid until it crystallizes out (XIII, 94), and our perceptions or our notions of others are formed, on supersaturation, with the instantaneousness of chemical reactions (III, 9; V, 99).

We are ourselves analysts of ideas, and our notions of other people are like a metal bathed in an acid which gradually reacts with it (IX, 246). Our social conceptions are a sort of amalgam (X, 133), and the meeting of two conflicting ideas in our minds, one of which we do not wish to express, is likely to be quite evident to a keen observer who will deduce the truth by the method of analysis or electrolysis (XI, 108).

Sleep is volatile and unstable (XI, 155), and the affect of alcohol is to render volatile all difficulties or obstacles (IX, 303). Our own brains are like crucibles where memories interact (XI, 67), but too often we tend to regard the minds of others as inert receptacles where no chemical reaction takes place (I, 112). Our bodies are retorts where the chemical reactions of illness and fatigue can be observed (IX, 129–30). An unpleasant experience is like a corrosive acid (XIII, 79–80).

In the world of society, women are like an amalgam (II, 71) or an unusual chemical compound (V, 59–60). In love, our relations with them are a series of chemical experiments (II, 70) in which new products are formed (IX, 271–72). Different women in contact may react violently like unstable powders (XIII, 306), and our modified notions of them are like chemical salts changed in nature as well as appearance by the action of another salt (XIII, 136–37). This conscious mingling of heterodox social elements can be done by hostesses in much the same way as an experimenting chemist mixes different chemicals (X, 290). A surviving beauty is as miraculous in society as the existence in nature of radium (XV, 109), for time is itself a chemical reagent (XV, 119).

The artist is a sort of experimenter in a laboratory. The raw materials for the experiments which he performs in his mind are indifferent in themselves (V, 107), but it is the transforming power of the high temperatures of his genius which dissociates and recombines atoms in new and exciting ways (V, 118). Vinteuil is a sort of chemist (XII, 75), and both Elstir and Bergotte are really alchemists in that they transmute the dross of everyday impressions into the gold of artistic works (XI, 227; XIV, 93).[1]

Inventions, Modern Science. For Proust, the contemporary advances in science which resulted in the perfection of such things as the automobile, the airplane, the telephone and the camera are a source of never-ending wonderment. What he has to say about such inventions remains fresh and accurate, but he displays such a naïve quality of delight in things which now seem to us so ordinary that the effect is to give his work in places an aura of artificial enthusiasm.

There is a side to man's nature which is mechanical. The energy of the young girls is as unthinking as that of a machine that is set in motion (V, 35). Marcel himself in his joy or his eagerness to act is like a machine vibrating on the spot and brimming over with energy (V, 229; IX, 253; XI, 31). His speed varies depending on his mood just like the different gears which control the speed of a car (II, 233). In sleep, these gears also change the speed (I, 151).

---

[1] The question of alchemy is closely related to imagery drawn from gold Cf. pp. 131–32. See V. E. Graham, 'Proust's Alchemy,' *MLR*, LX(1965), pp. 197–206.

L

Our social relations have something mechanical about them. Personal motives are a sort of internal engine over which we can have only a limited control (IV, 199). Frequenters of the salon of the moment are attracted there with the compulsion of a pneumatic machine (XV, 167–68). New manners or customs are like unthought-of refinements in inventions, but once popularized, they have a tremendous vogue (VIII, 118).

For Proust, the telephone stands for what once was considered impossible, against which prejudice was strongly opposed and which now is accepted as perfectly ordinary and common. Marcel makes use of Madame de Guermantes's advice in the latter sense (XI, 37), and he describes the idea of solitary homosexuals' being able to join organizations as progressing in the same direction (IX, 30).

Reality and our perception of it have the same relation to each other as the actual sounds transmitted over the telephone and the electrical reconstruction of them. We have difficulty in understanding how sounds can be carried from one city to another, but that is because we fail to realize that the gestures or words of others (whether ordinary individuals or authors) are not directly perceived but only indirectly as through a telephone (V, 198; XIII, 189). Imagination is to reality as imperfect as primitive telephones compared to the modern improved ones (X, 319).

Creative artists are like experimenting scientists, and the discoveries of a Vinteuil are just as remarkable as those of a Lavoisier or an Ampère (II, 180; XII, 75). The early productions of an artist are as inefficient as the early, unperfected inventions of a scientist (XV, 39–40). The imaginations of ordinary people are never developed to their full extent and they remain like primitive inventions (XIII, 94–95).

Proust refers three times to the phonograph. The accurate correspondence between the sound of Gilberte's voice in middle age and her voice as a young girl make the former sound as though it comes from a phonograph because of her changed appearance (XV, 104). A phonograph is an accurate imitation (VI, 12) but it leaves us as unsatisfied as an artificial storm at the Exposition (II, 224).

The invention referred to most frequently by Proust is that of the camera. The ideas associated with photography are very well suited to his conception of reality, partly because it is a visual manifestation and partly because of the techniques involved in taking and developing pictures.

Proust declares that our observation of others is similar to the taking of snaps with a camera (VIII, 172). The universe is dynamic and constantly changing but we immobilize it, falsely of course, by the series of still pictures which we are busy storing up in our minds (XIII, 78; XV, 129). Memory consists of reproducing the snapshots which we have filed away in our heads (XI, 184; XIV, 209; XV, 8, 93; V, 135–36, 153).

There is, however, a conscious intervention on the part of the individual, for his memories do not always coincide exactly with reality. It is as though the mind took a snapshot which is a negative and which it then proceeds to develop and print by the action of its own transforming fluids (V, 131; IX, 252; XV, 45). Indeed, the confrontation of memories with actuality (as, for instance, in the phraseology of a book) is often as unpleasant as the sight of a real photograph which is a less valid likeness of an individual than our real memories (XV, 31). The women we love are merely *une projection renversée, un 'négatif' de notre sensibilité* (V, 158).

In social relations Proust often draws on imagery based on photography. Charlus' manner of shaking hands takes as long as it used to take to pose for early photographers with their inadequate lighting (XIV, 159). Albertine smiles vaguely into the distance as though her picture were being taken (XI, 185), and a less brilliant salon is like a retouched photograph (XI, 252). Marcel's impressions of others and the fugitive expressions which he catches on their faces or which recur in his memory are like candid pictures (XIII, 96; VII, 17; XV, 103). Names, for him, are photograph-bearing identity cards (VI, 12). Albertine is like the photo-telephone of the future and in the sound of her voice is contained the image of her appearance (V, 200–1).

In one rather ineffectual image, Proust compares moonlight to *un doux magnésium continu permettant de prendre une dernière fois des images nocturnes* (XIV, 131).

LITERARY IMAGES

Even though images drawn from nature constitute the largest single category in *A la recherche du temps perdu*, images from literary sources weigh very heavily. This is not surprising, since Proust is a writer of wide reading and catholic tastes. He introduces figures drawn from literature and writing in the most disparate contexts. It would be of little value to analyze and classify all such images, but a cursory analysis of trends reveals some interesting features about Proust's methods and favoured sub-sources.

For Proust, the expression on people's faces is a sort of hiero-glyphic writing or code difficult to decipher (VI, 19; IX, 107; XIII, 13). His own memory often presents him with the same cryptic sort of word puzzles, but familiarity or the sudden apprehension of pattern in what had appeared formless and meaningless provides a key to the puzzle (V, 44; VI, 82; IX, 24; XI, 105–6, 110; XV, 22, 23). Anything incompletely understood or with a possible hidden meaning behind it is like secret writing to be solved. The manu-scripts of Vinteuil (XII, 74–75), Albertine's lighted window (XII, 159–60), the identity of the Princesse Sherbatoff (X, 40), the person-ality of Marcel or Morel (IV, 198; X, 215)—these are all enigmas challenging deciphering.

Proust uses the dictionary in rather a derogatory sense. The Guermantes clan are intelligent but only like a dictionary, or a travelling salesman (VIII, 88). Their conversation is of interest, in the manner of a dictionary of archaisms (VIII, 205). He also speaks derisively of literary criticism as opposed to creative writing. The Duchesse de Guermantes leads a sterile life similar to that of a critic (VIII, 109).

There are many common literary terms throughout Proust's cycle, and they remind one constantly that one is reading the work of a writer interested in his craft who regards everything that happens as possible material for his book. The days that pass are pages in the book of life (XIII, 104; XV, 16), and our memories are libraries storing up the books deposited in them (IV, 55; XIII, 158). Conscious recall is merely a process of seeking out these books or flipping over their illustrated pages (XIII, 116; XV, 15). People are like books or illustrations in books (V, 42; XV, 106, 138, 158). Madame de Guermantes is like an interesting old book (VIII, 203; XI, 40). A newcomer to society is an unpublished work (IX, 183). Fashionable dresses appear in limited editions (XIV, 43) and are as unreal as scenes from a novel (XI, 39, 40). Ordinary daily events are possible subject matter for literary productions. Marcel's love affair with Albertine is an allegory of all love affairs (XIII, 112) and it obeys the rules for courtly love (VII, 239). Saturday lunch at Combray could provide the nucleus for a great epic (I, 152). The young girls whom Marcel admires mix all the arts in their youthful pranks just like the early poets for whom there were no separate *genres* (V, 157).

Newspapers stand for that which is trivial or sensational. Their false tone of optimism is used to characterize a platitude uttered by Brichot (XII, 32). Gullibility is typified by Françoise's acceptance of the claims of newspaper ads (VII, 181), and Saint-Loup, when he receives improper suggestions, is as righteously indignant as reporters at the news of armed robberies (VI, 223). Brazen-faced lying is indulged in by newspaper editors (XI, 222), and reporters of no particular merit are said to be haughty and self-important (X, 232).

The abstract and complex relations of the world of society are compared by Proust to philosophical speculations. The salon of Mme de Guermantes is like one of Leibniz's superior monads (VIII, 120), and she herself excels all her rivals in the same way that the world of liberty exists above Kant's world of necessity (VIII, 118). Proust uses the same comparison for the Swanns (III, 99) and he compares the speculative and intangible relations in love between Swann and Odette and between the narrator and Gilberte to difficult philosophical concepts (II, 108, 247).

When we turn to actual literary references, we find that the author most frequently quoted by Proust is Racine. He draws extensive analogies between the hotel at Balbec and the setting of *Athalie* (IX, 223–24, 309–11; X, 158). Homosexuals like Charlus and Vaugoubert are compared to the socially ostracised Esther and Joas (IX, 86–87; XII, 149). The narrator himself is regarded by the director of the hotel as Esther is by Assuérus (IV, 108–9) and by Mme de Guermantes as Mardochée is by the same king (VII, 249). Françoise is like Aman in wanting Albertine-Esther banished (XI, 121) and she is like Joad in her dislike of Eulalie-Athalie (I, 149). The narrator in his farewell to the hawthorns is like Phèdre in his disregard of his person and the arrangement of his hair (I, 197).

Proust refers to other playwrights besides Racine and he generally does so in connection with the rôles which various individuals play during their lives in society. Bloch in his old age becomes a sort of Shylock (XV, 132) while Charlus is King Lear (XV, 76). Charlus and Jupien are like Romeo and Juliet (IX, 40–41). A jealous older lover is a kind of Harpagon (X, 76). The Duc de Guermantes changes from Jupiter to Géronte (XV, 195) and M. d'Argencourt becomes a sort of *moribond-bouffe d'un Regnard exagéré par Labiche* (XV, 76). Society queens *jouent à la reine . . . comme les reines dans Sardou* (VIII, 58), and Cottard in the Verdurin circle is like the marquis or the baron in Marivaux (X, 27).

Several celebrated literary figures are used by Proust to characterize individuals in his novel. Saint-Loup refers to his uncle Charlus as a Don Juan (IX, 120) and Proust calls him a kind of Don Quixote (IX, 72). Mme Verdurin speaks of Morel as Charlus's Dulcinea (XII, 96).

Proust assumes a certain general culture in his readers, which allows him to refer in comparisons to commonly accepted standards as expressed by well-known works of literature. Swann's concept of love is related to the *Princesse de Clèves* or *René* (II, 178). The narrator rejects a thought engendering apostasy *comme un dévot la Vie de Jésus de Renan* (III, 99). Something seemingly important which later appears quite trivial undergoes the same metamorphosis as Gulliver in his travels (XI, 222). A rapid *dénouement* in love is compared to the conclusion of certain tales by Balzac (XIII, 105), and to describe adequately the reading-room at Balbec, Proust says he would have to borrow from Dante (IV, 80).

Proust frequently paraphrases or quotes from other authors in his literary images without indicating the source. Here again he assumes that the reader will recognize either the characters referred to or the wording. A good example is the reference to *Phèdre* quoted above (I, 197). Others include references to the *Chartreuse de Parme* (VII, 246) and the *Fables* of La Fontaine (I, 268).

There are many fecund literary ideas which Proust appropriates for his images, sometimes seriously and sometimes facetiously. The barrier between the narrator and certain types of young girls he is attracted to is just as imaginary, he says, as the *abîme infranchissable* of Pascal (XIII, 332). The grandeur of the Guermantes family is founded by Françoise on the number and brilliance of its members just as Pascal founds the truth of religion on the reason and authority of the Scriptures (VI, 26).

Included in literary references, one should consider the figures of speech which draw on strictly historical material. Almost without exception, these deal with position in society, and the author referred to most frequently by Proust is Saint-Simon. Marcel's Aunt Léonie is as important to Françoise as the king at Versailles to Saint-Simon (I, 162–63). She regards class distinction much as the aristocratic memorialist did (III, 82), and Marcel's own mother feels the same indignation as Saint-Simon when she sees someone in the lower orders of society trying to raise himself (X, 208).

In love, Albertine or Gilberte or Odette follow the same progression as women in the court of Louis XIV. After a period of favour they assume the rôle of *entremetteuse* (XIII, 168). Their careers are of great interest (II, 254) and one can name the successive lovers of an Odette with as much assurance as if one were listing the Kings of France (XII, 120).

Servants hold a rôle in society like that of courtiers at Versailles (VI, 78). They conceal behind their nondescript appearances tragedies like those of the kings and queens in stained glass windows (I, 167). A Madame de Guermantes is of the age of Louis XV while her pompous husband is Louis-Philippe (VIII, 173). Monsieur de Norpois looks like Saint Louis (VIII, 178) and his memory is as phenomenal in its factual resources as certain obscure history texts (III, 65).

Marcel regards himself from a historical point of view. His jealousy behaves like a historian searching documentation in the facts accumulated in the mind (XI, 181), and reality often is as new and startling as the discoveries of an independent historian who has conducted his own researches (XIII, 12). Marcel looks at flowers like the humble memorialist who observes a king from an anonymous position in the crowd (I, 247). Our actions are remembered by others in the same way that letters or mementos of famous people are collected by their acquaintances (VII, 247).

Proust likes to base the idea of writing a book or analyzing the style of another author on images. An over-furnished salon is like a book from which the author failed to remove mere technical display (VIII, 89). In social relations, unless we flatter the tastes of others, we are likely to offend in the same way that the innovations of a new author are received with displeasure (II, 69). It is only one socially superior like Mme de Guermantes who is envied for whatever she does just like celebrated authorities whose works are felt to be the result of the exigencies they were exposed to (VIII, 107). Jealousy, sorrow or love are all books which we write ourselves and which we labour over at length (II, 192; XIII, 45; II, 247). Profuse details help to persuade us of reality (I, 75; II, 216) but their very fictional quality at times makes us doubt their importance (X, 332). However, it is not ambition that accomplishes results but laboriousness, and happiness is not a re-arrangement of old patterns but something new and unique (IV, 70–71). Joy is not the arbiter which preserves the future for us but rather *les sages réflexions du passé* (V, 63).

Folk Lore, The Arabian Nights. For Proust, the sudden remarkable changes which take place in the world of society either in the appearance or the rank of different individuals can only be related to the supernatural events of fairy-tales. The change in Saint-Loup after Marcel meets him (IV, 164), the presence of Mme de Villeparisis at Balbec (IV, 105, 106), the alteration in the attitude of Charlus on the occasion of his meeting with Jupien (IX, 22) and the various changes in the appearance of Mme de Souvré (XV, 95)—all these things seem to be the result of fairy-magic.

The dwellings of Mme de Guermantes (IX, 181; XIV, 198–99) and the Swanns (III, 104; IX, 186–87, 192) are like fairy dwellings to those who want to enter them or to those who joy in their power and their influence. Powerful hostesses like Mme Verdurin or Mme de Guermantes are like influential norns or fairies (IX, 111, 184–85; XII, 43, 58). The association of a name with a person breaks the enchantment which his appearance or reputation alone created (VI, 11, 12; XV, 161), and relations with others can change magically by very simple acts (I, 63). Bergotte's opinion that Marcel is intelligent transforms the attitude of his parents toward the author (III, 183).

Love and sleep are fairy states (XIV, 20; VII, 243; VI, 111; XI, 141), and food like asparagus seems to be beautiful maidens metamorphosed into vegetables but still able to perform magic (I, 166). Françoise when cooking is aided by supernatural powers (I, 165). Music is definitely a fairy-world inhabited by dryads or fairies of its own (II, 178; XII, 71, 72). Any creative artist is endowed with supernatural power which may be lying dormant like the Sleeping Beauty but which can be roused with the right stimulus (XIII, 232). For the narrator, the trees which he describes in writing are his awakening aesthetic experience and they remind him of druids or sorcerers (II, 280; IV, 147).

In space, men occupy a fixed position and they can only move at a regular, fixed rate. In time, however, they can move at supernatural speed and they can occupy space in more than one dimension. Proust extends this comparison by saying that men wear the mythical seven-league boots in the world of time (X, 171; XV, 230).

The comparison of witches or sorcerers is on a less noble plane than that of norns or fairies and Proust reserves it for servants or common folk. An old cook with her broom (IX, 228), a poor woman of the streets (VIII, 231), or the director of the hotel at Balbec after the guests have gone (V, 226), are like ghosts or witches. Foreigners with their different costumes and physical traits are like phantoms or spirits evoked by a medium (VII, 16).

Generally speaking, Proust has no use for spiritism. He says of the aged Legrandin that the few words he uttered *avaient l'insignificance de celles que disent les morts qu'on évoque* (XV, 92). He uses the trance into which a medium may go to describe the agitation of a violinist playing the little phrase of Vinteuil (II, 180), and he says that Françoise in her intuitive response to whatever affects Marcel is like a spiritist with extra-sensory perception (XII, 204). However, it is only in the tricks of heredity that we see magical transformations which might be attributed to sorcery, if such a thing existed (VIII, 238). Jealousy and the first manifestations of psychosomatic illnesses have the same sort of supernatural or hypnotic powers (XI, 127; VI, 104).

Proust refers very frequently to the *Arabian Nights*. Sometimes he quotes from it (VIII, 35), and the narrator himself is compared both to the Caliph (when he enters Jupien's extraordinary establishment (XIV, 167)) and to Scheherazade (in the daily ingenuity which his jealousy imposes on him (XI, 162)). The richness of style of the work is used to describe the symphonic texture of an orchestrated composition by Vinteuil (XII, 64–65). Also, the intricacies of the hotel at Balbec (IX, 311–12) and the rich complexity of Venice are compared to the magic atmosphere of the Bagdad of the *Arabian Nights* (XIII, 259, 273–74, 280, 281).

When following incognito a male who had attracted him Charlus compares himself to the Caliph of Bagdad who goes about the streets in disguise at night (IX, 18–19). He also says that he controls the 'Open Sesame' to society (VIII, 221), and this phrase is used by Proust in other instances where a metaphorical entrance sought in vain is suddenly found. Swann in society is like Ali-Baba (I, 30); Marcel's fierce jealousy when he discovers that Mlle Vinteuil is Albertine's friend is the magic formula which introduces the latter into his heart (X, 334). Sleep provides the key to other enigmas long puzzled over (XII, 173–74), and the involuntary memory is like a genie which opens the door vainly sought or miraculously transports the subject at request to far-distant scenes (XIV, 210; XV, 10).

For Marcel, furniture seems to be like the metamorphosized individuals of Persian fairy-tales (III, 187). Albertine is held captive by him just as the fairy-tale character who held *enfermée dans une bouteille la Princesse de la Chine* (XII, 230). In the lives of the young social set, the favourite restaurant plays a rôle *aussi important que les caisses d'étoffe dans les contes arabes* (VI, 186).

Proust uses a variety of Oriental expressions some of which probably have their origin in the *Arabian Nights*. A group of young homosexuals is called a harem (XIV, 157), and the inoffensive men with whom a jealous lover surrounds his mistress are referred to as *gardiens de sérail* (XII, 87). Albertine is called a *petite péri* (V, 39), and in conversation she declares—using this time a term relating to Japan—that another girl *a l'air d'une petite mousmé* (VII, 224). Such expressions, as well as the term *mameluck* which Mme de Guermantes uses (VII, 168), most likely come from Proust's close reading of his well-loved Oriental stories.

Knighthood, Hunting, Etc. Proust employs heraldic and medieval terminology in his descriptions of nature. The iris with its royal blades erect seems to bear a real sceptre (I, 186), and the steeple of the church at Combray is like an arrow aimed at the sky (I, 95). The rays of the sun (VI, 98) and the vibrant morning street noises are also like quivering arrows (XI, 9). Bells in the church steeple striking twelve noon seem momentarily to adorn with twelve symbolic rosettes a sonorous crown (I, 100), and at the entrance to the Bois de Boulogne the sumptuous foliage is like an oriflamme (II, 275).

In considering members of the *Faubourg St.-Germain* and families whose genealogy can be traced far back into history, Proust utilizes imagery which emphasizes feudal traditions, hunting and duelling. Saint-Loup is a feudal tower (XIV, 189), and other members of the upper set are said to offer alternately *l'aspect d'un tournoi et d'une forêt domaniale* (VI, 36). Their politeness is merely a part of their education, like horseback riding or fencing (VI, 158). Indeed, their manner of shaking hands makes you think they are handing you a foil, parrying a blow or dubbing you knight (IV, 163; VIII, 79, 80).

In particular, Proust associates members of the upper class with horses and equestrian skill, probably because of the prestige of the

Jockey Club. The Princesse d'Orvilliers wears a harness of diamonds and sapphires and shakes her head under its weight like one of the king's chargers (IX, 156). Mme de Guermantes, Mme de Villemur and the Princesse de Guermantes all behave in society with the grace and the skill of adroit equestriennes (VIII, 68; IX, 49–50, 149). For the Duc de Guermantes, the *Faubourg St.-Germain* is simply *un prolongement de sa cour, une piste plus étendue pour ses chevaux* (VI, 38). Even his vocabulary and the conversational figures of speech he uses are based on terms of horseback riding (VIII, 125, 258). Saint-Loup in manoeuvring along the back of the bench at the restaurant is like a skilled jumper at a horse show (VIII, 41, 43). Both he and his uncle Charlus treat inferiors like horses. Saint-Loup, in getting Marcel to show off in front of his friends, tells him how intelligent he is *en me bouchonnant comme un cheval arrivé le premier au poteau* (VI, 128–29). Charlus, in saying good-bye to Cottard, holds his hand and strokes it *avec une bonté de maître flattant le museau de son cheval* (X, 264).

The Duc de Guermantes is a hunter and his eyes are like targets in which the pupils are perfect bullseyes (VII, 56). His disapproving glances at the Duchess are like *deux pistolets chargés* (VIII, 133), and even the name Guermantes, when it is pronounced before the jealous Legrandin, causes his eyes to change as if they had been struck by a missile which caused the pupil to secrete a counteracting fluid (I, 174).

Classics, Mythology. One of the most significant features of this examination of the literary images which Proust employs is the revelation of the very extensive use he makes of figures drawn from classical authorities and Greek and Roman mythology.[1] One might argue that none of the images reveal any profound knowledge of classical literature and that most of them are of common currency. Indeed, it is debatable whether any of the images used necessarily proves first-hand acquaintance with original works. All that could be granted, but one would still have to admit that classical references form a large and extremely important part not only of Proust's literary images but of his images in general. One can count at least 146 of them.

Members of the Guermantes family and important socialites of the *Faubourg St.-Germain* are consistently spoken of by Proust as gods or goddesses. Their remote and lofty position makes them

[1] See J. Seznec, *Marcel Proust et les Dieux*, Oxford (The Zaharoff Lecture for 1962).

seem superior to ordinary mortals, and their apparently supernatural powers lead the narrator to think of them as members of the
Olympian race. The famous extended image at the theatre exploits
this comparison (VI, 47–49, 51, 63, 69).

Individual members of higher society are compared to specific
gods. The Duc de Guermantes is said to be like Hercules (VIII,
122) or Jupiter, particularly because of his frowning countenance
and the metaphorical bolts he hurls at the Duchess (VIII, 153; IX,
109, XI, 49, 50; XV, 199). He is compared especially to the gold
statue of Jupiter by Phidias (VII, 131). Charlus is also Olympian
(IX, 135; XI, 57). He is said to brandish bolts of lightning against
others (IX, 55), but he is more like an older Apollo than Jupiter
(VIII, 210). The Duchesse de Guermantes is a sort of water divinity
(IX, 182) or Minerva (VI, 59), and her cousin, the Princesse, is
more like Juno (VI, 69) or Diana (VI, 67). The sons of Mme de
Surgis are as different and as splendid as the sons of Jupiter by
different mothers, even though they have the same mother (IX, 117).
Even Odette and Mme Verdurin, when they achieve rank in society,
are compared to goddesses (III, 55, 63–64; IV, 50, 52; XII, 138).

Creative artists are compared by Proust to gods. Bergotte is one,
(I, 133) and he walks among mortals, as it were, in disguise (I,
138–39), while his works, as well as the works of other writers, like
a sort of collective Venus, only realize themselves completely in
the minds of their readers (XIII, 190). Françoise, in her wizardry
as a cook, makes of her kitchen a kind of temple to Venus (I, 102).

The acquaintance of members of higher society and creative
artists is intensely coveted by the narrator and so is that of beautiful
girls or women who attract his attention. Members of the *Faubourg
St.-Germain* are compared to gods and goddesses, and the same
figure is extended to all those individuals who rouse in Marcel
feelings of desire. This desire is compared to the perfumes uniquely
associated with Hera, Porthyraia, etc. (IX, 305). Albertine is a sort
of household god (XIII, 132) or invisible divinity (XI, 188) as well
as a redoubtable goddess of Time (XII, 230). Unknown milkmaids
or peasant girls are like goddesses from Mount Olympus walking on
earth now that the immortals no longer live above (XI, 172–73, 207,
208, 210; XIII, 86; XV, 159), and both they and Albertine and her
friends are compared to nymphs (V, 221; XIII, 90). All ordinary
men are said to have the silhouette of an ideal nymph intagliated on
the eye, but for homosexuals it is rather an ephebe (IX, 24).

Inventions which amaze and delight Proust also partake of this quality of desirability and remote incredibility and, for that reason, they too are compared to manifestations of the Greek and Roman gods. An airplane is said to be like a god (X, 211; XIV, 170), and Proust extends the metaphor considerably in his description of the telephone and its use (VI, 161–62; XI, 121, 123, 125).

Proust uses many classical images and he does so with a degree of freedom and naturalness that makes it quite obvious that there is nothing stilted or strained about their introduction into the context. Birds singing near the sea are Oceanides (X, 168) and children and bathers playing in the waves are Nereids (V, 229). The sportive sea itself is a Nereid (IV, 130) and the boxes which Mme de Guermantes and her friends occupy at the theatre are called *le royaume sous-marin des Néréides* (XIII, 214; XV, 181). A disagreeable young girl or the angry divinities of the telephone are said to be furies (XI, 78; VI, 162), and the renascent effects of heredity provide us with the only real phoenix (XIV, 134). The thermometer with which the grandmother's temperature is taken is a sibyl or one of the Parcae (VII, 148, 149). Albertine is a *bacchante à bicyclette* (V, 133) and Charlus, because of his sexual ambivalence is a sort of centaur (IX, 23–24). The progress from sleep to waking or waking to sleep is a sort of crossing of the river Lethe which is perhaps just our own blood (IX, 206, 208).

Proust also refers casually to many classical legends and he does so on the assumption that they are well-known to his readers. One or two, such as *avoir aux talons les ailes de Mercure* (VI, 115) or *un chasseur beau comme Endymion* (IX, 245) are almost proverbial, but the great majority, even though they draw on the familiar body of classical legend, explore original applications of these tales.

The story of Orpheus and Eurydice is referred to several times by Proust. Swann, in his desperate search for Odette in the different restaurants at night, is like Orpheus seeking Eurydice in the underworld (II, 24). The narrator, after the death of his grandmother, is left alone like Orpheus when Eurydice dies (VI, 165–66). In memory, however, he breathes again the fresh atmosphere of the past with the delight of Orpheus in the Elysian fields (XI, 36).

The leeches in the grandmother's hair at the time of her last illness remind the narrator of Medusa (VII, 193), and the doctor who attends her comes with his bag loaded with *tous les rhumes de ses clients, comme l'outre d'Éole* (VII, 181).

One of the important themes of *A la recherche du temps perdu* is the process of continuous change which is going on in people. The formidable concierge at the Swanns' becomes for Marcel, after he has the right to be admitted to their home, *une bienveillante Euménide* (III, 95). Gilberte, when he gets to know her, is so different from what she appeared to be that Marcel believes himself to have been a victim of mixed identity such as that which occurs in the Menechmes (III, 173). The narrator himself, in his later years, displays a facet of his character which is a sort of sage Mentor compared to the others (XI, 134). As a youth, among the young girls, he was more like Telemachus (V, 225).

Relations in love are illustrated by classical legends. Any loved one is like Janus; the face we see when they are about to leave us is attractive but the one we see when we possess them is dull and undesirable (XI, 225). Albertine is a vast and complex sea which Marcel tries in vain, like Xerxes, to beat (XI, 129). In his jealousy, he is being saved for special punishment, much as Orestes was saved from destruction so that he might avenge the murder of Agamemnon (X, 318). The punishments of jealousy are repeated on us *ad infinitum* like those tortures suffered in the underworld by Ixion or the Danaides (XI, 187).

A homosexual, though male, has hidden in his body the spirit of the young girl Galatea (IX, 32) and he waits on the sand like a strange Andromeda whom no Argonaut will ever deliver (IX, 39). Monsieur Nissim Bernard in mistaking a normal twin for his homosexual brother plays the rôle of Amphitryon without knowing it (IX, 323). Charlus is under the influence of Venus Androgyna (X, 76) and in his masochistic orgies at Jupien's establishment he resembles Prometheus being tortured on his rock (XIV, 146, 174).[1] When he is overwhelmed by Mme Verdurin in her salon, he is more like a terrified nymph being pursued by the god Pan (XII, 142).

In society during his influential years, Charlus is the complete autocrat. Offenders against him are greeted with *les philippiques les plus éloquentes mais les plus terribles* (XII, 40). When he is humbled, his downfall is as great as that of Oedipus, and the moral to be drawn from it as grave (XIV, 202–3).

---

[1] It is interesting to note that the narrator also compares himself while seated in Mme de Villeparisis's carriage, listening to birds singing, to Prometheus on his rock listening to the Oceanides (IV, 148–49). Speaking from personal experience, he says that an invalid removing cotton from his ears *vient de créer, non pas, comme Prométhée, le feu, mais le bruit du feu* (VI, 92).

Besides all these legendary references drawn from classical mythology, Proust has many figures which employ references to specific Greek and Roman writers and their style. Françoise, in quoting Mme de Villeparisis or in her deduced knowledge of the narrator's family, is as far from the truth as Plato who deformed the words of Socrates and believed in myths which were based on a false conception of the universe (IV, 121; VII, 225). Moreover, she cannot answer questions explicitly and she speaks *comme Tirésias et eût écrit comme Tacite* (VII, 226).

For Proust, refined literary or social taste is symbolized by the pleasure an initiate takes in reading or citing an ode of Horace (IV, 195; X, 280) or some Vergil (XIV, 62). The stereotyped remarks M. de Guermantes makes in society resemble those conventional phrases used by the Latin poets to fill out a hexameter with a dactyl or a spondee (VIII, 185–86). The style of Bergotte has a harmony similar to that of classical orators (III, 180), and the young girls known by Marcel shout in a sort of musical fashion which is like the declamation of Greek or Roman poetry (V, 175).

The classical writer referred to most frequently by Proust is Vergil. Brichot sees in Charlus a contemporary comment on Vergil's second eclogue (XII, 156), and the young girls, after the narrator knows them, change in appearance as though a semi-opaque cloud enveloped them *pareille à la Leucothoé de Virgile* (V, 222). Marcel's aunt cannot comprehend the true social position of Swann, and the idea of his relations with important people

> . . . eût paru aussi extraordinaire à ma tante qu'aurait pu l'être pour une dame plus lettrée la pensée d'être personnellement liée avec Aristée dont elle aurait comprise qu'il allait, après avoir causé avec elle, plonger au sein des royaumes de Thétis, dans un empire soustrait aux yeux des mortels, et où Virgile nous le montre reçu à bras ouverts (I, 30).

The *Avenue des Acacias* is like the *allée de Myrtes de l'Énéide* (II, 268), and the repetitious tortures of Ixion and the Danaides also probably come from Vergil.[1]

Marcel says that the compound names of German wines remind him of the sonorous epithets given to heroes in Homer (VII, 97). Odette in her luxurious robes is like a siren swimming in the water (IV, 26), but in her old age, her voice is rather sad, almost supplicat-

[1] See p. 162 above and also I, 228.

ing *comme celle des morts dans l'Odyssée* (XV, 112). The fogs at Balbec are like those of *le véritable pays des Cimmériens, dans l'Odyssée* (I, 178–79).

The changes which the years bring to our ideas and our notions of people are *aussi nombreux que les métamorphoses d'Ovide* (IV, 191). Albertine experiences various metamorphoses (V, 133) and so does Mme de Guermantes (VI, 33). For that reason Albertine is like a goddess with several heads (VII, 233). The voice of La Berma is like that of a nymph changed into a bubbling spring (VI, 57).

The voice of Mme de Cambremer, on the other hand, is gravelly, like that of Demosthenes with his mouth full of pebbles (IX, 277). The views around her Château of Féterne are like the beautiful models of famous monuments which Hadrian assembled around his villa (X, 174).

There are many other general classical references which do not readily fall into any set divisions. For the narrator himself, the *Côté de Guermantes* is like Mount Parnassus or the Helicon (VI, 15), and in his memory it floats, detached, *comme une Délos fleurie* (I, 248). The idea that the River Vivonne has a physical source is as incredible to him as the idea that there existed in the ancient world a spot that was supposed to be the entrance to the underworld (I, 231; XIII, 328).

An authoritarian way of speaking is said to be like a sort of Delphic oracle (I, 126; III, 33–34), and the conversation of M. de Guermantes presents living evidences of the past just like the contemporary geographical areas known of old by historians like Xenophon (VII, 70).

Proust compares the heavy sleep from which one wakens after taking drugs to the overfeeding of Hercules by the nymphs (VI, 106). Our own spirits, he says, are independent and recalcitrant like old Proteus (XI, 252). Ideas about aesthetics or any intangible subject are like goddesses who sometimes materialize and sometimes remain invisible (VIII, 25).

Pigeons with their varied markings are said by Proust to be like a goddess who merits different attributes depending on the appearance she has under given circumstances (II, 255). The furiously charging horses in the Bois de Boulogne are like the fierce chargers of Diomedes (II, 277), and the shadow of the carriage and horse which return Marcel and his ailing grandmother from the Champs-Élysées, projected against a wall, is like *un char funèbre dans une terre cuite de Pompéi* (VII, 174). The catastrophe of Pompei is also used by Proust to describe the immobility imposed by heredity (V, 175–76) and the wild atmosphere of air-raids during the war when individuals at any moment can be caught and immobilized in the acts which they are performing (XIV, 136).

Religion and the Bible. Much more startling than the number of classical references which Proust employs is the revelation of the extent to which he introduces religious and Biblical images in his work. Strictly speaking, of course, purely religious images as opposed to those clearly coming from the Bible should not be considered as literary images. However, it is not always possible to separate the two classes, and since they have the same ultimate source, they have been grouped together. The resultant statistics on that account ought not to be any less significant. There is a grand total of no fewer than 305 religious images in *A la recherche du temps perdu*, and this number would be increased considerably if one included references to Racine's *Esther* and *Athalie*.

Now, it is usual to think of Proust as half-Jewish and definitely agnostic; the Catholic side of his background is rarely stressed. Certainly the accumulated evidence to be derived from an examination of religious images in *A la recherche du temps perdu* does nothing to prove whether Proust was fundamentally religious or not, but it does indicate very clearly an intimate knowledge of the Bible and of the Catholic cult. This fact is extremely important.

In his images, Proust refers to all the important phases of the Catholic church calendar—Lent, Easter, Christmas, the processional of the *Fête-Dieu*, etc., as well as the forms of the mass and the church ritual associated with the different ceremonies. The aspect of all of them which he emphasizes most strongly is their unvarying form and the air of mystery and exultation associated with them.

In society, the fixed routine which characterizes the costume of a beauty like Odette (both in its appearance and in the manner in which it is put on) and the regular meetings of a salon like that of Mme de Guermantes lead Proust to compare both these phenomena to church ritual (IV, 49; VIII, 159, 160, 195). The narrator speaks of *la communion du grand monde* (IX, 101) and he declares concerning the salon of Mme de Guermantes that *la présence du corps de Jésus-Christ dans l'hostie ne me semblait pas un mystère plus obscur que ce premier salon du Faubourg* (VI, 35). Even servants, in their lower order of society,

M

follow a strict routine in their day and Proust speaks of the sacro-
sanct meals of Françoise and the other servants as a sort of *pâque
solennelle.* When the rites are finished Françoise, *qui était à la fois,
comme dans l'église primitive, le célébrant et l'un des fidèles, se servait un
dernier verre de vin* (VI, 19).

Proust extends the metaphor considerably. A salon or a set in
society is a church (VI, 16; XI, 252). To contravene its regulations
is to threaten its orthodoxy (I, 255; XII, 53, 98), and to break with a
salon is like a conversion (X, 99). The leader of a salon is like a
grand inquisitor who seeks always to extirpate heresy among the
faithful (II, 61). If necessary, dangerous individuals will be excom-
municated (IX, 65) or 'put on the index' (XII, 44). Important social
figures are treated with the deference due a bishop or the pope
(VIII, 197), and one genuflects before them (VIII, 91). Smiles or
greetings between members resemble at times the gesture of bene-
diction made by priests (IX, 107), and conversation may almost be
intoned like a chant (IX, 127; X, 201).

Bird songs remind Proust of church music because they start
early in the morning and seem to utilize the Lydian mode for their
rendition of Matins (XII, 232). Both laughter and sobs are like the
ringing of church bells (XII, 107; I, 55), and Proust compares at
some length the sound of street noises to the music associated with
the Catholic Church. The calls of vendors might almost be Latin,
and they resemble the liturgy sung in a Gregorian mode (XI, 144,
145, 146, 147, 157, 169, 170). The principal themes in Vinteuil's
music are like saints or angels (XII, 72–73, 214).

The partaking of communion is specifically used by Marcel to
describe the precious but regular daily kisses which his mother and
later Albertine give to him (I, 24, 43; XI, 94). He even refers to
them in connection with Albertine as his *pain quotidien,* a phrase
directly from the Lord's Prayer (XI, 10). When his mother kneels
before the dying grandmother, her face is a sort of ciborium in
which all her love is proffered (VII, 180). Marcel himself finds in
Albertine a religious experience which makes of her a mystic ideal
to which he brings all his doubts in order that he may be cleared of
them *dans l'abdication d'un croyant qui fait sa prière* (XI, 93).

Beautiful arrangements of flowers or effects of light on tables
are compared by Proust to relics and altars or repositories decorated
for special festivals. The association in his mind is an obvious one
and the flowers most often described this way are the hawthorn (I,

188, 190, 191), although chrysanthemums and artificial lights on tables at Odette's are also connected with altars (II, 10, 11; III, 126), and fruit trees with repositories and first communions (VI, 188, 189). The tables with their white cloths at Balbec are like altars ready to receive the sunset (XV, 17). Sunlight performs the same service for Marcel's commode (IV, 129), and before any of these exquisite groupings, he stops for a moment *en une courte station et le temps de faire mes dévotions à la 'vue'* (V, 48). Such scenes framed in the window are especially like relics when the shutters are closed hiding them from view (V, 49).

Anything precious and mysterious is associated by Proust with altars, and the Holy of Holies or relics, which are on it or near it. In the world of the arts, the stage where La Berma performs is consecrated to her like an altar (III, 22; VI, 53). The corner of the room where Albertine plays the piano is a sort of precious sanctuary (XII, 226), and the platform where the musicians perform the music of Vinteuil is an altar for the accomplishment of certain mystic rites (II, 181). La Berma herself is hidden behind the curtain of the stage like the Holy of Holies (III, 21–22). In the world of society, the Swanns' home is at first a forbidden sanctuary to Marcel (III, 102, 104). A society queen's forgotten glove is a precious relic (XII, 89), and a dress by Fortuny is more elaborately decorated than the religious treasures of St. Mark's in Venice (XII, 209). Genealogical connections with famous figures in the past or inherited habits of speech or thought are also like precious relics which are carefully kept and exposed to view (VIII, 186–87; IX, 300).

Proust uses other Catholic elements in his descriptions. The chicken Françoise cooks is like a golden chasuble *et son jus précieux égoutté d'un ciboire* (I, 167). Oyster shells with salty liquor in them are like *bénitiers* (V, 128; VI, 143). The rays of the sun are like a monstrance (I, 206), and eyelids half-closed in the bright sunlight *comme des veilleuses d'albâtre . . . se remplissaient d'une lueur rose* (VI, 180). The hall tree at the Swanns' is like the seven-branched candlestick of the Bible (III, 96). Marcel's great-uncle who, as a priest, assists at the services for the dead grandmother watches Marcel at the death-bed from behind spread fingers which hide his face like the grill of a confessional, but when he notices that he is being observed, *il . . . clôtura hermétiquement le grillage qu'il avait laissé entr'ouvert* (VII, 200).

The rich colours of stained glass windows are used to describe the effects of natural or artificial light. The sea, when illuminated, is like the sea in a stained glass window (V, 49), and the colourful dishes at Combray are like brightly-set apertures in a dull gray stone background (V, 170). The magic lantern projects similar colourful windows (I, 19), and the colours of the spectrum from a glass prism are as vivid as the stained glass in the Cathedral at Chartres (XI, 208). A ruddy-faced peasant gives the impression of being seen in the light of an illuminated stained glass window (IV, 72).

People are also compared by Proust to decorative or architectural features of churches. The Guermantes clan, and especially Mme de Guermantes and Charlus, are like the figures in the stained glass windows at Combray (VIII, 195; I, 239; XV, 199; XII, 78). The frequenters of their salon are the pillars of the temple or the gold statues of the apostles in the Sainte-Chapelle (VI, 36), and servants in attendance or merely procrastinating are like statues of saints in their niches (I, 77; II, 146). Théodore attending Marcel's Aunt Léonie is like one of the young sculptured angels attending the Virgin Mary in a *bas-relief* (I, 205).

Religious architecture is used by Proust to describe such prosaic things as an outdoor pump and the entrance to a grocery store. It is the fancy carving on them which makes him think of Gothic ornamentation (I, 102, 118). The same feature characterizes an elaborately iced cake (V, 169), and the bony structure of a fish reminds Proust of the form of a Gothic cathedral (IV, 118). More abstractly, the polyphonic structure of the music of Vinteuil is considered by Proust to be similar to the architectural rhythm of a cathedral in which the predominating themes expressed by certain statues placed high on the steeple resemble the principal theme of the music (IX, 231).

Individuals in all ranks of society from the very highest down to the very lowest are referred to by Proust in terms of the religious hierarchy. Their relatively fixed position, the set costume that goes with it, and their relations to those above and below them, all make this comparison a very effective one. Charlus is said to be a Jesuit or a pious ecclesiastic because of his lowered eyes (X, 221, 254). He is also referred to as a bishop (IX, 21; VII, 114), a Pope (XII, 150) and an apostle (XII, 157). His brother, the Duke, is also said to be like a bishop (XV, 229). Monsieur de Cambremer, on the other hand, resembles a sacristan (IV, 103), but his venerable mother, too, is more like a bishop, especially because of the accoutrements she carries (IX, 265, 285). Other members of higher society who are spoken of in terms of religious rank are General de Beautreillis (VIII, 140–41), Mme de Villeparisis (VIII, 179) and Monsieur de Vaugoubert (IX, 86). Cottard in his wartime uniform looks like a little boy dressed up in the costume of the 'Enfants de Marie' (XIV, 92–93). Servants and even prostitutes are compared to curés hypocrites, confesseurs papelards and detestable priests (VI, 201, 205; X, 272–73). Young attendants in a house of prostitution repeat the orders of the madame comme ces catéchismes qu'on entend les élèves psalmodier dans la sonorité d'une église de campagne (X, 273).

In their relations among themselves and in their family relations, individuals in society are often compared to saints or martyrs. A victim of jealousy, in particular, is said to be suffering martyrdom (X, 321; XI, 117), but a social snob is also a victim of his own principles (I, 174, 176). A virtuous woman like Mme de Marsantes is called a saint (VII, 89, 90), and a long-suffering wife like Mme de Guermantes is a sort of martyr (VI, 176; IX, 109). Marcel's grandmother in the midst of the resentment of other diners at Balbec when she opens the windows, remains impassive like Saint Blandine (IV, 94).

Authoritarian individuals are like prophets. Figures in society, and especially Charlus, because of his arrogant and peremptory attitude, are prophets (XII, 57; XV, 97). Literary critics, for the same reason, are self-appointed prophets who repeat messages no longer new (XV, 41).

Proust utilizes commonly much material from Christian legend in his images. The dining-room at Balbec is as precious and colourful as Heaven itself (IV, 93), and music introduces us to a sort of Paradise from which we fall like angels when it stops (XII, 70). Bergotte's books, on the shelves above his death-bed, watch over him like angels (XI, 233), and beautiful fruit trees in blossom are like denizens of Heaven (VI, 196). Women are compared by Proust to angels (II, 129; XI, 140), and homosexuals are said to have in their bodies angelic female spirits beating their wings toward other men (X, 132). Such an abstract quality as certainty is called an angel (I, 18), and death is said to be a powerful angel (VII, 171). Marcel's grandmother, in his mind, has an appearance as fixed and arbitrary as that of God the Father with his long white beard (XV, 157).

People who are socially enviable are spoken of as having a halo which sets them apart from the ordinary rank and file. For the narrator, Gilberte is a supernatural being because of her friendship with Bergotte, and Mme de Guermantes because of her position in the *Faubourg St.-Germain*. Both these individuals are said, therefore, to wear halos (V, 40; VI, 16–17). For less perspicacious folk, the members of the Verdurin circle seem to wear a prominent halo (X, 10), but for all of us *notre notion de la personne . . . y est embellie de l'auréole que nous ne tardons pas à lui rendre* (IV, 36).

Besides references of this sort to common but vague Christian legends, Proust has many images which refer specifically to the Bible, both in the Old and New Testaments, and the Apocrypha.

The creation of the world is used by Proust to describe the magnificent and mysterious formative powers of the artist Elstir (V, 86). Odette in her costuming and promenading is as assured and poised as the Creator accomplishing his work (IV, 48), and the arrival at a social function of Mme de Guermantes is like the creation of the world (VIII, 105).

The story of Adam and Eve is generally associated by Proust with love or desire. Swann's desire for Odette and Marcel's desire for Albertine are like the attraction Eve exerts upon Adam (II, 29; VII, 210, 220). When Albertine leaves Marcel, it is as though he were awakened, like the young Adam newly created who has to solve all his problems without the aid of predecessors (XII, 251). The narrator's erotic dreams are caused by a false position of his thigh *comme Eve naquit d'une côte d'Adam* (I, 13). The life and activities of Mme de Guermantes, for those who are not her associates, are like the forbidden fruit (VIII, 157) or Paradise denied (XV, 181).

Proust compares at some length the Cathedral of Laon perched on its hill-top to Noah's ark landing on Mount Ararat (VI, 14, 15). He also refers to a new mode in costume as *une espèce inconnue née du dernier déluge* (IX, 184), and he compares the atmosphere of companionship in a restaurant surrounded by cold winter fog to that which existed in the ark (VIII, 35–36).

Light effects, both natural and artificial, are compared to the luminous column which guided the children of Israel at night in the wilderness (V, 229; VIII, 27). The three blows sounded behind the curtain at the theatre to indicate the beginning of a play scatter the sea of spectators into their places much as the Red Sea parted for the Hebrews fleeing from Egypt (VI, 46). The Jews in *A la recherche du temps perdu* are particularly associated with this period of Jewish history. Bloch is chained to his heredity (XV, 83), and the personality of Rachel is *mystérieusement enfermée dans un corps comme dans un Tabernacle* (VI, 192).

The conduct of Françoise is governed by a code as arbitrary and as harsh as that of the Old Testament (I, 44; XI, 18), and her comments are as abrupt and bitter as if they came from Ecclesiastes (I, 149).

There are many well-known episodes in the Bible which Proust refers to casually. The Duchesse de Guermantes is regarded as being very precious *comme un Moïse sauvé des eaux, un Christ échappé en Égypte* (XV, 175–76). In analyzing the character of others and fixing it, particularly for homosexuals, the narrator sees in their appearance a sort of invisible writing which traces on them the fatal terms *Mane, Thekel, Phares* (IX, 23). In interpreting his own dreams, Marcel is both Joseph and Pharaoh (IV, 39). As he awakens, the bones of his body seem to assemble miraculously before him, probably like those associated with Ezekiel (V, 72).

Morel looks like a young David able to combat Goliath as he shakes hands in virile fashion (IX, 334). Homosexuals in general, however, are like Samson, condemned continually to turn a mill in a narrow circle (IX, 25). The whole question of homosexuality and Lesbianism is associated particularly with the cities of Sodom and Gomorrha and the sinfulness which eventually led to their destruction (IX, 13, 45; XI, 27). Also compared to Sodom and Gomorrha in their destruction are rain on a town in the distance (I, 206), houses which look as though they might have been burnt or exposed to a fiery rain (VI, 196), and the punitive elements in the life of a poet which cause him to undergo the most dreadful torments in order to 'bring back a few inhabitants of Sodom' (XII, 9). Ironically, the homosexual Charlus refers to himself as an inhabitant of Sodom (XIV, 177) and, in his relations with Morel, he compares himself to the archangel Raphael and the young violinist to Tobiah (X, 266; XII, 150).

There are, in Proust, and coming strictly from the New Testament, numerous references to Christ and His disciples, to His parables and miracles, and, especially, to His agony and death. Charlus and the young mechanic are both spoken of as apostles (XII, 157; X, 209; XI, 165), and when Charlus is at the height of his jealousy over Morel, the ordeal is referred to as his Calvary (X,

273). When Charlus spies on Morel in a house of prostitution, the terrified Morel who knows that Charlus is observing him, looks worse than Lazarus raised from the dead (X, 274). The narrator himself responds to Bergotte like a prodigal son in the arms of his father (I, 134), and in describing the effect on a deaf person of milk boiling over, he says that it is necessary to watch the pot and to take it off the flame as the waves rise, just as Christ stilled the storm in time (VI, 92). The narrator's own illness, in causing him to die as far as the world of society was concerned, performed the same function for his creative powers as the grain of wheat dying that it might bear much fruit. (XV, 227). An angry or pained expression, or the sun appearing in a stormy sky are compared to Christ's stigmata (VIII, 26; V, 49). Old age is a *chemin de croix* (XV, 193) and Marcel's Aunt Léonie, in a figure objected to by Gide,[1] presented to him to kiss a forehead in which *les vertèbres transparaissaient comme les pointes d'une couronne d'épines* (I, 77). The words which Odette says to Swann are felt by him to *garder vaguement comme le voile sacré, l'empreinte, dessiner l'incertain modelé, de cette réalité infiniment précieuse et hélas! introuvable* (II, 86). Flowering bushes are supernatural beings to the narrator but not unfamiliar ones; in considering them as such, he deceives himself just as Mary Magdalene was deceived in thinking that the figure she saw near the tomb was the gardener (VI, 195–96).

In referring to the future of Bergotte's writings, Proust mentions Pentecost where the apostles were endowed with the ability to understand all tongues (XI, 228). Finally, he refers to the Last Judgment as the revelation of ultimate truth. Reality, change, and the permanence and eternal truth of art are spoken of by Proust as being aspects of the final goal which an individual can reach and therefore *le vrai Jugement dernier* (XV, 23, 81).

Besides all the above references to the Bible and Catholic cult, Proust draws into his images early church history, references to other sects and religions, atheism and religious philosophy.

We have already examined numerous images which refer to art as religion and to the creators of art as religious figures. Writers, especially, are said to be like priests or the early Church fathers who know sin (the former by study, some of the latter by personal experience) and who therefore are able to understand all ideas and to establish a general moral rule for humanity (III, 163, 175–76).

[1] See Gide: letter to Proust dated 'Janvier 1914' in Gide: *Œuvres complètes*, VIII, 378.

During the war, the corridors of the Métro are as black as the catacombs (XIV, 171), and the frequenters of Jupien's establishment celebrate in safety, within its darkened precincts, rites as much frowned upon as those performed by the early Christians (XIV, 172). A different sort of *Cène sociale* is celebrated by Mme de Guermantes and her friends but it also resembles in its exclusiveness the secret meetings of the first Christians (VIII, 158–59).

The narrator compares himself to a naïve early theologian in his imagining Albertine offering satisfactory explanations for the causes of his jealousy (XIII, 119). He also says that place-names arouse in him a feeling of anticipation as eager as that of early Christians about to enter the gates of Paradise (II, 233). Rachel, as the mistress of Saint-Loup, has one good influence on him at least, for she teaches him pity towards animals *comme les premiers moines du moyen âge à la chrétienté* (V, 23).

Social ineptitude is compared by Proust to the awkwardness of a Protestant thrown into contact with Catholic custom (III, 152; VI, 97; VII, 42). Saint-Loup refers scathingly to the Verdurin salon as a sort of Protestant chapel or sect (X, 202). Homosexual relations are said to consist of rites associated with a different religion than Christianity or with the desecrated rites of the Black Mass (X, 185; XII, 254).

Persistence, generally speaking, is the characteristic of atheists, whether it be the obstinacy of those loved ones who deceive us by their lies (XII, 227–28) or the perseverance of searchers after truth in making known to others, even though they may themselves be dying, the truths which they have discovered (XI, 180–81). Marcel likes to imagine that Albertine in her last hours turned away from atheism to him—*de se confesser enfin à lui, de mourir en lui* (XIII, 114).

The human personality in its complex variety is very much like many-headed Oriental gods except that we only see one face at a time (V, 184). When an individual dies, the fact that he ever existed becomes a source of doubt for us *comme ces dieux des religions abolies qu'on offense sans crainte parce qu'on a cessé de croire à leur existence* (XIII, 228). Souls are used by Proust to characterize what is light and intangible but persistent, such as the filagree shadows of trees in the sunshine (XIV, 56) or the subconscious organic memory of scent and taste (I, 68).

In the realm of religious philosophy, Pascal is the only writer referred to by Proust. The difficult abstract questions which Pascal raises are used to describe the complexities of social relations and the reasons for their existence (VI, 26; X, 138). Marcel later discovers that the abyss which he thought existed between him and the young girls, for example, was in itself as imaginary as Pascal's abyss (XIII, 332).

From all the above examples, it should be manifest how important a rôle religious imagery plays in Proust's work. There is further evidence to be deduced from a study of the imagery drawn from paintings, sculpture and music which treat religious themes, but it merely strengthens the observations already made.

As in the case of images drawn from the Classics, it might be argued that none of the images drawn from religion reveals any professional study of doctrine or any first-hand acquaintance with other than the common heritage of religious knowledge. All this can be admitted freely without denigrating Proust's abilities. After all, he was not writing a treatise on theology, and the bare fact that he included in his work such a large body of religious images indicates what an important rôle religion played in the background of his thinking.

Geography, Travelling. Some of Proust's references through images of travelling and geography are no doubt the result of personal experience. Figures of speech mentioning Venice, Switzerland and Holland would fall into that category. On the other hand, many others, including those that are strictly theoretical, can be classified only as literary references. For that reason, all images which involve references to countries, modes of travel or the business of geography have been grouped together here.

For the narrator, the desire to travel and to see new places epitomizes all desires. Seeing La Berma act (III, 19) or penetrating into the salon of the Guermantes (VII, 246) is like undertaking a voyage long dreamed about. These experiences may in fact be as disappointing as the revelation of a new city (VI, 35). The same is true for love, because it also is like a journey or an outing, whether it be normal love (II, 71, 214; III, 199; IV, 40; IX, 211) or homosexual love (XIII, 320). Love is also like a road or path (VIII, 8).

Life itself is like a voyage and our passage through time is similar in many ways to passage through space (V, 223; I, 172; IV, 83; XV, 137, 154). Life passes through different latitudes to the extreme cold of old age (V, 158). Most obviously, our day-dreams

(XI, 143–44) or real dreams (I, 14; X, 150, 153; XI, 99, 151), the reading of books (XV, 31) and seeing of plays (III, 31) are like journeys, and we are conscious, when we leave them, of having travelled away from the ordinary routes of everyday living. Days can seem as long as those at the North Pole in summer (V, 52–53). Associations which occupy us during a particular period of time are like a journey abroad (XII, 11). Practice of a secret vice has the same effect (XII, 12). Some people age faster than others and it is as though they had taken express trains toward their destination (XV, 105). Memory is a sort of voyage in reverse or return journey which takes us over routes we have covered before (XIII, 175, 176, 177).

Other people are embarked on a similar sort of journey to our own, and for that reason, they can be compared to vessels, countries or even roads and routes. The young girls who attract Marcel's attention are like countries he would like to visit (I, 13; IV, 140). This is true especially for Gilberte (XIII, 327) and Albertine who reflects in her manners the geographical peculiarities of Austria. Other individuals who incorporate in themselves unique geographical characteristics are Françoise (I, 44–45), Mme de Villeparisis (VII, 14) and Mme de Guermantes (XI, 41–42).

Names in general are associated by Proust with geographical phenomena. Guermantes is like a mountain to be explored (VIII, 174) or a geographical abstraction similar to the equator, a pole or 'the east' (I, 183). Paris place-names permit of the same sort of exploration (VIII, 12).

Oddly enough, it would seem, the concept of a departure for a journey or a prolonged trip represents for the narrator all that is sad and miserable (II, 27, 243; VI, 149). And strange hotel rooms stand for the ultimate in unpleasant unfamiliarity (I, 19; IV, 78).

Individuals are as devious as highways (V, 161) or a crossroads in the forest (XV, 206). Our contacts with them are like the junctions of different roads (VI, 194)—never the same for those who approach a goal by variant routes.

Even ideas in our minds present us with a sort of crossroads where we must make a choice (XIII, 156), and the attainment of truth is the ultimate aim which we pursue (XII, 170) despite the fact that halts are forced upon us like unscheduled train stops (XI, 183). Outward appearances are as incidental as the railway bench on which we read a novel (I, 215).

Aesthetic subjects are related by Proust to the three-dimensional environment of geography. The acting of La Berma (VI, 62) and the music of Vinteuil (XII, 58–59) are like new and strange lands, and every creative artist is, in his own way, an inhabitant of a land that is unique to him alone (XII, 68, 69). The eternal variety of art (and indeed of nature itself) makes its contemplation similar to a journey (IV, 91, 92; V, 90; VIII, 26). Performers of music are like roads or short cuts which introduce us to new lands (XII, 77). Charlus plays an intermediary rôle between society and artists similar to that of the reindeer utilized by the Eskimos; lichens and mosses which cannot be absorbed directly by humans are transmuted by the intervention of an agent (VIII, 226).

The method of travel that Proust refers to most frequently is that by rail. Movement at social gatherings is similar to the distracted movements of travellers in a station (II, 149), and relations there are often about as cordial as those between strangers thrown together in the same compartment (X, 40) or in a railway buffet (IV, 100). The type of conversation one hears under such circumstances is also used to characterize that of those who are waiting for the grandmother's death (VII, 202). Meaningless social smiles are as omnibus as the public railway service (X, 178).

Proust also refers to travel on foot and travel by coach or carriage as well as by boat and by plane. Memory, in particular, is related to all these modes of transportation. Very early childhood memories are as near the ground as a stroller who is resting beside the river bank (I, 226). The effortless involuntary memory is like a carriage which rolls over smooth grass lawns or a plane which takes off from the ground and floats smoothly in the air (XIV, 200).

Besides all the above references to modes of travel, Proust also refers specifically to various parts of the world and to their inhabitants.

Primitive instincts or emotions are compared to those of savages. Françoise in her ability to sense innuendo is like a primitive savage (I, 45; VI, 76), and the cruelty of the members of the Verdurin circle toward Saniette is like that of cannibals (X, 91–92). Cottard regards Charlus as a wild savage (X, 264), and Bréauté considers Marcel as some sort of aborigine because of his lack of social prestige (VIII, 64).

The exclusive *Faubourg St.-Germain* is regarded by the narrator as an exquisite oasis or an exotic shore (VI, 36, 37). Love or desire is like a thirst or a drought which is assuaged by the loved one or a letter from her. This, too, is like an oasis or a welcome rain (VI, 149; V, 39).

The changed appearance of people in old age leads the narrator to compare them to the dwarf trees or giant monkey bread trees one finds in one or other of the extremes of latitude (XV, 80). Certain shrivelled-up women are like Turks (XV, 103).

Two of the relatives of the Duc de Guermantes are compared to Swiss alpinists because of their appearance and because their residence is situated on a height (VIII, 231, 232, 235; IX, 161–62). The Trocadero also reminds the narrator at times of Swiss scenery (XIV, 84), and an effect of the sun on water makes it look like alpine meadows (IV, 91).

Splendour and amazement are the impressions called up in the narrator's mind by Venice or the sight of certain other lovely Italian cities. He uses this comparison to describe the Fortuny creation which Albertine wears (XII, 209, 211, 240–41, 245). For Françoise, the charms of Combray are like those of Venice (VI, 28), and for Marcel, Rivebelle holds the same sort of exotic beauty (V, 229). The excitement which a social gathering promises (IX, 182) and the dissipation of jealousy (II, 25) are also as emotionally stimulating as the brilliance of Italian skies and seas. Even the pangs of jealousy are not unpleasant to Swann *comme au morne Parisien qui quitte Venise pour retrouver la France, un dernier moustique prouve que l'Italie et l'été ne sont pas encore bien loin* (II, 214).

THE ARTS

Everyone reading Proust has a favourite set of images which he would like to consider as uniquely important, and since practically all images recur in some numbers, it is very easy to build up supporting evidence, provided one overlooks other sets of images which are perhaps more numerous. Even a strictly impartial count can be misleading, of course, because it weighs as equally significant a rather common image and one that may be brilliant and startlingly new. How to reconcile this discrepancy without allowing the subjective element to intervene has been the major problem of this study and it becomes particularly acute when we turn from literary images to images drawn from the world of the arts.

No one needs to emphasize Proust's interest in painting, sculpture, music and the theatre. His knowledge of the techniques of each of these art forms and, what is more significant, their underlying philosophies is that of a passionate *amateur*. He relates the different fields of expression to each other and shows the unity of purpose and method which exists behind apparently divergent techniques and media. The one art form to which all the others are related and which, both objectively and subjectively, stands first as a general source of images is painting.

Painting. We have already drawn attention to the fact that Proust is a great lover of nature. Pure nature images constitute the most important single large class in *A la recherche du temps perdu*, and as a category they also overflow into learned references drawn from botany and zoology and artistic images drawn from painting. Proust loves to compare nature to art, and in these comparisons the emphasis is on the beauty of nature which can be described only in terms of those near-perfect and permanent works of art which are the acknowledged standard of all that is wonderful and lovely, rather than on art itself. These works of art were inspired by nature in the first place and they are the only lasting unchanging records to which can be related the recurring transient phenomena of nature.

Any beautiful view seen through a window which frames it reminds Proust of a painting hung on display. It may be a cloud effect which reminds him either of a pastel (IV, 69; V, 52) or a detailed drawing by Pisanello (V, 49), or it may be the white-capped sea or a line of snow on the window itself which resemble the enamel work of Gallé (V, 49; VIII, 19; X, 172). A butterfly on the window is exactly like the identifying emblem Whistler added to his paintings (V, 52), and a line of windows or reflecting mirrors on bookcases inside a room present a varied series of paintings resembling a museum showing, or the different panels of a series on a given subject (V, 49, 51, 52).

The sea, either seen through a window behind people or through trees in the distance, is like a painted backdrop, a tapestry or Japanese *cloisonné* (IV, 91, 101, 160; I, 228–29). A vessel in the distance appearing to be of almost the same misty colour as the sea gives the effect of an impressionistic canvas (V, 51).

Any time of day presents us with effects similar to those of paintings. The first soft light of dawn is like a delicate pastel (I, 251; VI, 107) or a travel poster (IV, 65), but the fiery sun surrounded by barbed rays is like the stylized representations one sometimes sees (X, 334–35). The golden light of the sun at Florence is similar in effect to an Angelico (II, 227), and bright sunshine with light reflected from water at Venice reminds one of Chardin and Veronese (XIII, 258–59). Twilight is more like subdued yellow and blue Persian art work (II, 275) or soft water-colours (XV, 13). Moonlight plays strange artistic tricks with perspective because of shadows and reflections (I, 49).

Spring is the season of the year which provides the greatest profusion of artistic effects (IV, 133). Rain then seems to varnish the leaves of the trees (I, 207), and a similar result is achieved by the warm light which Odette's umbrella throws on her (IV, 53). It is blossoms and flowering shrubs, however, which account for the greatest numbers of comparisons with paintings.

Sometimes flowers are vaguely referred to as *chefs-d'œuvre* (I, 189; II, 269), but more often the images are specific. The pink hawthorn in contrast to the white gives the narrator the same joy as a full colour painting compared with the pencil sketch of it (I, 189). 'Snowballs' remind him of the linear shrub drawings of the Pre-Raphaelites (IV, 45), and a double row of chestnut trees with their orange flowers in full bloom against a relatively neutral background looks like an unfinished painting in which they are the only part to have had the colour added (II, 274). Roses are like 18th-century paintings of flowers (VII, 14) while lilacs and buttercups are more reminiscent of Persian and Oriental art because of their colours (I, 185, 226). Cornflowers in a field seen from a carriage are like the same identifying mark of authenticity which 'certain ancient masters' (as well as Whistler, apparently) added to their pictures (IV, 137–38).

Within buildings and in the city, light effects also remind Proust of paintings. A dimly-lit stairway or dining-room is like a painting by Rembrandt (III, 99; V, 46). The village of Combray seen from a distance is similar to primitive medieval paintings of walled circular towns (I, 71). In Paris, on the other hand, houses in poor quarters are like an exposition of Dutch pictures (VIII, 231), and the smoky railway station of Saint-Lazare provides as terrifying a background as those used by Mantegna or Veronese in their crucifixions (IV, 57).

Exotic foreign costumes in Paris during the war seem to make the architecture an unimportant painted backdrop for the more interesting groupings of costumes in the foreground. This is like the style of Carpaccio (XIV, 85, 128).

One often hears it proclaimed that illustrations in a book are disappointing because they never live up to the mental pictures one has built up around familiar or well-loved characters. With other writers than Proust, this is no doubt almost always true, but in his case the argument really does not hold. His system of mental images is a visual or pictorial one, as we have already remarked many times, and he does his very best to make us see the characters in his book exactly as he sees them. To do this, he compares them to what he considers well-known portraits familiar to most of his readers. The only limitations on the prospective illustrator of Proust's works are his own ability as an artist and the complex and constantly changing appearance of any one individual. It might be necessary to paint a series of portraits of any one person in order adequately to illustrate the complexity of his particular character, but there is no reason why, at a given moment, his exact appearance cannot be delineated.

People in all ranks of society are compared by Proust to portraits or figures in group paintings.[1] The servants in the restaurant at Doncières are like peasant figures in a painting by Breughel or one of the other Flemish masters (VI, 119, 120). The head waiter Aimé resembles standard portraits of the Prince Eugene (VI, 202), and various members of the retinue at the Saint-Euverte establishment remind Swann respectively of portraits by Mantegna, Goya or a Cellini bronze (II, 144, 146, 147). Gilberte's governess is like the portrait of Jeffries by Hogarth (V, 80).

The two servants who are compared at some length to paintings are Françoise and the kitchen-maid. They are related particularly to the contrasting figures of Envy and Charity in Giotto's frescoes in the Arena at Padua (I, 114, 115, 116). In addition, Françoise is also compared to portraits of Anne de Bretagne (IV, 63), representations of 'La Justice éclairant le Crime' (VII, 227) and dignified entremetteuses in paintings of the old masters (XI, 174).

In higher society, various members of the Faubourg St.-Germain are compared to paintings. Oddly enough, Mme de Guermantes herself is only vaguely referred to as a portrait, a chef-d'œuvre or a

[1] Cf. M. E. Chernowitz, Proust and Painting, New York (1945), pp. 52–62.

toile de maître (VII, 244; VI, 176–77; VIII, 244). Monsieur de Guermantes, however, is compared specifically to the Bourgmestre Six of Rembrandt (IX, 104), and the Princesse de Guermantes is said to be like a beautiful model (IX, 50–51) or the exquisite little emblem already referred to which Whistler and certain other artists used to sign their paintings (VI, 50). Charlus resembles a grand inquisitor painted by El Greco (XII, 9); the Duc d'Aumale, a medallion of Henri IV (VI, 47). M. de Beausergent is like an old engraving of a haughty courtier (VI, 67), and the Princesse Mathilde resembles a portrait by Winterhalter (III, 143). Other important members of the upper class, not always identified, are said to be like 'figures in a picture' or 'living historical pictures' (II, 147; IX, 155).

Swann delights in finding in his acquaintances resemblances to celebrated pictures (II, 15), and it is the similarity between Odette and Botticelli's painting of 'Zipporah' which persuades him she is beautiful (II, 27). Her life when he is not around is like a series of studies of smiles by Watteau (II, 36). The same predilection characterizes the narrator Marcel. For him, Madame Swann is a more delightful and mysterious person than *La Gioconda* (III, 126). As a child, his father in night clothes reminds him of Gozzoli's picture of Abraham (I, 55), and in later years he compares both his friend, Saint-Loup, and his mistress, Albertine, to paintings. Saint-Loup has the noble gestures of an historical portrait (VI, 89) or an antique frieze (VIII, 44) and the harmony of a restful landscape (IV, 169, 170). This same surprising comparison of a person to a landscape is also applied to Albertine and especially to her hair (XI, 86; XII, 226) which also reminds him of Velasquez' painting of an Infanta (XII, 213). Other features of Albertine are also related to art. Her cheeks are like the rose enamel of a delicate miniature (V, 220), but the perspective of her features seen from near at hand makes Marcel think of figures drawn by Michelangelo (V, 205). Albertine's thigh is like the neck of the swan in Leonardo da Vinci's painting of Leda (XIII, 138), and certain expressions of her face are like the same artist's caricatures (XI, 96). She is also compared to a portrait by Latour (XII, 185) and it is said that if she were to appear in a painting carrying her '*diabolo*', future commentators would have as much difficulty identifying it as present commentators looking at the objects held by allegorical figures in the fresco at the Arena in Padua (V, 149).

N

The narrator compares the band of young girls to figures in an ancient fresco (V, 40, 223) or a primitive painting (V, 171). He surrounds himself with them, he says, much as Rubens surrounded himself with female companions who became models for goddesses in his pictures (V, 224–25). Any one of them or any peasant who inspires desire is like *un vrai Titien à acquérir avant de s'en aller* (XIII, 274).

Swann himself is compared by Marcel to one of the magi in a fresco by Luini (III, 181). M. Nissim Bernard is said to look like ancient representations of King Sargon on Assyrian friezes (V, 14, 15), and Jews in a group form a cortège like those seen in ancient works of art (IV, 172; IX, 136). Their types are exaggerated like stylized illustrations for the New Testament or the *Arabian Nights* (IV, 172).

Besides comparing people to paintings, Proust also compares them to painters, and this category of images is restricted almost entirely to the elaboration of social relationships. Any person who is an expert in his field is said to be like a painter, whether it be Françoise as a cook (III, 72), Charlus as an authority on protocol (XII, 36), or beautiful women like Odette or Mme de Guermantes in their mastery of dress and manners (VI, 175–76; XIV, 113–14; XV, 184–85). People socially prominent in certain circles are also said to be artists; M. Verdurin (X, 178–79), Swann (III, 9)—although in his capacity as Odette's husband he is like an artist delighting in a rather unworthy milieu (IV, 11)—, Cottard (VII, 187). Rapid, comprehensive glances, such as those exchanged between homosexuals or servants calculating tips given to others, are like those of a painter sketching (XI, 185; XII, 205).

The pictorial quality of Proust's mental images is strikingly illustrated by his choice of synaesthetic images to concretize proper names. *All* words present visual images, like paintings, to him (II, 229), but proper names are singularly detailed in form and colour. Some are as vivid in hue as posters (II, 229). Others are like portraits in sombre colours of the *belle médaille de la Renaissance* Proust so frequently refers to (IV, 184; VIII, 192). The name Florence is like one of Giotto's paintings (II, 232), and a name of ancient coinage is like a lasting work of architecture which we see today just as it was in paintings done hundreds of years ago (XIII, 208). Even voices with their distinguishing auditory characteristics present to the narrator visual images like paintings (IV, 174, 175).

The effect of heredity is similar to painting. A child is like a copy of an original (IX, 121) and not always a very good one (III, 170). Each of us is like a painter copying from a pre-arranged design the person we *are* rather than the person we would like to be (VII, 12).

Marcel uses images drawn from painting in describing his own mental experiences. Dreams are, of course, visual, with nightmares fantastic albums (VI, 106), and the figure of Sleep itself projected in a dream is similar to Giotto's figure of Envy (VI, 178). Memories especially are like a collection of paintings (XI, 31). Some of them are mere sketches (II, 82) and others are worn and indistinct like faded frescoes (VII, 210; XV, 63). Most memories have been repainted by us many times (IV, 37), and the related series of memories concerning particular incidents in our lives is like the paintings on an altar piece (XV, 139–40) or the interlinked strokes on a single picture (VIII, 188). Reality compared to memories is like an original masterpiece as opposed to engravings or prints of it (I, 224), but the involuntary memory has the power to draw forth from the little tubes of paint the exact shade and character of the real object (VI, 12). Even the imagination, and particularly the imagination in love, is like painting (XI, 83). Hope is like an artist's canvas (IV, 35), and anticipation works like an artist whose sittings are limited and who must therefore prepare himself thoroughly in advance (I, 42). Possessions of the loved one, or the desire of them, makes them seem more precious than valuable works of art (III, 96). Happiness through love, Marcel says, *c'était une chose à laquelle j'avais constamment songé, une chose toute en pensées, c'était, comme disait Léonard de la peinture,* cosa mentale (III, 92). Trying substitute pleasures with another individual than the one really loved is like going to the Louvre instead of visiting Venice (XIII, 166).

When Proust uses images to describe the techniques of the different forms of creative art, he draws his source material consistently from painting. The work and methods of Elstir are compared to those of Leonardo da Vinci (V, 194) and Carpaccio (VIII, 51). There is a direct relation here and also in the description of stage make-up for plays or ballet as a form of painting (VI, 216–17). When acting itself is compared to painting, however, the relationship is not so obvious. The reasons for the superiority of La Berma on the stage are as difficult to analyze as the qualities that make the Mona Lisa such a provocative painting (III, 31). La Berma is like a painter of great murals (III, 20) or the impressionists who subordinate detail to overall effect, and in her masterpieces she is recognizable just as one recognizes in different pictures the distinguishing characteristics of the great painter (VI, 61, 62).

Music is also like painting. Its style may be as pure as that of Raphael (XI, 199), and because of its contrapuntal structure, it seems to partake of three-dimensional qualities. A theme making its appearance in the harmonic framework of the composition is like a charming view seen through a half-opened door in the background of one of Pieter de Hooch's paintings (I, 294). There is as striking a difference between the themes of Vinteuil's sonata and his septet as between a grave angel of Bellini playing a theorbo and a scarlet-robed archangel of Mantegna sounding a trumpet (XII, 72–73).

Literature, as an art, has many things in common with painting. Style has to be polished and perfected so that visual pictures may be created in words just as clearly as in painting (III, 164; XI, 232). Models are necessary and the writer has to observe just as eagerly and just as closely as the painter (XV, 59). Both artists need many models before they can portray one abstracted but perfectly typical example of a species (XV, 58), and both need a broad perspective on life to inspire them to work (XV, 214). The painter paints to be seen from a distance and the writer writes for posterity and not for his contemporaries (III, 130). Both must 'load every rift . . . with ore'. All these ideas are very startlingly combined in the following significant metaphor which refers to the well-known painting 'Le Déjeuner sur l'herbe' by Manet: *l'herbe drue des œuvres fécondes, sur laquelle les générations viendront faire gaiement, sans souci de ceux qui dorment en dessous, leur 'déjeuner sur l'herbe'* (XV, 218).

Sculpture. Whereas in the field of painting Proust uses images very widely in referring to nature, people, introspective phenomena and the various arts, in the field of sculpture he restricts his comparisons almost entirely to those with people and the effect on them of age and heredity. What is more significant, perhaps, is that he hardly ever refers to specific statues even though his references to paintings are generally to particular works by well-known artists.

Occasionally, it is true, Proust will compare an effect of nature to sculpture. Pigeons on the ground are like antique sculptures just dug up (II, 252), and the impression left by fog or mist over parts of the sea is to make the section visible resemble those polished statues which jut forth from an otherwise unfinished block of marble (IV, 130). Sometimes also Proust compares a musical

composition or a work of literature to a piece of sculpture (III, 129;
XII, 222) and very occasionally he mentions specific sculptors. The
first episode in Dostoievski's *Brothers Karamozov* is said to be *mystérieux, grand, auguste, comme une création de la Femme dans les sculptures
d'Orvieto* (XII, 223). Françoise as a cook is like Michelangelo working with inspiration in his chosen medium (III, 24, 40).

Other people in our minds or our dreams are like statues or
pieces of marble suitable for statues in a quarry (XI, 154; XII, 102).
Names can conjure up works of sculpture just as well as paintings
(IV, 73), and both habit and memory are like sculptors fashioning
statues—the one lot rigid and set (XI, 81), the other lot varied and
unusual (XV, 31). Fatigue is like a sculptor immobilizing the body
in order to take a mould of it (V, 69).

It is when he talks about people, though, that Proust likes to
draw on images which relate them to sculpture. The young men at
Balbec seem to the narrator like equestrian statues of demigods (IV,
104), and the band of young girls are like Grecian masterpieces
(V, 35) except that the stone from which they are carved is that
indigenous to the district from which they come (V, 177).

Any attractive young girl is regarded by Marcel as a desirable
and beautiful marble statue (XI, 172; XIII, 138; XV, 158), but it is
Albertine who symbolizes as a sort of little statue in his memory the
happy hours he spent at Balbec (VIII, 15). She is as French as the
peasant figures carved on the Church of Saint-André-des-Champs
(VII, 236). Her hair is arranged like that of a church statue (VII,
217), and when she rides her bicycle in the rain, her mackintosh
clings to her body as though a sculptor were taking its impression
(IX, 336–37). Free, Albertine is a triumphant Victory; captive, she
is only a ponderous slave (XII, 212).

For the narrator, the Duchesse de Guermantes is also a beautiful
bit of carving, but in Dresden china rather than stone (VI, 17; XIII,
325). He imagines her holding in her hand all the castles of which
she is lady, just like the formalized statues of benefactors at the
doorways of cathedrals (XI, 36).

Other ranks of society are also compared to sculpture in *A la
recherche du temps perdu*. The beautiful women loved by the Duc de
Guermantes are likened to statues (VIII, 124; IX, 71), and the
narrator finds in the *bourgeoisie un atelier merveilleux de sculpture la plus
généreuse et la plus variée* (V, 98). Madame Verdurin (II, 20, 60) and
Morel (X, 251) are both compared to statues and, within lower

ranks, Aimé (X, 163) and other servants (VII, 27; X, 194) and even a prostitute (IX, 237) are said to resemble products of the sculptor's art.

Young girls appear to be modelled in clay (V, 171), and their parents are, in a very real way, the sculptors (V, 98), since features which at first appear vague and soft (VII, 216) have an inherent form predetermined by heredity (III, 170; XV, 210). Certain traits may come from one or other of the parents, retaining their sculptural quality (IX, 113), and even mental preoccupations are handed on from one generation to the next so that they continue to shape and model modes of thought (VI, 159).

As individuals mature, the ductile clay hardens into stone and with old age it may even wear away or crumble (VII, 26, 30; XIII, 152; XV, 101, 105). This process affects all mortals from beautiful women (VII, 25) and the vain 'dandy' (XV, 97) to the great actress La Berma (XV, 168) and the social giant Charlus (IX, 10; XIV, 201). It affects duchesses (IX, 92) as well as ordinary women (V, 172) and it affects Marcel's own grandmother in her final illness and death (VII, 180–81, 207) as well as the vain and selfish Legrandin (XV, 91). Death is the great sculptor who with the help of illness and old age gradually immobilizes his models (XV, 106).

Architecture and Ruins. Buildings, with their three-dimensional character and their complicated inner ramifications, provide an excellent source of visual, concrete images for Proust. Foods of all descriptions are compared to vast, elaborate buildings (V, 86; XI, 160–61), and the physiognomy of individuals is said to be architectural in its lines (V, 68; XIII, 236; III, 150). Dresses are like great works of architecture (IV, 50) and even a coiffure may resemble a tower (II, 251).

The world of society is like a great building (VIII, 188), and individuals within it also seem to be architectural in nature (XV, 98). The very name *Guermantes* is like a feudal tower dating far back in French history (VI, 14).

In the world of the arts, musical compositions (XII, 212, 214) and novels (XV, 54, 220–21) are said to be constructed like monuments or great cathedrals.

The narrator speaks of his own life as a building (XI, 98) where memories are the furniture. Reverie and recall both have the effect of restoring parts of ancient buildings or reconstructing on ancient foundations (VIII, 182; XI, 30; I, 244, 251). Fatigue has the power to disarrange furniture so that the mind resembles an apartment on moving day (IX, 143), and even such emotions as hatred require suitable foundations on which they may be built (IX, 73).

Quite logically, ruins are used by Proust to describe people who have grown old, like the Duc de Guermantes (XV, 192–93). Names (VI, 13) and ideas (X, 157) fall into ruins as we grow accustomed to them or forget them, just as quickly as do emotions (XIII, 331). The conversation of other people is like a ruin which permits the skilful restorer to attempt a reconstruction of the thought back of the expression (V, 199).

Music. From the realm of music, Proust draws a surprisingly large number of images, and they reveal evidence of a detailed technical knowledge that is not paralleled for any of the other arts.[1] We already have ample proof of the fact that Proust makes no concessions to his readers in any of the areas of specialized knowledge which he taps, but in music his learned references must be especially difficult for readers without formal training.

Some musical terms used by Proust are common enough. To understand references to a voice or a sound that is said to be *pianissimo* (XIV, 204), *forte* or *fortissimo* (VIII, 213) does not require any particular musical background. Also, it is easy to comprehend what is meant by a dynamic *crescendo* in the intensification of the sun's light (II, 240) or the *diminuendo* which the anticlimactic use of three adjectives in Mme de Cambremer's letters invariably produces (X, 106). It is not so simple, however, to see what is meant when Proust says that sleeping bears the same relation to waking as an *andante* movement to a *prestissimo* when a quarter-note in the one lasts as long as a half-note in the other (XI, 150), or what is indicated when the narrator declares that the sound of train wheels or church bells can be grouped rhythmically in different ways *entendant selon* [*sa*] *fantaisie d'abord quatre doubles croches égales, puis une double croche furieusement précipitée contre une noire* (IV, 68).

The falling pitch of a speaker's voice (VIII, 211) or a sequence of consecutively weakening adjectives is like a descending scale, except that the latter fails to end on the common chord (X, 283). On the other hand, Bergotte, in the skilful and sonorous endings which he

[1] See Florence Hier, *La Musique dans l'œuvre de Marcel Proust,* New York (1933) and G. Piroué, *Proust et la musique du devenir,* Paris (1960).

contrives for sentences, is like the composer of an overture who effectively repeats several times the final cadence which concludes the work (III, 158). Repetitious bird calls are like cadences and the pigeon's cooing resembles a transposition into the minor of the rooster's crowing (II, 232).

Memories of former happy times, which, just because they are past, are now sad in retrospect, are also like a transposition of the original into the minor (XIII, 177). When they fade and disappear, however, they become like the pivot chord which prepares for modulation to another key (XIII, 223). Indeed, any change of mood is like modulation to a different key (II, 227).

Charlus, in his conversation, uses musical terms and he suggests to the narrator that since their friendship is not to develop, they should part on a perfect cadence without any dissonance (VIII, 219, 220). A jarring element of any kind is said to be dissonant (IX, 299), even though beauty results from the augmentation and diminution of intervals rather than from simple progressions (XI, 155). The same notes in sequence are completely changed for the musician by rhythmic or harmonic variations (IV, 77–78). We see simple rhythm in Mme de Cambremer's keeping time to the music with her head nodding like a metronome (II, 150) or in the monotonous phrases with which certain individuals always begin sentences (XI, 198). A more complicated but subtler form analogous to that of a triumphal march is found in the rhythm given to one of Elstir's pictures by the inflexible vertical line of church steeples in a city (V, 92–93).

A few of the terms Proust uses are drawn from singing. When a name is pronounced, the first syllables are 'attacked' (VII, 97). Charlus uses the highest register of his voice when he makes insolent remarks (VIII, 211), and Elstir, at the Verdurins', is forced to employ *falsetto* when he reaches the top of his range (II, 55). Feeble imitators of Mme de Guermantes are, in reality, singing the same tune an octave below her (XII, 40), but the effect of perspective on the church tower at Combray illuminated by the sun is to make it appear more lofty, like a tune sung *falsetto* an octave higher than normal (I, 92).

Other terms used by Proust come from the art of the piano. Repeated sounds an octave apart remind one of a blind piano tuner (XI, 169), and an unpleasant voice is said to need tuning (XIV, 128). A keen ear is like that of a piano tuner or a competent musician (IX, 85; XI, 221; XII, 129). To describe something sustained, whether it be a feeling of joy, a memory, or a lingering ray of sunlight,

Proust employs the metaphor of the *sostenuto* pedal on the piano (IX, 299; XII, 239–40; VI, 177). Alternate loud and soft sounds which result for the invalid from the withdrawal or insertion of cotton into his ears are compared to the use of the two pedals on a piano (VI, 91). A prolonged smile is like a sustained G sharp (VIII, 56).

Besides the voice and the piano, there are other instruments for musical expression which Proust refers to. Faint sounds are compared by him to muted violins (I, 50), and the partition between Marcel's room and that of his grandmother at Balbec is as sensitive as the resonance box of a violin (IX, 209). The narrator regards his own body as a similar sort of delicate instrument (or possibly a harp (I, 159)) whose strings are tightened or loosened by the weather or the season of the year (XI, 29, 30). Albertine asleep responds in just the same way to the narrator's touch, as indicated by the pitch of her breathing (XI, 140).

Vocal sounds such as words and laughter and the timbre of voices remind the narrator of musical instruments. The young girls and the women known later in life by Marcel all have voices which seem to be produced by distinctive regional instruments (V, 176, 186; XI, 124–25), and the laugh which Charlus has inherited is like the tone of the particular small trumpets for which Bach wrote in his works (X, 101–2). Bergotte's laugh is a noisier sort of trumpet (I, 126), and Charlus' normal speaking voice also partakes of clarion-like quality (X, 304).

The narrator finds a barrel-organ or hurdy-gurdy unpleasant, and he uses it to characterize a feeling of worry or discord (IX, 240) and to describe the tangential quality of the imagination (VI, 50). The lift-boy at Balbec is compared in some detail to an organist playing his instrument (IV, 81, 82; X, 206).

When it comes to the performance of music, most of Proust's references are to the piano and the orchestra. The certainty of Saint-Loup's social intuition in a new situation makes him like a mature musician reading at sight (VIII, 43) or a great pianist giving his own inimitable style to the simplest music (IV, 160). His obvious social pre-eminence makes him (like his uncle Charlus) a sort of orchestra leader (VI, 129, 220; XIV, 204). The director-general of hotels who visits Balbec is also like a conductor (IV, 114), but Françoise and the other servants who ignore the bell which summons them upstairs are like members of an audience at a concert who do not hurry back to their seats when they hear the orchestra beginning to tune up (VI, 32).

The narrator hears in street noises or a snatch of song, themes and motifs for an orchestral composition (XI, 143; VI, 9, 170). Flies in summer give the effect of a sort of chamber music (I, 117), and the muttering of Françoise when she is disgruntled is like a part of the orchestration of the day (XII, 205). Nature and flowers are orchestral in their texture (XI, 9–10, 32; I, 188, 189; II, 232–33, 268), and even the detailed workmanship of a blouse of Odette's, because of the care lavished on it, is similar to the intricate orchestration of a great composition (IV, 49). Memory with its rich context is like an orchestral work with themes and counterthemes (VIII, 23; XV, 21), but recognition of a person, like a theme, depends on its orchestration, and the changes brought by age, like a new setting, may make the melody unrecognizable (XV, 105).

In voices and conversation, the narrator discovers further analogies with musical performances. Charlus, when angry, speaks as loudly as a full orchestra playing *fortissimo* (VIII, 213), but when he calms down the effect is that of a gentle *scherzo* after the violent opening movement (VIII, 216). Françoise in her persistent gossip is like a composition with repeat marks in it which send you back consistently to the beginning of the *andante* (VI, 26). (One finds similar '*reprises*' or '*da capo*' signs in dreams (XIII, 151).) Polite trivialities are like a preliminary counted bar in music during which nothing is played (VII, 104). The conversation of Mme de Guermantes, on the other hand, has the charm of a French folk song (XI, 40), and its effect on hearers is like that of music (VIII, 198).

Literature is also a form of symphonic writing. In tone, Bergotte's work resembles the unique style of a particular composer (I, 130). His conversation might be said to be 'disorchestrated' since he puts all his creative efforts into his writing (III, 158), but here he and his fellow artists have the advantage enjoyed only by composers as distinct from performers, i.e. they are able to play at one time on the keyboard of several different centuries (VIII, 48).

Love is like music in its pattern and structure. The young girls Marcel admires are like phrases in a musical composition (V, 33–34), and desire is like a refrain running through one's head (V, 68). Jealousy is also like a repeated musical phrase where the melody remains the same and only the words differ (VI, 207). Love itself is like a song, and if we begin in the middle with a certain woman, she knows what comes next without having to go back to the beginning (I, 266).

Innate tendencies of any kind are compared to inherited musical aptitude. Homosexuality (IX, 29), coarse instincts which can be refined by the beneficial influence of environment (VIII, 84), and one's racial background (IV, 104–5) are all compared by Proust to the particular musical urges which are our individual heritage.

Among the images drawn from music in Proust's work, there are numerous references to specific composers and compositions. The two musicians most frequently mentioned are Wagner and Beethoven, with the former holding a slight edge.

It has often been pointed out that Wagner's method of composition with its recurring *leit-motifs* bears a very close relation to Proust's own style. The narrator finds reality a complex pattern of multiple interconnected themes which are very like those used by Wagner (XIII, 37, 38), and he refers familiarly to many of the Wagner operas. Sudden apparitions in the political world are like the appearance of Lohengrin descending from his swan boat (VII, 69). The beauty of sunlight through stained glass windows has the same quality of joyous reserved pomp as parts of the score of *Lohengrin* (I, 240), but the evolution of reality seems to bear as little relation to the sources from which it grew as *Tristan* does to *Lohengrin* (XIII, 319; VIII, 202). Mechanical sounds such as the telephone bell, a squeaking door and air-raid sirens remind Marcel respectively of the shepherd's pipe in *Tristan* (IX, 169), the orchestral accompaniment to parts of the Pilgrims' Chorus near the end of the overture to *Tannhäuser* (VIII, 17), and the cry of the Walkyries (XIV, 78, 79, 102). Charlus conducts himself in society like the Margrave whose entrance in *Tannhäuser* is made to the accompaniment of the famous march (IX, 66), and Marcel, in the unfamiliar home of his adored Gilberte Swann, feels more ill at ease than if he were in the laboratory of Klingsor, the magician in *Parsifal* (III, 125). Young girls are like the *filles fleurs* in the same opera (VIII, 54–55).

The sound of the wind blowing the trap in the chimney of Marcel's room reminds him of the opening of Beethoven's Fifth Symphony (VII, 209), and it is probable that he has the same work in mind when he describes the way he and his grandmother used to knock back and forth between their rooms at Balbec (IV, 87). Fresh air is breathed by Mme de Cambremer with the same joy as that of the liberated prisoners in *Fidelio* (IX, 277). The repeated

phrases which characterize Beethoven's preparation for the introduction of a new theme are like the glances the homosexual Charlus
directs at Jupien (IX, 13). Morel, in a state of embarrassment, is
said to be redder than if he had played consecutively all of Beethoven's sonatas (XII, 133). In society, the opposite poles of propriety are symbolized by dancing the boston and listening to one of
Beethoven's posthumous quartets (IX, 53).

Numerous other composers are referred to incidentally by
Proust. In the diplomatic relations between Norpois and his
counterparts, the formal questions and answers are like the stylized
phrases in a Mozart concerto (III, 37). Norpois at times keeps his
face inexpressive, and then one has the impression that he is listening
to a sublime Bach aria or an exquisite string quartet, or (if his voice
comes back) that he will sing *un chant innocent et mélodieux de Mendels-
sohn ou de César Franck* (XIII, 267, 268, 269). A silence is also compared by Proust to the one in the Barber of Seville which succeeds
Lindoro's music and thereby awakens Bartholo (VIII, 53).

The street noises already referred to are compared by Proust to
parts of *Boris Godounov* and *Pelléas* as well as religious music (XI,
144, 145, 146, 147). Winter with its cold winds which make doors
and windows screech produces sounds like refrains written by
Fragson, Mayol or Paulus (XI, 70), whereas gentle summer breezes
are more like the long phrases of Chopin (X, 143). To these long
phrases from Chopin Proust also compares the leisurely progress of
the band of young girls (V, 35). On the other hand, love, with its
precipitous *dénouement*, resembles in form a Ballade by Schumann
(XIII, 105).

Theatre. When we turn to images drawn from the theatre, we
again find in Proust's work a wealth of references, but this time they
are almost entirely non-technical and they are very obviously
constructed from the point of view of a spectator in the audience.[1]
Proust refers to specific actors and specific rôles and scenes in plays
he knows, as well as to such things as make-up, scenery and the
externals of acting, but throughout all of it, one gets the impression
that his observations somehow lie alongside the real business of
acting and that they do not penetrate beyond the surface.

[1] Cf. J. G. Linn, 'Proust's Theatre Metaphors'. *Romanic Review*, XLIX (1958), pp.
179–90.

Almost all of Proust's theatre images are directly associated with people. Relations between individuals, and the pre-conceived idea we have at a given moment of the position and function of any one person makes it seem that they are playing a variety of rôles. The world of society (in its very broadest sense) is nothing but a theatre where 'one man in his time plays many parts' (IX, 332; XV, 9, 140).

We see this principle clearly illustrated in *A la recherche du temps perdu* in the lives of Odette (II, 271, 272; III, 126; XV, 196), Saint-Loup (VI, 215), Albertine (V, 115; VII, 228; XI, 82, 214, 215), and the narrator himself (III, 208; V, 70, 153; VIII, 142). A new evolution in the development of an individual is said to be like a character waiting in the wings for his cue to come on stage (V, 155; IX, 118; XV, 132). In the final scenes of this play of life, characters are so altered in appearance that they seem to be wearing disguises (XV, 75, 77, 81, 98) or masks (XV, 90, 107), and the last character to appear is, of course, Death (VII, 169).

Women especially are like actresses because they consciously assume studied mannerisms which conceal their true character (XII, 91; VI, 34; I, 236) and they use their voices much as great actresses do (VIII, 137; X, 64, 65; XV, 107). They are equally jealous of their rôles (XII, 93, 94).

Servants, however, also play fixed rôles, and the unique setting of the hotel at Balbec, with its numerous attendants whose movements are rigidly prescribed, reminds Marcel of the choruses in Racine's *Esther* and *Athalie* (IV, 131; XIII, 155; IX, 223, 224, 309, 310, 311; X, 158). As a servant, Françoise is a star in her own right both because of her jealous regard for her prerogatives and because of her unequalled ability to express her ideas through a word or two or through gesture (III, 74; V, 160; VII, 178, 190, 227; IX, 174).

Diplomats are also like actors on the stage (III, 71; XIII, 312), and the assignments given to them are like rôles distributed by a casting director (XV, 111).

Affectation of any sort is like an assumed rôle. M. or Mme Verdurin expressing gaiety are like theatre masks (II, 65), and Charlus, who conceals his homosexual desires behind a face that is expressionless except for the eyes, plays a rôle that is quite the opposite of his true nature (XII, 11, 109; IV, 199; X, 160). Gestures and especially formal greetings or presentations are like theatrical gestures (II, 271; IV, 53; VII, 100; IX, 62).

In the realm of social relations, the ramifications of the use of images drawn from the theatre are so extended and so complex as almost to defy logical analysis. Persons regarded as unimportant by others are said to be like marionettes (I, 164), while those who are positively ludicrous are compared specifically to characters from a Guignol (IV, 83; XV, 78). Anything mechanical like the chattering receiver of a telephone (VI, 163) or the serving of a banquet by servants (VIII, 68) is reminiscent of Polichinelle and the puppet theatre, but the exaggerated atmosphere of Paris during bombing raids is more like *vaudeville* (XIV, 79).

Anything invariable, whether it be a daily platitude uttered by the *maître d'hôtel* (XIV, 68) or the routine of Marcel's undressing at night as a child is like a theatre performance (I, 64, 65).

There is an important distinction between performers on the stage and the menial workers whose business it is to take tickets, change scenery or show patrons to their seats. For Charlus and the other members of the *Faubourg St.-Germain*, Mme Verdurin belongs to this latter class (XII, 79), and the repulsive 'marquise' at the public washrooms is like a circus clown who takes the tickets before going on-stage (VII, 161).

Members of superior classes or those whom we desire as friends or lovers are like great actresses and actors even though what makes them attractive may be no more intrinsic than the false jewels worn on the stage (X, 26–27). To Marcel, his mother entertaining Swann is like an actress performing, and, for that reason, he fears that Françoise will be unable to pass her his note (I, 44). Both Gilberte and Albertine are actresses whose private life behind the stage is hidden from him (III, 127; XII, 227; XIV, 13). The Princesse de Guermantes (VI, 52), her cousin the Duchess (VI, 70–71) and the author Bergotte (III, 180) are like celebrated stage artists.

At the same time, members of higher society and those we love are also like spectators in privileged seats in a theatre. The Duchesse de Guermantes (II, 153) and her brother-in-law, Charlus (IV, 198; VII, 110), are both spoken of as though they were lordly spectators at a play. Albertine has access to Marcel's heart and she introduces there various people and places just like someone taking a theatre party through the entrance wicket (XII, 229).

Perhaps the key to this apparently contradictory situation is provided by the narrator where he describes the guests at Balbec who,

... au milieu de cette rangée de chaises redoutée où eux-mêmes tout à l'heure, d'acteurs devenus critiques, viendraient s'installer pour juger à leur tour ceux qui défileraient devant eux (V, 32).

In our relations with others, we are continually pretending to feel emotions we do not feel and we try to give the impression that we are deceived by similar pretense on the part of others. Jealousy, in particular, sets the stage for the performance of these comedies (XII, 196, 198–99, 204), but propriety in social intercourse often makes similar demands (VIII, 236).

Plays are based on life and it is not illogical to compare the incidents in our existences to those in plays. Indecision is a 'drama' in Albertine's heart (XIII, 245), and the whole of her brief life is like a fast-moving tragedy (XIII, 104). A sudden change in the pattern of Marcel's existence is *un coup de théâtre* (XV, 74), and the episodes he witnesses during his life, such as the encounter between Jupien and Charlus, are much more exaggerated and actually less credible than the most far-fetched play (IX, 16).

People as well as the background against which they move are compared by Proust to scenery on the stage. The perspective of the faces of Swann and Rachel is like painted backdrops (IX, 118; VI, 216), and the faces of the young girls remind the narrator of those effective but very simple props used by the designer Bakst to give an illusion of reality which is strikingly beautiful (V, 219). The streets of Combray are the setting for the simple drama that goes on there (I, 68–69, 184).

For a deaf person, everything he sees is like a representation on the stage, since sound, which is a quality essential to reality, is missing (VI, 92, 94). For the same reason, dreams with their inconsistency are like theatre performances (XIII, 151).

Among his many theatre images, Proust occasionally refers to specific actors and actresses. Saint-Loup, who inherits homosexuality like his uncle Charlus, is similar to an actor who takes up the rôle formerly played by a Bressant or a Delauney (XIV, 82). Marcel's mother and father, in repeating phrases used by Norpois, are like spectators trying to recapture the intonation of Bressant or Thiron in a particular play (III, 71), and the ultimate in social triumph, *i.e.* managing to lure Mme de Guermantes to a fête, is like having Sarah Bernhardt come to a gala (XV, 123–24).

Proust frequently uses images which involve specific plays or rôles and even particular scenes in those plays. As we have already noted, the dramatist most often cited is Racine.[1] The narrator uses imagery drawn from *Phèdre* in describing himself (I, 197) as well as the actress La Berma who is always associated with this rôle (XV, 168–69). Figures of speech based on *Esther* and *Athalie* are used for a great variety of purposes and we find them employed in connection with such disparate characters as the following: Mme de Guermantes (VII, 249), Françoise (I, 149; XI, 121), the homosexuals Charlus and Vaugoubert (IX, 86–87; XII, 149), and the hotel director at Balbec (IV, 108–9).

Molière is the next most frequently employed source of specific images. The stylized mannerisms of members of society are compared to the artificiality of certain comedies of Molière (IV, 117; IX, 54). Charlus is compared to Scapin (IX, 126) and his brother the Duke, in old age, is a comic Géronte (XV, 195). A possessive homosexual is similar to Harpagon (X, 76), and even Swann, in later years, has something ridiculous about him that reminds one of Mascarille rather than Solomon (VII, 15).

Charlus and Jupien are compared to Romeo and Juliet (IX, 40–41), and when he grows old, Charlus himself is rather like King Lear (XV, 76). These references to Shakespeare, along with two comparisons which emphasize the difference between reality and imagination by comparing the actor who plays the rôle with Hamlet (XIII, 284) and the Danish port of Elsinore with the setting for the play (VIII, 182), constitute the whole of Proust's references to English drama.

In *A la recherche du temps perdu* there are various other incidental references to specific plays and authors. M. d'Argencourt in old age is like a *moribond-bouffe* of Regnard exaggerated by Labiche (XV, 76). Marcel's Aunt Léonie watches a sort of '*spectacle dans un lit*' (Musset) from her bed at Combray (I, 161), and Cottard, in his relations with Mme Verdurin, is like a character from Marivaux (X, 27). Society queens are compared to the queens in Sardou's plays (VIII, 58), and Mme de Cambremer, when she listens to music, has eyes which sparkle *comme ceux de Latude dans la pièce appelée* 'Latude ou Trente-cinq ans de captivité' (IX, 277). Mme Verdurin, in her relations with others, is like a cruelly realistic play (XII, 46, 47, 48).

A few theatre images in Proust's work are associated with nature rather than people, but they are very few. The corolla of a

[1] See p. 153 above.

white rose is compared to a theatre box (XIV, 27), and the pale moon is said to be like an actress who is not playing a rôle and who tries to make herself inconspicuous in the theatre as she watches her colleagues on stage (I, 198–99). Night produces effects like stage scenery (III, 78), and the sun, when it appears from behind Marcel's curtain in the morning, is like an actor bounding onto the stage (X, 334–35).

Finally, Proust uses the theatre image to describe one of his hypotheses as to the nature of intelligence. He suggests that it may be something unique similar to the single stage in a theatre which is seen and shared by all the spectators (III, 175).

Ballet. Before leaving the world of the arts and the section of it dealing with the theatre, we might consider separately those images which Proust draws directly from ballet. As far as scenery in ballet (as distinct from regular plays) is concerned, no attempt has been made to differentiate the two. For that reason, some of the references above to scenery actually refer to scenery in ballet, *e.g.* those of the designer Bakst.

Mme de Guermantes is like a prima ballerina in society (VI, 42), and Albertine in her different apparitions is like a star of the dance illuminated in a variety of ways (V, 221). The young girls in general have the grace of dancers (V, 33), and any peasant girl who attracts Marcel's attention is like one of those ballet representations of the Temptations (XI, 213).

In formal gestures, especially, Proust sees analogies with dance forms and he actually uses a few technical terms from ballet. The mechanical offering and withdrawal of candies by the hostess at a party is *réglé d'avance comme le pas d'une danseuse qui tour à tour s'élève sur sa pointe et tourne autour d'une écharpe* (VI, 51). Charlus is as talented in the social graces as an artist developed by Diaghilev (X, 64), and both he and his brother (as well as other members of the Guermantes clan) have such an elaborate ritual of greeting that the narrator refers to their movements as *pas graves et mesurés* or *entrechats* (VIII, 82; VII, 198).

SOCIAL AND DOMESTIC ENVIRONMENT

Many of Proust's images are drawn from personal experience, even though they cannot be termed strictly introspective. He refers, for example, to childhood and school-days and to a variety

o

of games and pastimes associated with these periods of life. He also refers to specific studies, but these images we have considered separately above under the sciences and literary references. From later periods of life, he draws references to social customs and the hierarchy which governs rank. Along with these images we have also included those connected with the law—crime, judges, prison, etc. And finally, he refers to more mundane matters such as dress, costume, food and cooking.

Childhood. By suggesting that the images Proust draws from childhood are a direct result of personal experience, we do not intend to imply that they are necessarily memories of his own childhood. Some of them no doubt are, but others may only be the fruit of careful observation.

Proust regards infancy in two ways: it is the age of innocence and purity, but it is also the age of ignorance. For Marcel's mother, for example, the grandmother's life is as free from stain as innocent childhood (X, 327). For the narrator himself, however, the restricting 'cradle' of thought is something to be broken away from as soon as possible (I, 117–18).

In spite of this fairly clear-cut dichotomy, Marcel utilizes both categories of images to describe himself. When he feels at peace within the shelter of his grandmother's arms, he is like an infant sucking at its mother's breast (IV, 85). Similar states of beatitude are made vivid by comparison with his feelings when his mother kisses him good-night as a child (I, 249). Feelings of delight are compared to those experienced by a child born in prison when it discovers the exciting foods that exist outside the confines where it has been living (IV, 138–39). They are also compared to the excitement of a child who is about to investigate his New Year presents (III, 124; XIII, 260) or that of one who learns that he is going to have a party (V, 98). Anguish, on the other hand, is related to the feeling Marcel experienced when as a child he lost his grandmother in a crowd (VI, 165).

The narrator's memory is like childish collections of stones, insects, etc. (I, 242). Habit is a nurse which carries him like a child in its arms (I, 159). The involuntary memory turns back the pages of the book of life to childhood (IV, 146–47), and Marcel becomes again the child he was at the time of the experience stimulated by the organic memory (XV, 31).

Relations in love are compared by Proust to the tender, protective love which exists between parent and child. For the narrator, Albertine is at times the child (XI, 86, 142, 189; XII, 257), at times the mother (X, 329). For Swann, it is always Odette who is the child (II, 27, 43, 88), but for Charlus, it is sometimes he who is the parent (X, 241, 251; XII, 50) and sometimes his paramour, particularly when Charlus himself is old and helpless (XIV, 202, 203). Rachel is the child in her affair with Saint-Loup (VI, 147), though the narrator himself declares that in love generally men merely project the pleasure which they feel in the company of a woman in the same way that children project their affection towards a pillow or a flower or anything which pleases them (XIII, 100).

In social relations some people are compared to children or regarded by their fellows as children. These references, generally speaking, are unfavourable. Marcel's great-aunt does not realize Swann's high position in society and she treats him as a child treats a precious *objet d'art* (I, 51). The Duc de Guermantes in the Dreyfus Affair regards Swann as a child who has betrayed his heritage (IX, 104–5). Saniette (I, 275), Aimé (X, 205–6) and Mme Verdurin (X, 118) are in turn compared unfavourably to children. Françoise tends to regard the dying grandmother as a child (VII, 194), and both she on that occasion and the Princesse de Luxembourg, who treats Marcel and his grandmother as children (IV, 123, 124), are regarded with scorn. States of social embarrassment are compared to the attitudes of punished children (IV, 131; V, 124).

All of the above references are directly related to people, but Proust occasionally uses images drawn from childhood to describe nature. The grandmother in her love of naturalness surreptitiously removes stakes from the roses in the garden just as a mother runs her hands through her son's hair which the barber has flattened down too much (I, 25). Curtains seem to provide a cradle for the rising sun (IX, 211), and the silent passage of a swan is as startling as the discovery at night that a child whom one thought asleep has its eyes wide open for a moment, smiling up at you (VIII, 10).

Games and Toys. In this section, some of the references to card games, lotteries and gambling are definitely not at the level of children's amusements, but it seemed reasonable to consider together all images drawn from the same kind of source.

We may consider together, first of all, images which utilize the kaleidoscope, the magic lantern and the stereoscope.[1] They have this in common that they all rely on the same essential feature, *i.e.* the effect of light. Here again our attention is forcibly drawn to the predominantly visual quality of Proust's imagery, and, within that category, to the importance of images emphasizing light.

Only once does Proust actually use the kaleidoscope to describe a purely visual phenomenon. In this particular instance, it is the vagueness of the dark at night when one opens one's eyes from sleep that is thus described (I, 12–13). Otherwise, the kaleidoscope stands for the changing picture of the world of society (III, 112, 113, 116; VII, 15; XV, 41) or the confused changing picture we may have of the real nature of the personality of another individual (XIII, 127).

In the narrator's mind, the projections of the magic lantern stand for the beautiful and the imaginative even though these pictures may not correspond to reality. The world of dreams (VI, 104; XIII, 151–52), an exquisite but unreal view at night (XIV, 57), Elstir's paintings (VIII, 50) and Marcel's vivid memories of Albertine (XIII, 140), Mme de Guermantes (VI, 11) and Combray (I, 72) are all like projections of the magic lantern. The passage of the days is like a succession of images thrown by the magic lantern (V, 69), and an aesthetic experience like music conjures up visual pictures for the narrator similar to those of the lantern (XII, 24).

The actual lantern itself, or physical details such as shadows of people or inaccurate focussing, intrude on the enchantment of illusion, and this is like the disparity between imagination and reality. In the world of dreams, it is the body of the sleeper (XIII, 151–52); in the world of art it is the painter Elstir himself (VIII, 50). Jealousy is like an inaccurate adjustment of a reflector which casts terrifying shadows on the wall (II, 111), and a person's real nature, contrasted with Marcel's preconceived ideas about it, is like an object on which it is difficult to focus the reflector (VI, 45).

The stereoscope is used by Proust to illustrate the process of inner evaluation which examines the comments or the appearances of others and gives to them a sort of consistency or third dimension (VII, 230; VIII, 201). He uses the same idea to describe individual impressions of stage scenery and settings for plays (I, 104). Each person has, as it were, unique criteria for judging, and he alone is

[1] Cf. Roger Shattuck, op. cit., pp. 7 et seq.; Howard Moss, op. cit., pp. 10 et seq.

conscious of them in the same way that only one person at a time can look into a stereoscope.

The narrator compares his need for action to the energy of a spinning top which, when released, bounds in all directions (I, 209). Familiarity with names and people causes their original colour to fade so that they become gray like a bright top quickly whirling around (VI, 13). On the other hand, the contradictory statements which Albertine makes to Marcel are as violently opposed as the adjacent colours of a top which has almost stopped spinning (XI, 120).

There is, in Marcel, an attitude of scorn toward the women who have the power to seize men's affections. These women are never completely possessed or understood by their lovers who control only a sort of inner doll which is a more or less inaccurate mental representation of the women they love (VII, 240). Dolls are mechanical, but Odette, who had so many lovers during her life, really becomes an inert and helpless doll only in her old age (XV, 109).

Women are also like collections: no matter how many of them one has or has had, there is always room for one more (VII, 218).

Some of Proust's images are drawn from the circus or similar spectacles designed primarily for children. The boat in Elstir's painting seems to be leaping up and down like horses on a merry-go-round (V, 90). In old age, the Duc de Guermantes totters as though he were walking on tremendously high stilts (XV, 229), and Mme de Franquetot watches an agile pianist with as much trepidation as if he were a trapeze artist performing high above the ground (II, 150). Saint-Loup watches with the same anxious preoccupation Marcel's conversation before the acquaintances Saint-Loup wishes him to dazzle (VI, 130), and when a rude journalist refuses to put out a cigar that bothers Marcel, it is Saint-Loup who administers to him a *pièce d'artifice* (VI, 223). The agility with which Dr. Dieulafoy accepts his fee is similar to that of a sleight-of-hand artist (VII, 204), and Bergotte, when Marcel first meets him, is like a magician (III, 149). A similar image is elaborated on considerably in the description of Charlus in the card room at Mme Verdurin's party (IX, 116).

In social relations, Proust often uses games as a source of images. The result of the juxtaposition of supposedly important social situations with mere pastimes or even silly childish amusements is to lend a degree of ridicule to the social world. Even love and jealousy is a sort of game of hide-and-seek (XI, 27), and when Mme

Verdurin covers her face, supposedly to laugh, it is as though she were the one who is 'it' (X, 118). M. de Vaugoubert is projected from one group to another in a social evening like a helpless tennis ball (IX, 101), and the betrayal of Charlus after the Verdurin party is conducted by the participants like a hiding game (XII, 131). Marcel gets a point across to Legrandin's sister by addressing her mother-in-law, just as in billiards one sometimes aims at the cushion rather than directly at a ball (IX, 276–77).

Cards and card games are used in a variety of ways by Proust. A figure in a stained glass window is compared to a King in a card deck (I, 86, 87). M. de Guermantes is Mme de Guermantes's unwitting aid (just like an accomplice in a card trick) in providing her with material for sallies of wit (VII, 67). Françoise, in her ability to predict the future, is like a fortune-teller with cards (XI, 138). Writing literature is similar to playing cards in that one must accept and make the best of what is dealt (V, 119). In his early efforts, however, the narrator is like the victim in a card trick who always draws a blank card, no matter what he does (VI, 182).

Life in society is itself a great gambling game in which one tries to win the stake or the lottery (VIII, 239; III, 55–56). Our knowledge of its different aspects is like a jig-saw puzzle which we piece together (XI, 109).

School, College, Academic Institutions. Proust sees in the supposedly mature social world analogies with academic institutions and the rather unpleasant experiences of students in study and examinations and their relations with their teachers.

A social group, whether it consist of business associates (III, 37; IX, 99), members of the same salon (III, 216; VIII, 179; IX, 94; X, 28) or servants (VI, 205, IX, 243), is like a restricted academic body—a school, the Institute, the Society of Bibliophiles or the Academy. People with interests in common are like students of Sanskrit or lecturers in the *Collège de France* (IX, 39), and social giants are like erudite scholars in obscure fields of knowledge (IV, 136).

Teachers, lessons and examinations are disagreeable enough, and Proust uses them to characterize unpleasant situations. The domineering attitude of Norpois with Mme de Villeparisis in her old age is like that of an angry teacher (XIII, 265), and the restaurant owner with a limited repertory of comments is like a mediocre teacher of recitation (VIII, 35). The difficulty of interpreting the significance of the comments or expressions of others is as great as that of translating a Greek lesson (V, 144), but the practice of *thème et version* makes one more conscious of reality, as for example in the examination of a typical piece of church architecture (IV, 143). Ignorance of protocol is greeted by a *maître d'hôtel* with the frown of an examiner who receives a wrong answer (VIII, 29). Disappointment of any kind is like the disappointment of a candidate who does not get a chance to perform adequately (IV, 75) or who fails in an examination (VIII, 18), and an ambiguous situation is as embarrassing as an oral question where the answer is not known; the only possible clue is in the expression of the face of the interlocutor (XV, 107–8).

The effect of careful observation or interest is somewhat the same as the case of the student who reads and re-reads a lesson at night; Sleep erases with its sponge the blackboard of Day's impressions (XI, 150), but in the morning the lesson can be recited by heart perfectly (III, 128; VI, 56).

Compliments in society are passed out with as little emotion as that of a chairman distributing prizes (VIII, 197), and like them, they are less a reward for past achievement than encouragement for the future (IX, 85). Older people take as much satisfaction from surviving longer than their fellows as prize winners over surpassing their classmates (XV, 146).

From school experience Proust also utilizes gymnasium instruction in addition to all the academic subjects we have already examined. A haughty society queen draws herself up as though she were performing a particular kind of exercise to develop the thorax (II, 152). Writing is considered as necessary and as healthy for the creative writer as exercise for other men (XV, 51), and the narrator, considering himself inept at this sort of expression, admires other writers much as a clumsy child enjoys someone who is good at gymnastics (VII, 184).

Social Customs and Behaviour. The rules of polite conduct and the traditions associated with proper behaviour under given circumstances are things that have been passed down from one generation to another, evolving or being modified in the process. More or less intangible, they are absolutely rigid and are understood by all educated people. In describing social relations, Proust delves again and again into this common fund of limited social situations, and he pursues his favourite tactic of making concrete and specific something which would otherwise remain vague and elusive.

The idea of the embarrassment experienced by one's appearance at a party in a lounge suit when everyone else is in dress clothes is used from the point of view of the wearer to describe the self-conscious discrepancy between Jupien's appearance and his conversation (VI, 23–24), and from the point of view of the hostess to describe Albertine's nervous laughter which tries to cover up for an indecent suggestion made to her by the narrator (VII, 238). How to react to new music in public is as difficult as knowing what to do with a strange utensil at the dinner table where one looks to one's neighbours for a cue (XV, 170). We cover up our personal thoughts like a discreet woman smoothing down her skirt (VII, 90), and in the presence of strangers it is as impolite to withdraw into oneself as it would be to open then and there the present they have brought (XIII, 161).

Proust uses many common social situations to describe in quite a precise fashion an incidental fact which often appears far less significant than the image he selects, but which is made much more vivid by this technique which borders very often on satire.

When a discreet guest smiles in approbation at the scapegoat Saniette, he does it as unobtrusively as if he were passing a note in public (X, 15–16). Mme Sazerat, after the Dreyfus Affair, acknowledges the unavoidable greetings of the narrator's family but she does so as if there had been a broken engagement (VII, 182) or as if Marcel's father were a criminal or worse (VI, 184, 185). Charlus looks at other homosexuals as though he and they were children whose parents had quarrelled and for that reason had forbidden them to speak to each other (X, 240–41). Even nations in their disputes are like relatives or servants who have quarrelled with their affiliates (XIV, 97).

Relations between friends or relatives can vary all the way from the intensely formal exchanges between Gilberte and Marcel near the end of their friendship, which are like official toasts and replies (IV, 44), to the patronizing attitude of Mme de Villeparisis towards her nieces whom she treats just like servants (VII, 46–47). This same lady is no more considerate of the feelings of her old lover, M. de Norpois, than if she were passing him a cup of tea (VII, 54), and Mme de Guermantes is as annoyed at having to acknowledge

Marcel's daily greeting as someone approached a second time by a beggar to whom charity has already been extended (VIII, 58). Françoise at times shows her annoyance with the narrator as eloquently as someone who thought he had received a present made of gold only to discover later that it was a cheap imitation (V, 21).

Many other ordinary social experiences are related by Proust to more exalted situations with the result that the satire is directed at the images rather than at the original experience. Albertine toying with her '*diabolo*' is like a hostess who continues to crochet during visits (V, 200). Saint-Loup is as protective of Marcel in public as an anxious mother whose daughter is making her *début* (VI, 125). Using current slang or abbreviations shows as much affectation as for members of the *bourgeoisie* to refer to important members of society by their nicknames (XIV, 48, 52). At Balbec, Marcel overhears a woman speaking of Albertine in just the same way as one would speak of a younger member of the La Rochefoucauld family (V, 46).

Frequently of course, the satire is directed at the original experience, but here the persons with whom the images are associated are often themselves social climbers and of the type so disliked by Proust. The Princesse de Parme and her associates conduct themselves in their box at the theatre as if they were in a private salon (VI, 46). Her curiosity is excited by the narrator at the Guermantes home and she covets him just like a new sort of table decoration (VIII, 94). The socialites visiting the Verdurin salon for the first time feel that they are slumming in a place like the *Boîte à Bruant* (XII, 54). Forcheville who marries Odette for her money and her position likes to think of himself as similar to the millionaire who charitably supports and rehabilitates a common prostitute (XIII, 196). Even the relations between Mme de Villeparisis and the narrator's grandmother at Balbec are not dissimilar from the sort of camaraderie that one sees among equals in a barber shop (IV, 118).

The useless preliminary exchanges between homosexuals make the narrator think of someone who is about to point out to another that he has a thread on his coat or to ask him if they have not met before somewhere else (IX, 12–13). These preludes are like the formal parties given for engaged couples (IX, 13).

Society and nature might seem to have nothing in common but Proust does refer three time to images drawn from social customs in connection with his descriptions of nature. Sunlight on his desk is like an invitation to a party (II, 251), and blossoms on fruit trees and hawthorns are like wedding gowns or the decoration associated with rural weddings (I, 154; IV, 133).

Castes, Noble Hierarchy. In a small rural town like Combray, notions of rank or caste are quite different from those which operate in the world of society in the capital. In Combray the castes are as rigidly separated as those in Hindu society, making it impossible for one to love from one class to another (I, 28). They are determined very largely by one's income (XIII, 273). In Paris, on the other hand, people move up and down in society and, within their own little circle, the same relative categories of rank are applied as in the world of society generally (VIII, 221; X, 92; XV, 87). For this reason, even a servant like Françoise (VI, 28) or the son of a furniture merchant (V, 47) is like a prince to inferiors within their circles.

When Marcel falls in love with Gilberte, her parents are like the king and the queen for him (II, 277; III, 180), and their home and the entertainments they enjoy are like the background of Versailles with its pleasures and protocol (III, 96, 103, 184). In society, Odette is a sort of queen for those who surround her (IV, 50, 52), and Swann, before his unworthy marriage, is regarded by those who know his position as a sovereign or a prince (I, 203; II, 147; III, 107). The Cambremer family feel that they are royalty compared to the Verdurins (X, 291). Mme de Guermantes holds spiritual sway over her salon (XV, 177), and the Duke is like one of the great lords at Versailles (VIII, 55). In the *Faubourg St.-Germain*, however, it is Charlus who is the real ruler. He is compared to a Duchess (X, 263–64), a member of the royal family (VII, 251), Monsieur, the brother of Louis XIV (IX, 78), and the monarch himself (X, 263, 265).

The royal rank associated with the position of Charlus in the exclusive circle of high society is carried over into the realm of homosexuality. Young men are greeted by him as if they were princes at Versailles (XIV, 159), and Morel is spoken of as his morganatic spouse (X, 290). When Ski, Brichot and Cottard succeed in making Charlus talk about homosexuality, they are as pleased as if they had persuaded the Empress to talk about her reign (X, 241). Actually when Jupien and Charlus talk about other homosexuals in the feminine, they are following a procedure similar to that which applies to the term of address for a prince (IX, 19).

The exaggerated concern which any person shows for another leads the narrator to suggest that the first person regards the second as a sovereign or a noble. Marcel's mother treats his father with that kind of deference (III, 49), and Andrée makes of herself a fawning courtier in order to please Albertine (V, 193). The narrator himself recounts with obvious pleasure the same sort of obeisance made to him by a lordly-looking servant (VIII, 54).

Finally, Proust suggests that a great creative artist is like a ruler and his output *comme un royaume clos, aux frontières infranchissables* (VI, 152).

Commerce. In Combray, castes were rigidly determined by income, and even in the world of society, rank and the polite exchange of formalities are regarded as financial resources which one manipulates according to the desire for personal gain (I, 259; IV, 153–54).

Such intangibles as memories (XV, 144), anticipation and desire are spoken of as financial credits or dividends (V, 133). Even the taste for different types of literature goes up and down in cycles like stocks on the Exchange (IX, 275).

On a lower plane, invitations and the satisfactions of homosexual love are like a pension or an income from a business (IV, 31; X, 75).

The Law, Crime, Etc. In the life of any individual there are manifestations which are similar in kind to those which characterize the typical criminal. Françoise shows a feeling of guilt when the narrator surprises her suddenly (IX, 163), and she and other servants, like ex-jail birds, instinctively recognize each other for what they are despite disguises or subterfuge (X, 160). Jupien and Charlus are more like criminals because of their illegal sexual activities (XIV, 168; XII, 127; IX, 17, 153), but in love and jealousy all men partake of the same qualities. Marcel trembles like a criminal at the sight of Mme de Guermantes (VI, 175), and the scenes he makes for Albertine are based on lies which, like a criminal, he thinks he has ordered so that he will never be caught (XI, 221). In his sense of premonition about her departure, he is like an assassin who is filled with fear even though he knows he will never be discovered (XIII, 22). The same insane desire to speak of his 'crime' motivates Swann in his jealousy over Odette (II, 168), and the protestations of Gilberte that she really loves the narrator are like the repeated statements of a criminal that he is actually innocent (III, 195).

Bloch is as much ashamed of his Jewish blood as a son of the fact that his father is a criminal (VII, 86). The Dreyfus case created the same sort of furor, but, like the marriage of Saint-Loup and Odette's daughter, the outcome of both is eventually accepted, just as one finally forgets whether a girl's father was a criminal or not (XIV, 45, 46). The Duc de Guermantes is as wicked as a criminal towards the Duchess, but he manifests certain signs of humanity in his use of polite formulae at least (VIII, 47).

We are all criminals in that we hide our true nature from others. Our personalities are not available to others like public documents (I, 31), but sometimes we have an absurd desire to confess to someone else, just like a murderer who admits his crime for no reason (VII, 32). More often, we live behind pretense, touching and retouching the alibi which we have built up for others (III, 64). The narrator himself, when he feels the utter nothingness of his thought, experiences the pangs of conscience of the secret criminal who is praised for his good actions (I, 234).

The prison image is used by Proust to describe the effect of silence for a deaf person (VI, 148–49). Also, for the narrator, going to sleep in strange surroundings is like the tortured imprisonment of Cardinal La Balue who could neither sit nor stand in his cage (IV, 83). Both Swann and Marcel treat their loved ones like prisoners because of their jealousy (III, 169; XII, 208); Part V of the novel bears the significant title: *La Prisonnière*. Charlus, just before his betrayal by Mme Verdurin, is entrusted to Brichot, like a man under guard (XII, 106–7).

There are other images drawn from legal sources which Proust uses in his work. Logical conclusions or conclusions deduced from connected bits of evidence are similar to the opinions arrived at by an examining magistrate. Certain remarks by Charlus, for example, reveal in this way his homosexuality (X, 132), and in his jealousy the narrator uses the same approach with Albertine (XI, 69). Brichot pursues a topic with the same persistence as a magistrate (XII, 122), and Mme Verdurin has the same self-satisfied smile as a judge (X, 129). Mme de Saint-Euverte at her garden-party is, once a year, a sort of supreme magistrate (IX, 95). Charlus, when he speaks authoritatively, is like a lawyer arguing (XII, 95) or a member of parliament (X, 120–21), and servants who enter the names of guests in the guest-log are like notaries (II, 146).

Legal images have a way of recurring in connection with Charlus and his homosexuality and in connection with the narrator and his jealous love-affair with Albertine. Charlus is as crafty in his conversation as a witness sub-poenaed to give testimony (X, 236), and Marcel in his jealousy is like a police agent or a detective (XI, 28). In order to create an angry scene, well-verified documentation is necessary (XI, 109).

The narrator also uses legal images in connection with introspective processes. When one wakens from sleep, in order to orientate oneself to the situation, he says one must be as discreet as a suspect summoned before a judge who knows some details about the case (XI, 151). The narrator compares La Berma's acting to an important person coming without any thought of gain to testify in favour of an innocent person, and he fears for both of them that the public will not be polite enough (III, 27). He also compares the difficulty of identifying a person after the passage of many years to the difficulty a witness has in identifying the guilty person in a police line-up (XV, 87–88).

In his desire to write, the narrator sometimes tries to do without the drugs or alcohol he takes to control his asthma, but this makes him so ill that he submits again to them *comme une victime qui se laisse voler de peur, si elle résiste, d'être assassinée* (VI, 182). For doctors, an invalid who recovers against their prediction is like a freed criminal flaunting himself before the judge who had condemned him to death (IX, 57). In love, as well as the worlds of society and politics, there are judges, victims and executioners; the victims are generally so spineless that one can hardly bear resentment against the executioners (II, 205; IX, 132). An imposing doorman makes Marcel think of an executioner (IX, 52), and cruel critics of an actress are executioners (VI, 212).

Military Hierarchy, Battles, War. One would like to see in the images Proust draws from army life evidences of his own personal experiences during his period of military service. Actually, however, the figures of speech which he employs do not reveal any special knowledge which would not be known to any cultivated writer.

Proust uses images drawn from military life in describing social relations especially—relations between lovers or homosexuals, and more casual relations within the framework of the social hierarchy.

Love is, above all, a war or a battle (XIII, 25; XIV, 151) in which the lovers are opponents (XI, 33; XII, 190–91). This is just

as true for homosexual love as for orthodox love (XIV, 131).
Quarrels and jealousy are similar to single-handed combats, and
lovers enter them like soldiers, with the hope that they will survive
(IV, 13, 14; VI, 149; IX, 297; XII, 199, 200, 201; XIII, 59). Rivals
in love are also like combatants who enter the struggle (X, 324–25),
and the one who gains his point is the victor who dictates the
conditions of peace (X, 258). A smitten lover is like a wounded
soldier (XI, 14).

Even minor interchanges in love are connected by the narrator
with military terms. Charlus' significant glance at a desired youth
is like a parting shot fired by a retreating soldier (IV, 187), and his
hand on the narrator's shoulder is as brutal as the recoil of a '76'
(XIV, 137–38). The envelope of a letter from Mlle de Stermaria (a
letter of refusal, incidentally) falls at Marcel's feet like the casing of
an ejected shell (VIII, 18). Odette's lies enter Swann's heart (the
heart being *le théâtre d'opérations* (IX, 16)) like a horde of invaders
(II, 196).

In the world of society, any salon leader is like a great general
and strategist. Both the Verdurins demand implicit obedience
from their followers (X, 21, 87) and they do not announce their
objectives until after they have gained them (III, 215; X, 12). A
frequenter of their salon, such as Saniette, is a mere private or
common soldier (X, 87, 91). The Cambremers regard themselves as
an important military family whose château has been occupied by
invaders when they rent it to the Verdurins (X, 68, 69, 71, 72). Mme
de Villeparisis at Balbec is like an ambassador abroad (IV, 99), and
Mme de Saint-Euverte in planning her garden-party resembles a
general preparing for a great military action (IV, 92, 93). Mme
Swann acquires a salon much as a general in a colonial war acquires
territory (II, 110, 111).

Charlus as a social leader and a homosexual is frequently associated with military images. He is said to look like a musketeer of the
time of Louis XIII (X, 306), and his sexual aberrations are well-
known away from his immediate environment, *comme certains coups
de canon qu'on n'entend qu'après l'interférence d'une zone silencieuse* (X, 53).
He speaks without regard to his hearers much as a bomber releases
his missiles indiscriminately (XIV, 126), and conversation with him
is like a military engagement (IX, 124). When Charlus is finally
subjugated by the Verdurins, his defeat is a military one (XII, 141).

Certain military figures are themselves associated with military images. The laugh of the Grand Duke Wladimir is like the roll of a military drum (IX, 77–78), and the monocle of General de Froberville rests in his eye like a shell splinter which has caused a wound (II, 148).

Any specialist with superior knowledge is like a military strategist. Françoise as a cook (III, 72), the director-general at Balbec (IV, 114), Cottard as a doctor (VII, 179), even Marcel's father in his ability to guide the narrator and his mother home from their long walks at Combray (I, 157), are all like great generals to be admired. Bergotte is as lofty in rank to the narrator as a colonel to a private (III, 191), and his very name makes him tremble like a shot fired at him (III, 149).

Marcel frequently uses military imagery in connection with himself. As a child, the ringing of the bell on the gate which indicates a visit probably from Swann, is greeted like the signal for a military engagement, and the grandmother makes a sortie to see who the assailant may be (I, 25–26). The narrator's relations with servants are those of military opponents, but it is they who continually encroach on his precincts (VI, 78; VII, 189). At Balbec, he feels as ill at ease as a new recruit being outfitted for service (IV, 99), but later at Rivebelle he and Saint-Loup are more like triumphant heroes (V, 57). His relations with M. de Chenouville and his presentation to the Prince de Guermantes are like military operations (IX, 164, 282).

Illness is like a military engagement, and Proust compares neuropaths to soldiers who have so often disregarded peril that they never even perceive a fatal wound during the heat of battle (III, 85–86). The final struggle between Death and Life which takes place in the grandmother's feeble frame is like a war (VII, 149, 177).

Art in general is as complex and as unpredictable as war (XV, 35). New forms of art seize and use the arms of their predecessors (IX, 274). To evaluate the true significance of the acting ability of a great artist like La Berma, for instance, is as difficult as to appraise the relative significance of a great military engagement in a war (III, 30–31). Art has issues at stake, just like war, and the creative writer must fix on them and decide them to his own satisfaction if he is to accomplish anything (XV, 52–53).

Reality itself is like an enemy which attacks us by surprise (XI, 203; XII, 234), and we must re-group our forces to meet its challenge

(IX, 23). To penetrate to the true nature of others is as difficult as to locate the camouflaged outposts which have been carefully placed in a field by a vigilant foe (IX, 172). Even for himself, the narrator realizes that his personality changes and evolves to such an extent that he is not always one person but rather *le défilé heure par heure d'une armée compacte* (XIII, 92).

Women, Love Affairs. For Proust, love is the most exciting experience in life, and to it he compares the most important fundamental questions of existence—aesthetic and emotional experiences which transcend the world of every day and place us in contact with great inner truths.

Manifestations of the involuntary memory are the most precious experiences of the narrator's life, and he says that they seem to make everything else completely unimportant just like a passionate love affair (I, 65).

For Swann and the narrator, music is desired in the same way as the satisfactions of love (I, 284; V, 60). Vinteuil's music seems to caress or kiss them just as a lover would (II, 33, 177; XII, 63), and Swann regards Vinteuil's sonata as a sort of *confidente* of his real love for Odette (II, 67). Marcel feels the pangs of love when he sees the celebrated actor Maubant (I, 105), and he feels that characters in a play, because of their ephemeral quality, put us into contact with the great questions of reality, personal identity and death, just as love affairs do (VI, 210–11; XV, 223).

Marcel is infatuated with the style of Bergotte, even though he thinks that what attracts him is the subject matter. This situation is analogous to that of a man captivated by a certain woman who frequents a particular place of entertainment; he goes there thinking he wants to see the entertainment whereas it is really the woman he desires (I, 130). To suggest that he will love other women later is as unthinkable as to suggest to Marcel that he will prefer other authors to Bergotte later in life (I, 135). Beauty of style in literature varies like feminine beauty (III, 154). The first edition in which the narrator reads a work is like the first dress in which one saw a woman (XV, 33). Love is a strong passion which excites the whole organism, and nothing can divert it. The narrator compares his youthful search for beauty to the persistence of a lover (V, 30). In war, patriotism is a similar passion (XIV, 100) while the effect of drugs on Marcel is to make his heart beat fast *comme à un premier rendez-vous* (XI, 231).

Family love may be so strong that it, too, can be compared to passionate love. The narrator's grandmother caresses her relations with her glances (I, 22), and Marcel's desire for his mother's goodnight kiss is like that of a lover for his mistress. When Françoise agrees to carry a note to her to get her to come and see Marcel in bed, the boy is as grateful to the servant as a frustrated lover whose friend undertakes to put him in contact with the object of his affections (I, 47). His disappointment when his mother does not come is as great as that of a poor girl who has sent word up to her lover (or ex-lover) and who waits in the lobby even though there is no answer (I, 48–49).

Relations in the world of society are like an attenuated form of love-affair. Mme Verdurin, when she succeeds in breaking up Charlus and Morel, is as happy as a former mistress who succeeds in preventing the imminent marriage of her ex-lover (XII, 139). Conversation at dinner in the Guermantes home is as full of banalities as that of timid lovers (VII, 38). Charlus regards Mme Verdurin's establishment as scarcely better than a house of prostitution (X, 58), and M. de Guermantes treats Marcel's father with the effrontery of a courtesan (VI, 39). Marcel's early preoccupation with Mme de Guermantes is like a love affair (VII, 241) but, after his later experience in the world of society, he cynically concludes that *dans la vie mondaine, reflet insignifiant de ce qui se passe en amour, la meilleure manière qu'on vous recherche, c'est de se refuser* (XII, 210). Doctors are like mistresses whose word you cannot trust (VII, 172), and the patient is like the lover who is alternately filled with doubts and hope (VII, 171).

Homosexual relations are always spoken of by Proust in terms of clandestine love affairs (XII, 7). Charlus (X, 75), Jupien (IX, 18) and Morel (X, 249) are all spoken of as 'tarts', and Charlus is said to consider sexual inversion as just as dangerous for too youthful lads as prostituion for women (X, 241–42). Charlus is like a hypocritical woman who is scrupulously modest in dress but loose in morals (IV, 203; VIII, 222). He is only interested in erotic liaisons in which the 'mistress' is a man (XII, 108, 140), and once one is aware of it, Charlus' vice is as apparent as the condition of a pregnant woman (IX, 23). An extreme homosexual has as much difficulty regaining prestige in society as a woman who has been involved in scandals (IX, 35).

The narrator is never sure whether Albertine is a Lesbian or not.

P

She knows all about Lesbianism but he thinks that she may only have informed herself concerning it *comme une femme qui épouse un homme de lettres . . . afin de [lui] complaire* (XIV, 19). When she sees other Lesbians, she discreetly looks away, like a man who sees his former mistress with another lover (IX, 319).

Both Charlus and Legrandin are compared to women (X, 59, 61; XIII, 302), and Bloch is as sensitive about his Jewish blood as a 'tart' (*cocotte*) about her profession in a respectable milieu (V, 15). Charlus is also compared to a misogynist because of his apparently hostile attitude towards youths (IV, 200).

Finally, the process of fertilization which the rare flower belonging to the Duchesse de Guermantes must undergo is compared to the courtship and marriage of a young maiden (IX, 8, 9).

Food, Cooking. It seems rather prosaic perhaps to turn from love and women to food and cooking, but the relation between the two is far closer than might at first appear. Love or desire is a strong appetite like hunger and thirst. The narrator speaks of homosexuals attracted to each other as starved (XI, 25–26). He also says that he is starved for Albertine (V, 196; XIII, 62) and other young girls (III, 204; V, 156; XV, 156). The pleasure of satisfying love is like partaking of nourishment (VII, 236; XI, 69–70), and both kisses and the young girls whom Marcel frequents are compared to food (X, 200; V, 112).

We have noted in the preceding section how Proust compares aesthetic experiences to love affairs. Now love is an appetite which can be satisfied with the proper nourishment, just like any other appetite, and Proust completes the third side of this triangle by comparing aesthetic experiences to the taking of food.

Mme de Cambremer, when she talks about music or art, waters at the mouth (IX, 266). This is rather ludicrous but it is true to a degree of all aesthetic experiences. The narrator regards nature (III, 124; V, 50), newspapers (XIII, 188) and books (I, 58) as food. He says that it is as difficult for him to decide between two plays to see as to choose between two equally delicious desserts (I, 105). The distinctive vocabulary of Mme de Guermantes is like an unusual regional dish from Brittany (VIII, 146), and the narrator savours it as well as the style of Bergotte which makes a similar appeal to his palate (I, 134). Stories and experiences provide food for his imagination and his own future writings (VIII, 176; XV, 48), and he says that characters and situations in his book are composite, much like Françoise's famous beef jelly which is made from numerous pieces of meat (XV, 213).

In polite society, there are various situations which are reminiscent of the preparation and serving of food. An amusing story by Mme de Guermantes is served up like a dish (III, 40–41), but when it is repeated, it is like food heated up again or served cold the next day (VIII, 105, 145). In her old age Mme de Guermantes's stories are still considered the best, but actually they have deteriorated like pastries from a celebrated maker which one continues to order because of the name (XV, 177). To bring together socially distinct types is as daring as to experiment with standard recipes (III, 117–18). M. de Bréauté presents the narrator to the Prince de Guermantes much as he would pass a plate of cakes (IX, 74), and social snobs look with disdain at others much as they would reject an unattractive dish (IV, 97). Even music, especially if it is unfamiliar music, must receive the approbation of members of society just like a new way of serving food (II, 157).

Proust is very prone to comparing people to food. We have already noted examples of this above in the case of the young girls and Mme de Guermantes. To these, we can add several other interesting examples. Mme de Guermantes's cheeks in old age are compared to nougat (XV, 96), and Andrée's face when she is annoyed is like spoiled syrup (XI, 74). Céleste Albaret compares the narrator's own complexion to the interior of fresh almonds (IX, 315). Mme de Cambremer is a delicious honey cake when she is in a good mood (IX, 269), and a hard Normandy biscuit when she is huffy (X, 68). Charlus is like a curious box of oriental fruit, and the idea of tasting it (or him) turns one's stomach (X, 226). Mme de Gallardon looks like a pheasant cooked and brought to the table with its feathers on (II, 151).

Another thing Proust often does is to compare particular expressions on individuals' faces to phases of eating or digestion. Saint-Loup, when he smiles in a self-satisfied way, looks like someone *qui a bien digéré* (VI, 145). When Françoise is righteously indignant, she moves her lips like someone finishing off a tasty bite (VI,70). Her sorrow at the death of the grandmother affects her much like indigestion (VII, 201). As the narrator reproaches Albertine in his jealousy, she looks as though she were sucking with delight a piece of barley sugar (XI, 126).

Many aspects of daily life are compared by Proust to food or the odour of cooking. We have already noted the case of the rosy sky, like salmon, above the blue sea which is the color of mullet (V, 50). The steeple of the church at Combray is compared to a crisp golden loaf of French bread (I, 93), and the same comparison is used conversationally by the curate when he describes the town (I, 147). Pink hawthorn blooms are as precious as pink biscuits or cheese mixed with strawberries (I, 190) and they smell like almonds or frangipane (I, 156). Inside a closed building, the odour reminds the narrator of *pain bis* (VI, 90), and the exciting combination of odours from the fire and the various objects in the room at Combray is like a *gâteau provincial, un immense 'chausson'* (I, 74). The fog outside reminds him of spun sugar (VIII, 15).

There are other objects which are compared to food or utensils used for preparing food. Françoise's bonnet looks as though it were made from spun sugar (I, 77) or biscuit (I, 79), and a white porcelain bowl looks like hardened milk (XV, 35). The porch of the church at Combray is likened to a skimming ladle (I, 85).

Even proper names suggest to Proust foods or regional sweetmeats. Pennedepie is *savoureux et durci comme certain fromage normand* (X, 297), and Coutances reminds him of butter (II, 230–31).

Before leaving images drawn from food and cooking, we must consider a few images which refer to wine even though the question of intoxication will be left till a later section.

Spring is the season of the year which seems to have the effervescent quality of wine (XII, 260). This same characteristic is used to describe the nascent patriotism in time of war which sends Morel's blood coursing through his veins (XIV, 91).

In society, rank is comparable to name and year of wines. The Guermantes family are like a precious old wine (VIII, 180) while unimportant folk are mere dregs (IX, 96). The younger set who have no notion of Mme de Guermantes's real worth regard her as a Guermantes *d'une moins bonne cuvée, d'une moins bonne année* (XV, 176).

INTROSPECTIVE PROCESSES

Quite apart from the images of the preceding section, many of which depend on observation as well as experience, there is a general class of images in *A la recherche du temps perdu* which can be said to be derived largely from introspection. Pre-eminent in this section are figures of speech based on illness, the effects of drugs and alcohol and old age and death. True enough, some of these categories contain images based on observation, but the reason they have been grouped together in one class is that the primary emphasis seems to rest on their introspective quality.

Bodily Sensations. Under this rather vague sub-heading we have included a number of images which depend for their effect on certain bodily sensations not included under any of the other headings such as illness, drunkenness, hunger, love, etc. For example, friendship as compared to love is said to be like a feeling somewhere between boredom and fatigue (VIII, 22).

Sensations of touch can vary all the way from extreme pleasure to pain. Charlus loves to talk about Morel and to touch him in this way when he cannot actually touch him physically (X, 129-31). On the other hand Proust declares that the death of millions of strangers in war does not affect us as much as an unpleasant draft (XIV, 97). The intellectual activity of the young dandy, Octave, is just a mild sort of itching (V, 140), but the force of memory on the narrator is sometimes as strong as a real blow (IX, 237). He even shudders involuntarily at the sight of a compromising document as at the sound of a shriek (VII, 227).

Proust uses other involuntary movements to describe spontaneous or repeated physical phenomena. The young girls cannot prevent laughter any more than a sneeze (V, 175). The water heater at Doncières seems to have the hiccoughs (VII, 211; XV, 36). Marcel's acknowledgment of Gilberte's greeting is as instinctive and subconscious as the details of walking and how one foot is placed after the other (II, 247). When he becomes Albertine's lover, her existence seems to bear as vague but intrinsic a relation to his as his arms or legs (XII, 157).

Misconceptions or false hopes are compared by the narrator to mirages. The style of Bergotte deceives him at first into considering it wonderful (III, 61). He believes his own recovery from the illness that besets his later years is imminent, and this is as great a mirage as the conviction of the French people that the war will end any day (XIV, 181). Actual ignorance is like being blindfolded. This is how most people read the newspaper (XIV, 69), and one might say that the jealous man acts as though he were blindfolded (XII, 121).

The effect of the imagination or reverie is almost like hypnotism

(XII, 82–85), and when the narrator looks at beautiful flowers he is filled with sensations akin to visionary experiences (I, 191).

Sleep also partakes of the qualities of hypnotism or visions. When the narrator reads a book he is as oblivious to other things as if he were asleep (I, 123). The dissipation of jealousy brings as great a relief as a deep sleep (XI, 116–17). Dreams, on the other hand, resemble states of amnesia or unreality. We remember little of the vast complexity of impressions our dreams offer us, and this is just as true for reality (III, 128). The conscious efforts of our memory to recall specific images are just as frustrating as dreams which involve people we dislike and which never include loved ones we have lost (III, 79). The uncertainty of our memory is similar to those half-somnolent states between waking and sleeping (XV, 18) or sleeping and waking (IX, 202).

Illness and its Treatment. When one pauses to consider in Proust's work the vast body of images derived from pathological sources one is both amazed and appalled.

Of course it is true that even those who are only acquainted with Proust by hearsay know all about his asthma and his exaggerated hypochondria. And anyone who has read *A la recherche du temps perdu* realizes that psychosomatic illnesses are the central factor in the lives of the narrator and his aunt Léonie and that, according to him, the book would never have been written except for a prolonged absence from society imposed on him by his illness. Illness and death are the most important elements in the life story of Swann, Bergotte and the narrator's grandmother and, from one point of view, the whole grandiose work might be said to be the revelation of the cycle of life with its precipitous impulsion toward death.

All this is self-evident, even though it probably constitutes the most controversial aspect of Proust's work. What even the most careful readers of *A la recherche du temps perdu* do not realize, however, is the extent to which Proust uses images derived from illness and its treatment in widely diversified connections. In the examination of images associated with love in the preceding chapter, we have had some slight indication of how this class of images permeates certain themes, but in the following section we will see very clearly how vast are the ramifications of it.

It is not surprising that Proust should be interested in medicine and illness. After all, his father and his only brother were both physicians of some considerable prominence and Proust himself, as a youth, must have been continually exposed to medical terminology. His references to anatomy and disease are frequently quite technical and even if they are not always exactly accurate, they do vividly illustrate the point in question.

Proust uses the image of the doctor to illustrate the position of the person who has superior knowledge or superior power. The scholar Brichot has glasses like a laryngologist's reflecting mirror (X, 18). Morel as a musician is like a great surgeon who must not upset himself before he operates (XI, 244). In society, both the Duc de Guermantes (VII, 198) and his brother Charlus (VIII, 208; XII, 41, 86) are like learned and busy physicians because of their prestige. His degree of authority carries over into the area of homosexuality as far as Charlus is concerned (XII, 116), but rank anywhere is analogous to rank in the field of medicine, even though the ignorant are uninformed about it (X, 54). The narrator regards Swann as a great doctor because of his social pre-eminence as Gilberte's father (III, 98). A jealous lover, because of the power he possesses, is like a ruthless surgeon (II, 194). Nonetheless, we do not blame him for our suffering in love (XI, 115). Actually, each individual in love is his own doctor (IV, 41).

In treating illness, the most important factor as far as the doctor is concerned is diagnosis. Very often diagnosis can be made instantly without X-rays, auscultation or taking the temperature. The narrator finds himself able instinctively to recognize homosexuality in this way in Charlus (IX, 86; X, 132) and Vaugoubert (IX, 85). When Charlus is at Balbec, his symptoms are scarcely perceptible, but the keen doctor could predict from them coming catastrophes (X, 236). In later years, the symptoms of the malady are very plain (XI, 253; XII, 9, 10). In himself, the narrator is aware at different times of physical upsets, but he is unable to pin-point them as 'infatuation with Mme de Guermantes' (VI, 146) or 'effect of intermittent memory' (XIII, 179). It is only later that he is able to diagnose the cause of his state. Norpois is just as helpless in trying to diagnose Odette's unhappy situation before Swann marries her (III, 52).

A doctor can take a patient's temperature in trying to diagnose an illness, but in the case of love, for example, a mistress's demands for money give no better a picture of her complete life than a list of temperature readings would (VII, 213). The political situation is just as elusive, and individual factors in it are of no more importance than an X-ray of a patient which must be collated with a number of other factors in order to arrive at a diagnosis (VII, 78–79). The narrator himself in appraising people (particularly with the idea in mind of including certain features about them in his book) describes his method as X-raying (III, 199; XIV, 33).

The doctor always has an examining room where he makes certain tests and asks questions of his patients. Proust borrows from this procedure to describe how Rachel, as a prostitute, begins to strip in the presence of clients, stopping only if told to do so just as though she were preparing for a medical examination (VI, 192–93). The young males who condescend to relations with Charlus profess to dislike women *comme ils diraient au médecin qu'ils ne prennent jamais d'alcool et n'aiment que l'eau de source* (XII, 20). For the narrator, a feeling of novelty is as unpleasant as waiting in a doctor's office (IV, 81).

Of course, medically speaking, the ideal procedure is to prevent disease from developing. The narrator suggests that reality and imagination should be separated in order to avoid further difficulties in the same way that certain doctors recommend indiscriminate removal of the appendix in children in order to prevent later trouble (V, 97). Inoculation and vaccination achieve the same ends, but they are rather disagreeable. Françoise avoids learning how to use the telephone just as certain people avoid being vaccinated (IX, 168; XI, 123). Nevertheless, the effects of immunization are lasting, and Proust uses this figure to describe involuntary predispositions towards certain reactions, e.g. the influence of Bergotte's thinking on his readers (III, 159); fashionable 'boredom' in the Verdurin circle (X, 203); the subjective impulsion, in love, of individuals towards certain types (XV, 63).

Doctors may experiment on others (XV, 136), or they may experiment on themselves (II, 113; XV, 55) in order to discover more about the nature and treatment of diseases. In any case, they must decide very carefully what remedies to apply (this figure is used of Saint-Loup's indecision as to how to cure Marcel's unhappiness at Doncières (VI, 88)), and they must be alert to the various courses which an illness may follow. (This latter figure is employed especially in discussing war and battles (VI, 138, 140; XV, 151)).

The anatomy of all normal human beings is similar, and there are certain kinaesthetic phenomena which they have all experienced.

These feelings can only be described introspectively and while they are not illnesses or disease, they are variants from the healthy norm. For example, Proust compares falling autumn leaves to the yellow spots that sometimes dance before the eyes (II, 273). Extreme fatigue (VI, 110) and the impact of a reality contrary to that which was assumed (XIII, 77) cause the narrator to experience a feeling of dizziness. The re-echoing in his mind of certain remarks by Albertine which are grounds for jealousy is like the humming in the ears that we all sometimes hear when a sudden silence falls (X, 334). His intense excitement at the thought of visiting Venice gives him the feeling of nausea that one sometimes has with a sore throat (II, 236).

The influence of heredity on character development is affected by factors as invariable as those which govern physical development. In the child we have certain glands which no longer exist in the adult (V, 78), and our personalities continue to change according to pattern in just the same way that our body tissues are replaced (XIII, 220–21). Proust feels that he can describe these and other social phenomena in his book, basing his observations on the slightly variant types it has been his lot to meet, with as much accuracy as the anatomist who describes normal organisms on the basis of the continually varying ones he has examined (XV, 26, 50).

In a purely anatomical description Proust compares the features contributing to the originality of the loved one to the distinguishing characteristics of the individual lozenges of skin (V, 159). He also compares 'Envy' in Giotto's picture to an illustration in a medical text showing the effect of depression of the epiglottis by the doctor's instrument or a tumor (I, 114). In a rather far-fetched image, he compares the elevator in the hotel at Balbec to *une cage thoracique mobile qui se fût déplacée le long de la colonne montante* (V, 45).

The number of things that can go wrong with the human organism is infinite, and, in speaking of variations from the norm, Proust utilizes in figures of speech minor physical upsets, serious diseases and major physical and mental maladies.

One's manner of falling in love or being betrayed in love is compared to one's way of catching cold (XIII, 16, 107), The beneficial influence of his friend Saint-Loup has the same effect on Marcel as a doctor who takes a troublesome grain of sand out of his eye (VI, 109). Extreme fatigue immobilizes the narrator in the same way that seasickness does (XV, 219), and the insistency of certain themes in musical compositions seems to make them almost resemble migraine headaches (XI, 197; XII, 72). Toothaches are used to describe unpleasant experiences like jealousy (XII, 27–28), nightmares (I, 43), the jarring on the ear of a mispronounced word (VII, 224), and embarrassing social situations (II, 135).

All sorts of common social phenomena are referred to by Proust as illnesses. Snobbery is one (X, 80; XI, 15) and avarice and adultery are others (X, 80). War is a serious malady that attacks the whole state (VI, 220–21; XIV, 120). The popularity of certain puns or modes of expression is like an epidemic which must run its highly infectious course (VII, 72; X, 95). Even homosexuality is like a hereditary illness or predisposition towards illness in certain families (XI, 26; XIII, 324). If one symptom disappears, others take its place (IX, 37).

Love is the great illness which attacks all members of the human race. Certain symptoms can be cured eventually (XIII, 218) but it is only to give rise to others (XI, 104), and when the malady is running its course it assumes an overweening importance in our lives.

Love and jealousy can scarcely be separated and they are sometimes spoken of vaguely by Proust as a malady or an illness (II, 86, 136, 200; III, 54, 120). More specifically, he refers to them as nervous maladies (IX, 253) and he cites in particular asthma (XI, 34–35) and eczema (II, 87). This leads him to conclude that, like them, jealousy has its source less in persons than in places (III, 121).

The germs which cause disease are very tiny, just like the things that cause love (II, 169; IX, 260). Nevertheless, their effects are drastic, and love is as serious as cholera (II, 169), tuberculosis (II, 123), leukemia (XIII, 278), paralysis (XIII, 244) or heart disease (III, 93; XI, 118; XV, 55).

Love is also associated by the narrator with real wounds or operations (II, 123). Experiences which rouse all the doubts in him about Albertine's possible lesbianism are like a sharp point in his heart (IX, 257; X, 326) or the probing of a surgeon trying to remove a bullet (XIII, 101). Odette's lies are like knives cutting Swann (II, 200), and his jealousy is a deep wound (II, 197).

The narrator speaks of his falling in love with Albertine as the receiving of a wound (XII, 63), and as he gradually recovers from it, the effect is the same as that of a wound healing but leaving a scar (XI, 34; XII, 231; XIII, 88). The same figure is used for Swann's love for Odette (II, 82, 196, 199) and for the narrator's infatuation with Mme de Guermantes (VI, 145). A quarrel or a definitive separation is like an operation that must be performed coolly (XII, 239). While the wounds of love are healing, they are covered with dressings and if something occurs to re-open the wound, it is as though the dressing had been wrenched off (XI, 178; XIII, 19).

Love and jealousy are like physical torture (II, 83, 200; XI, 127, 135). The man who suffers from them and recovers is like an individual who has a limb amputated and learns to walk with crutches (XIII, 44, 94).

The figure of an operation is also used by Proust to describe the sort of effort that is necessary to break habits (IX, 210–11). Bergotte has produced his books with such labour that he seems to have been operated on for them (VII, 186). Dressings are used in descriptions of monocles which are removed and changed in somewhat the same way (II, 162; X, 146–47).

The anaesthetics which are used by doctors in operations are generally employed by Proust to describe a state of inertia or somnolence. Habit is a sort of anaesthetic (I, 20), and the narrator can do things automatically while his mind is on something else, just as a patient under a local anaesthetic can watch the operation without feeling anything (I, 39). Sleep is an anaesthetic (VI, 103) and so is preoccupation (I, 42). While listening to music, Swann appears to be under the influence of an anaesthetic (II, 32).

In the treatment of disease, the doctor can use medicine and drugs as well as the more drastic procedure of surgery. Drugs like morphine and cocaine have a double effect. They relieve pain or distress, and in this connection Proust uses them to describe the effect of habit (IV, 89) and sleep (V, 71; X, 154). Besides this, however, they give a sense of profound pleasure or even intoxication. It is this feeling which the narrator experiences when his mother kisses him good-night (I, 49) and which Mme Verdurin derives from music (XII, 34).

Women contain in themselves all the potentialities of soporific drugs (IX, 159–60; XIV, 151). The satisfactions of love or the calm memories of the loved one are similar in their effect to a sedative (XIII, 43, 87, 88); jealousy or disappointment, on the other hand, act like caffeine or the lack of a needed sedative (IV, 15; XIII, 40, 62, 83–84). Homosexuals are also like drug addicts (IX, 31–32; XIV, 112).

From drugs to poisons is just a step, and Proust uses many figures of speech which are based on poisons and their antidotes.

Habit is anodine as contrasted with the poisonous effects of novelty (XIII, 157), and familiarity with the defects in character of our acquaintances has the result of mithridatizing us against them (IX, 80, 81).

It is in love and jealousy, however, that the poison image is most frequently used. The loved one is like a beautiful but poisonous flower (XIII, 238). Her lies are poison (II, 195), and jealousy of her is like those poisons whose effect is cumulative (IX, 252). One absorbs daily doses of the noxious drug until such a hypersensitivity is built up that the least extra quantity would be fatal (XI, 103–4, 211). Even after a long interval of time, the drug could not be tolerated (III, 188).

Memory is like a pharmacy full of calming drugs and poisons (XII, 235–36). There, at times, the poison of jealousy has been sublimated (IV, 35) or evaporated (XIII, 227), but at other times it has its full harmful power (XIII, 154). Generally speaking, though, abstinence from drugs or poisons weakens their potential effect (IV, 29).

Our bodies have the power of secreting counter-poisons against the suspicions of jealousy (XIII, 73). Most often, we find the antidote for the poison in the very women we love. This is true for Swann (II, 195) as well as the narrator (X, 323).

Proust uses mental illnesses as well as physical ones in the figures which he draws from pathological sources. The intense preoccupation which a musician (I, 289) or a writer (III, 162) has with his art is akin to insanity. Habit, with its unvarying routine, resembles the fixations of madmen (XI, 53; IX, 264), and for the narrator, other people must be admitted to be as unreal as the furniture which an insane person talks to and believes alive (XV, 18).

Because of their idiosyncrasies, Marcel's grandfather treats his sisters-in-law as mad (I, 35–36), and the Duchesse de Guermantes has to be as courageous in dealing with the choleric Duke as those who look after maniacs (VIII, 152).

Charlus, in his homosexual preoccupations, is like a maniac (IV, 187; VII, 251, 252; XII, 8–9; XIV, 175). Marcel in his phobias about Gilberte and her family is regarded by Norpois as mad (III, 63, 66). His love for Albertine is also like insanity (IX, 294), and Saint-Loup believes him the victim of hallucinations when he sees the picture of the woman he professes to love (XIII, 30). In addition, his fixation about his mother's good-night kiss has all the symptoms of a certain type of insanity (I, 37).

In describing personal reactions, the narrator frequently draws on pathological images which refer to loss of some power or other —amnesia, aphasia, blindness, etc. Sleep and forgetting are common forms of amnesia (XI, 150; XIV, 18), and when Marcel experiences flashes of memory, he feels like a victim of amnesia just recovering from his illness(IX, 225–26). Habit and sleep are paralyzing influences (II, 262; XI, 152), and a false sense of security seems to petrify the intelligence (XI, 27–28). In order to forget Albertine, Marcel thinks he would need to relearn all the seasons he associates with her just as a victim of hemiplegia has to learn all over again how to read (XIII, 85).

Marcel regards the three trees which form the basis of his early aesthetic experience as loved ones who have lost the power of speech (IV, 147). They seem alive to him. He attributes the inability of other people to perceive certain things to a sort of atrophy of unused faculties (IX, 86). An obvious truth, he says, is so apparent that *même un paralysé, atteint d'agraphie après une attaque et réduit à regarder les caractères comme un dessin, sans savoir les lire, [l'] aurait compris* (X, 106).

In many of his images, Proust draws on the state of being an invalid. This is quite distinct from having an operation or suffering from a disease or insanity or taking drugs or medicine. It emphasizes the sick person's condition with the limitations it imposes on him and it is more concerned with the incidentals of illness such as diet, debility and convalescence.

Unrequited love is an illness (IX, 148), and separation from a loved one is a malady which many have experienced in common (XIII, 29). The residue of love is similar to the rheumatism contracted out-of-doors on fine summer nights (XIII, 136). Love itself is a chronic illness (XI, 25, 186) or susceptibility to illness (IX, 260), and a beautiful woman is looked after as carefully by her admirers as an invalid (IV, 48). The woman loved really is an invalid more than her lover realizes (V, 217).

When one is in love and jealous, one is like an invalid who cannot prevent himself from probing the very source of his pain. This is true for Marcel (XII, 247–48) as well as Swann (II, 200). In social relationships also, a recalcitrant person is regarded by a companion as an uncooperative invalid (V, 158). Visits to a salon and its leader are like visits to a sick person in her room (III, 216).

Homosexuals are like invalids (XIV, 173) and this is particularly true for Charlus in his old age (XIV, 112, 202). Their illness, however, is largely mental and they are compared to neuropaths (X, 222). This figure of neurasthenia is also applied to André's conception of love (XIII, 230), Mme de Villeparisis's attitude toward her social deterioration (VII, 12) and Marcel's notions about aesthetics (VI, 54).

Beautiful girls are like the delicate fruits which tempt the invalid's palate (V, 177), and the music which Swann associates with his love is like a dish specially prepared for an invalid (III, 133). Literary and musical style are compared by Proust to invalid diets and regimes which are designed to encourage good health (III, 160, 190–91; I, 285). In social relations the Duchesse de Guermantes speaks of her pleasurable anticipation as an invalid speaks of eating an orange (VIII, 256). Recovery from the malady of love is first indicated by the improved appetite for other things (II, 127). It is well on the way when the invalid puts on weight from the spiritual food of other activities (II, 119).

People in society are like invalids in their fretful peevishness and the vagaries of their whims (VIII, 110; X, 176, XIV, 49). Character defects are like an intermittent illness (X, 286–87), and undesirable associates are as loathsome as dread diseases (V, 25). Mme de Guermantes avoids women as though by doctor's orders (VII, 35).

The narrator's own moods fluctuate like his temperature (I, 247). For him, grief has the effect of a terrible fever (IX, 215), but pleasant memories are like the little balloons of oxygen which relieve a patient's discomfort (VI, 13) or huge soothing compresses on his heart (X, 196). A dream is an imaginary illness (VII, 240–41).

Certain tastes in literature are like pathological states (III, 34, 163), and a new way of writing or painting is as painful as treatment by an oculist (VII, 185). The carefully worded notes of M. de Norpois are as non-committal as medical bulletins (XIII, 270).

Drunkenness. Closely related to illness and medicine is the question of drunkenness. It is associated particularly with drugs, and Proust treats it mainly from two points of view.

First of all, he uses the fatuous appearance of drunks with their sentimental but transitory enthusiasms to describe superficialities. Bloch in society (IV, 180) and Marcel in analyzing the vivid intensity of emotions he feels under a variety of circumstances (VIII, 201; X,

218, 328) are said to experience the momentary but meaningless tenderness of drunks for a neighbour or the waiter who pours the drink. The narrator also compares his preoccupation with the present to that of drunks (V, 63–64).

In addition to this class of images, Proust also uses the rather revolting appearance of drunks to describe unpleasant people. Charlus is often *ivre de fureur* (X, 274), and Saint-Loup, in concealing from the narrator his homosexual leanings toward Morel, speaks with *une voix d'alcoolique* (XIV, 14). A repulsive specimen in Jupien's establishment is huge and his face is *couverte de taches rouges, comme un ivrogne* (XIV, 168).

The second point of view from which Proust regards intoxication and which he employs in images arises from the ecstatic experience which the sensation brings. From that point of view, music is like drunkenness (XII, 215). Communion with nature, fatigue and the suffering of love all modify reality as much as intoxication with liquor (VI, 209, 199; XIII, 126). Sleep is a sort of drunkenness (V, 70), and Mme de Marsantes is inebriated by the conversation of the narrator since he is the friend of the son whom she adores (VII, 130).

Old Age, Death. The logical term of illness and all its adjuncts is death. Indeed, Proust declares that *la mort est vraiment une maladie dont on revient* (IX, 234). At the same time, death is one of the great mysteries of this life and even Proust can find nothing pleasant to say about it. Death is fundamentally sad (IV, 148) and there is no sorrow like that associated with grief and mourning (XIII, 176, 218; VIII, 20).

Habit is a sort of progressive death by slow degrees (IV, 89, 90). In a lesser cycle, day dies only to be resurrected in evening's artificial lights (V, 52; VIII, 16). Reminiscences of people live on in our memories after the individuals themselves die, but the memories also finally die, making impossible any sort of resurrection (IX, 147; XIII, 193).

Old age is in many respects like death. The narrator compares his unswerving persistence in pursuing a fruitless aim to the unreasoning stubbornness of old people (XIII, 187). This rigidity of action is finally immobilized completely in death, and the narrator compares the aged Princesse de Nassau to an embalmed corpse (XV, 147). A salon that has seen its day and is now frequented only by elderly remnants of a disappearing generation is like a quiet cemetery (XV, 111). From the same point of view a book is like a cemetery where the names of individuals around which it is built are long since illegible (XV, 53). Forgetting is symbolized by the cemetery (VIII, 98; XIII, 83), but it begins in the process of retrograde obliteration which old people experience (XIV, 51).

There are certain phenomena of old age which are used by Proust to describe everyday experiences. Fatigue and sexual overindulgence are like senility (XV, 218; IX, 243). The sudden consciousness of a change in appearance or one's own attitude is like the shock an older person or an invalid experiences when he looks in the mirror and sees his altered looks (VI, 172; XIII, 275–76).

Jealousy in love is like the last fatal illness before death. Odette's confessions to Swann are cradled by him like hideous corpses (II, 204), and she herself is like a dying person watched over and cared for by a faithful relative (II, 182). The narrator compares both Albertine (XII, 245) and himself to dying individuals because of jealousy (XI, 208; XIII, 122, 149–50). When he visits her in her room just before she leaves him, she looks like a shrouded corpse lying on the bed (XII, 197). Albertine's trunks remind Marcel of coffins (XI, 14; XIII, 21).

Marcel compares to a sort of death his disappointment over missing his mother's good-night kiss. He speaks of turning down the bed as digging his own tomb and putting on his night-gown as donning a shroud (I, 44). When his mother tenderly indulges him, he feels he is receiving the forbidden foods which are no longer denied to a dying person (XIII, 257).

The narrator also compares himself and his desire to write to a fatally wounded soldier (IV, 218–19) or a dying mother (XV, 222) who realize their condition but think only of the wife or the son they are leaving behind. The evolution of the different manifestations of Marcel's personality is like a series of deaths which leave him unmoved personally like a casual friend amid the real grief of close relatives at a funeral (XIII, 220, 211). It is only when the involuntary memory operates that he is really moved as a son who has remained calm throughout the ceremony is moved to tears at a sudden and unexpected tribute to his father (XIII, 21–22; XV, 28).

It is the process of time evolution in general which Proust associates with death. Saint-Loup back from the battle front is like an invalid doomed to die (XIV, 76, 77). The kitchen-maid whose

term of confinement is fast approaching is like a dying person who
can think only of the thing that is causing her death (I, 115). Friendship runs its course and dies (IV, 159) in a pale imitation of what
happens to love. And finally, in society, people come and go. Like
Charlus, some of them manifest very early the ultimate source of the
cause of their death (XIV, 127), but in old age they all stagger and
stumble as though they had one foot in the grave, and their faces
are like those of the dead or the dying:

> Certaines figures sous la cagoule de leurs cheveux blancs avaient
> déjà la rigidité, les paupières scellées de ceux qui vont mourir, et
> leurs lèvres, agitées d'un tremblement perpétuel, semblaient mar-
> monner la prière des agonisants (XV, 96).

IV

TECHNIQUES

Hamlet: *Do you see yonder cloud that's almost in the shape of a camel?*
Polonius: *By the mass, and 'tis like a camel indeed.*
Ham: *Methinks it is like a weasel.*
Pol.: *It is backed like a weasel.*
Ham: *Or like a whale.*
Pol.: *Very like a whale.*

—HAMLET (III, 2.)

In the detailed examination of Proust's images set forth in the preceding two chapters of this study, certain characteristic techniques
have already shown up very clearly.[1] Attention has been drawn, for
example, to the visual and materialistic quality of the images in
A la recherche du temps perdu and to a few unusual features such as
those groups of reciprocal images where, for instance, young girls
are compared to flowers and flowers, in turn, to young girls. The
reader has undoubtedly noticed for himself many other recurring
stylistic devices and, in this final chapter, it only remains for us to
underline the unique technical procedures which characterize Proust's
use of images.

The more one reads an author, the more one becomes accustomed to his manner of seeing. The treatment by the oculist is
painful at first, but afterwards one sees the world in a new and
exciting and wholly consistent fashion. In Proust's case, the effect on
a reader is that he sees resemblances where none were apparent
before, and the most disparate objects are drawn together by
features which they have in common. Moreover, the reader's
subservience to the author is such that in all but the most blatant
cases, the similarities are accepted as reasonable and even logical.
Some of them are so obvious, once they have been considered, that
the reader wonders why they were never pointed out before.

In the case of aural sensations, especially, Proust selects images
which are consistently logical. Natural sounds are like bird-calls,
and the murmur of wind or water is compared to musical effects.

[1] On the general question of Proust's technique, the reader is referred to the admirable chapter by Stephen Ullmann in *The Image in the Modern French Novel*, pp. 124–238.

The sound of applause is like a storm and in music, in turn, we can hear natural sounds if we but listen.

Other sounds are also analyzed logically and the particular comparison which Proust selects is always felt to be accurate. The sound of rain on a window is like the sound of sand falling on glass, and an airplane in distance is like the buzzing of a wasp. The noise of storms or trains is like the roaring of wild animals, and a car starting up produces the same sound as that of a knife being sharpened.

In the field of visual images, Proust has countless examples of what we may call logical figures. All of the comparisons between people and paintings or statues which they resemble, for example, are logical. Here we accept the accuracy of the writer's observation, and by his statement that a particular person looks like a certain celebrated portrait or a standard type of portrait from a set period in history, we are assisted in picturing that individual.

Many visual images employed by Proust involve comparisons never made previously, but once we examine them, we admit on our own their veracity, even though they force us to consider familiar objects in a way never before experienced. The corolla of a white rose is actually like a *mignonne baignoire minuscule de Nymphenbourg* (XIV, 27), and in a real theatre, from below, the upper galleries seem like

> ... de grosses bourriches piquées de fleurs humaines et attachées au cintre de la salle par les brides rouges de leurs séparations de velours (VI, 65).

The result of this sort of thing is to destroy entirely our sense of perspective and any ideas we may have had about the relative size or importance of experiences in life. Proust insists that there are truths just as important in a soap advertisement as in Pascal's *Pensées*, and a life-time of study may not be as revealing as an hour or two of transcendental experience.

> To see a world in a grain of sand,
> And heaven in a wild flower;
> Hold infinity in the palm of your hand
> And eternity in an hour ...

this is just as true for Proust as for Blake.

In the realm of more abstract conceptions, Proust continues to use logical images. The excellence of a family name, like that of wines, depends on its age (VIII, 180). Man, because of his ability to live in the past as well as in the present, is like an amphibious creature (XIII, 145). The effectiveness of these images is readily apparent, and it results from a similarity of content in the subject and the source of the image that justifies our using the term logical.

In both of the above images, we can also notice Proust's consistent tendency to render as concrete or materialistic ideas which are abstract or vague. Even in the realm of specific sensory impressions, he loves to turn transient auditory sensations into visual phenomena and he declares in turn that a visual impression, such as that of a colour, has a positive organic effect on him; it seems to cut into his flesh like a knife (XII, 63).

Proust never lets stand general or vague expressions such as 'She was amazed', or 'She was tender toward me'. He consistently renders them materialistic and specific, so that we find examples such as the following:

> 1. Elle avait eu l'étonnement, l'embarras et la honte de quelqu'un qui a devant lui à table un instrument nouvellement inventé dont il ne sait pas l'usage et dont il n'ose pas commencer à manger (IX, 279).
> 2. La tendresse qu'elle me prodiguait était comme ces aliments défendus qu'on ne refuse plus aux malades quand il est assuré qu'ils ne peuvent guérir (XIII, 257).

Why he chooses the particular specific images he selects, we have already discovered from our examination of imagery related to themes.

There is no need to emphasize the number of instancs of *audition colorée* (colour vision) we meet in *A la recherche du temps perdu*. They are evident everywhere.[1] In addition to music and proper names, tastes and odours also present strongly defined visual sensations to Proust. To a certain extent, names and music also suggest odours or tastes, and the vocabulary of Mme de Guermantes, for example, is like a quaint regional dish made from an original recipe (VIII, 146).

Above all, however, it is to the field of visual imagery that Proust turns in preference. The narrator declares that for him words

---

[1] Note the following examples of *audition colorée*: I, 19, 62, 231; II, 230–31; IV, 76; V, 33, 35; VII, 38, 39, 97; VIII, 58, 59, 66; IX, 192, 283; X, 297; XIV, 15; XV, 181. On the general question of synaesthetic images in Proust, the reader is referred to Stephen Ullmann, *Style in the French Novel*, Ch. V; 'Transposition of Sensations in Proust's Imagery', pp. 189–209.

and names are like photographic identity cards (VI, 12) or the pictures one hangs in a classroom when teaching children to identify objects and their names (II, 229). When he hears Albertine's voice, the effect is always the same: *dans le son se découpait nettement l'image visuelle* (V, 201). The comment by M. de Guermantes that two individuals are related historically causes the narrator to see a series of paintings *pareille à celles que peignaient Carpaccio ou Memling, depuis le premier compartiment où la princesse, aux fêtes des noces de son frère etc. . . . jusqu'au dernier où elle vient d'accoucher, etc.* (VIII, 187). Here, from the point of view of technique, we cannot separate the mode of thinking of Proust the writer and Marcel, the narrator.

Many of Proust's images, as well as being concrete or materialistic, are general and therefore universally true. It may seem paradoxical that an image should be specific and general at the same time, but an illustration will indicate what is meant. Albertine, when she looks away from a Lesbian because she is with Morel, does so *avec le même genre de discrétion qu'un homme qui voit son ancienne maîtresse avec un autre amant* (IX, 319). This image tabulates exactly the attitude of Albertine, and the simile makes the statement much more effective than a bald statement of fact would be. At the same time, how a man looks at his former mistress when she is with a new lover is something we have all seen or experienced or something we can easily imagine. It has a certain amount of universal content that brings it within the ken of every conceivable reader, and it is images of this sort which abound in Proust's work and which help to bring a very unique view of life to the comprehension of all readers.

It follows directly that all of Proust's images have the effect of making straightforward statements or descriptions more vivid. His favourite device is the use of what we might call a sort of hyperbolic imagery. Servants and persons in society are compared to members of the royal hierarchy at Versailles. Love is a terrible illness and the man in love is like a criminal or a drug addict or a person likely to die from a fatal wound or a horrible malady.

Proust likes especially to elaborate smaller things and to give them a grandeur and an importance that is not theirs naturally. A cake is *gothiquement historié de sucre* (V, 169) and a fish is *une polychrome cathédrale de la mer* (IV, 118). Françoise preparing cold jellied beef with carrots is like Michelangelo carving a great piece of sculpture, and a chicken has golden skin like a chasuble. Rosemonde's nose has surfaces like a great tower rising from a powerful base while La

Berma behind the curtain of the stage is hidden from Marcel's view like the Holy of Holies.

In the case of religious imagery, in particular, one sometimes has the impression of actual blasphemy in certain of Proust's images. Certainly not in the case of those images associated with the arts, since we already know that aesthetics is really a religion for the narrator. And probably not even in connection with those images associated with love, although it is something of a shock to have the good-night kisses of Marcel's mother and of Albertine referred to as *pain quotidien* or *viatique*. But when a deaf person turning off the heat so the milk will not boil over is compared to Christ stilling the waves of the tempest (VI, 92), or when the narrator says that the presence of Christ in the communion is no greater a mystery for him than that of the salon of Mme de Guermantes, surely we are justified in protesting.

Many of Proust's hyperbolic images are highly ironic, and it is just the ambiguity of interpretation which they permit that will always allow of more than one interpretation of the attitude of Proust himself. This is particularly true for his images about society. Servants who act like higher members of the royal hierarchy or the religious orders may be exposed to ridicule just as much as social lions who meet in secret communion to celebrate rites denied to the uninitiated.

Some of Proust's images are quite clearly and devastatingly sarcastic. The picture of Charlus and Jupien as Romeo and Juliet is biting, and the picture of Mme Verdurin as a leader as demanding as Christ or the Kaiser (X, 21) exposes her to ridicule. When it is said that Forcheville felt that in marrying Odette, the widow of a Jew, he was performing the same act of charity as a millionaire taking a prostitute off the street, censure is clearly directed at the interested count.

When Proust allows himself to become bitter, he is sometimes amusing but seldom as effective as when he is more impartial. Vituperation is not in the tradition of great art, and there is nothing provocative about a Mme Verdurin, who,

> . . . juchée sur son perchoir, pareille à un oiseau dont on eût trempé le colifichet dans du vin chaud, sanglotait d'amabilité (I, 278).

Fortunately, such moments are rare.

In his desire to render his thought more concrete and more vivid by the use of images, Proust often chooses quite extraordinary comparisons, but most of them, it must be admitted, are very effective. The portrayal of Swann's jealousy, which,

> . . . comme une pieuvre qui jette une première, puis une seconde, puis une troisième amarre, s'attacha solidement à ce moment de cinq heures du soir (II, 92),

is vivid, concrete and hyperbolic, but it is also, and above all, artistically satisfying.

Who ever thought of the eye as a sort of bird's nest, with its soft surrounding eyelashes, but who would not be willing to admit that the image, as Proust uses it, is effective (XI, 86)? And surely the comparison of Andrée's hands to obedient dogs seems far-fetched until one sees how skilfully Proust employs it (V, 187)! The writer's mind as a mineral deposit of which he alone is custodian and exploiter is a very apt figure, the implications of which are easily grasped (XV, 216). So, too, is the identification of Marcel's concept of Bergotte with a stalactite which he has *lentement et délicatement élaboré . . . goutte à goutte* (III, 150).

It is only occasionally that Proust actually defeats his own purpose by choosing images that are utterly fantastic. In these cases, attention is diverted from the subject matter to the image itself so that the whole point of introducing an image becomes distorted or lost. Even here, however, the appraisal of an image remains largely a subjective matter, and what jars or annoys one reader may be casually accepted by another. And there is nothing to guarantee that the validity of an image objected to today may not be acknowledged or acclaimed tomorrow. Such are the effects of Proust's lesson on relative judgments!

All the same, it is difficult to see a church steeple as a brown cushion against the yielding sky (I, 93). Also, we gain nothing from the description of the blows Saint-Loup administers to the offensive journalist as *un phénomène astral* in which the narrator sees

> . . . des corps ovoïdes prendre avec une rapidité vertigineuse toutes les positions qui leur permettaient de composer . . . une instable constellation (VI, 222).

The fault here is that Proust, in pursuing his bent for hyperbole, exceeds the vague and flexible limit which separates the artistic from the precious. He is carried to this extreme in his description of the telephone with its *Vierges Vigilantes* (VI, 161–62; XI, 121, 123, 125), and he is certainly mocking what he recognizes as a tendency of this sort in himself when he introduces into Albertine's conversation the amusing description of ice-cream as architectural in its form (XI, 160–61). At the same time, many of these over-refined figures remain in his writing, and we are justified in refusing to condone a train as *le laboratoire charbonneux*, . . . *la chambre magique qui se chargeait d'opérer la transmutation tout autour d'elle* (II, 235). The description of the temperature thermometer is also over-precious (VII, 148–49).

In what Proust calls *le démon du pastiche*, writers of parody seize on idiosyncrasies in authors and ridicule them by emphasizing only their excesses. Now it is true that there are some very artificial and far-fetched images in Proust's work, but we must not give them undue prominence. In Chapters II and III we have seen literally hundreds of interesting and pertinent images and we must not allow their significance to be outweighed by twenty or thirty poor ones. Unusual images characterize *A la recherche du temps perdu* but fantastic ones do not.

While we are on the question of defective images, we ought to mention another class which does not conform to the pattern of the majority of Proust's excellent images. This class may be called learnèd or abstruse images, and figures of this sort fail because they are not apprehended by the 'average' reader.

We have already remarked that Proust, in his selection of images from academic sources, makes no concessions to the reader as far as factual information is concerned. Frequently he states quite clearly the source of his image, but sometimes he quotes or paraphrases without acknowledging it, and it is here that images for that reason occasionally lose their full flavour.

Presumably most people would recognize references to *le cor* . . . *le soir au fond du bois* (III, 78) or a *spectacle dans un lit* (I, 161), and the paraphrase of Phèdre's great opening speech would be known to every school boy (I, 197). More oblique references to the conclusion of *L'Education sentimentale* (III, 70), and to the quixotic voyage of Des Esseintes in *A Rebours* (III, 199) would be less easily apprehended, however, and casual references to *un embarquement pour Cythère de la passion* (XV, 63) and to the loved one as a Melusina (III, 171) or a Puss-in-Boots as opposed to a Viviane (IX, 304–5) really require an explanation.

On occasion Proust also employs faulty mixed metaphors. In Chapter I we noticed the example of the Cambremer family 'anchored' where they had never hoped to be able to 'pitch their tent' (XIII, 291). One might add to this case that of Charlus *qui* bouillonnait *depuis longtemps contre quelqu'un,* and who then *le* clouait *de désespoir* (XII, 141), and the narrator whose imagination receives *un vigoureux coup de fouet* from comments by Charlus, which, in turn, *l'avaient aiguillé vers la cousine d'Oriane* (VIII, 225–26). The effect of such a juxtaposition is to restore their full power to faded metaphors and to cause an unpleasant clash of opposing ideas.

One of the fundamental principles behind Proust's use of images is his desire to show us as many facets of the personality of an individual or as many contrasting elements of an experience or a situation as possible. He will choose images from any source that suits his purpose, and in connection with one person or one emotion, he will utilize figures of speech from any number of different spheres.

The most important philosophic idea behind Proust's conception of the nature and meaning of life is one that he shared with Bergson —that mental and chronological time do not coincide, and that man, caught up as he is in the stream of time, is a continually changing and elusive entity.

For Bergson, words themselves are hard fixed symbols, and the great problem in writing is to overcome the resistance which they offer. This may be accomplished partly by the use of a great variety of images. A single image is as crystalline a thing as a word, but widely differing images directed around one object or one idea give it a relief or a multi-dimensional quality that allows us to transcend the fixed limits of words.

The following quotation from *La Pensée et le mouvant*[1] might well serve as an epigraph to any study of Proust's use of images:

> Nulle image ne remplacera l'intuition de la durée, mais beaucoup d'images diverses, empruntées à des ordres de choses très différents, pourront, par la convergence de leur action, diriger la conscience sur le point précis où il y a une certaine intuition à saisir. En choisissant les images aussi disparates que possible, on empêchera l'une quelconque d'entre elles d'usurper la place de l'intuition qu'elle est chargée d'appeler, puisqu'elle serait alors chassée tout de suite par ses rivales. En faisant qu'elles exigent toutes de notre esprit malgré

---

[1] Pp. 185–86, quoted in Paul Foulquié et Gérard Deledalle, *La Psychologie contemporaine* (Presses Universitaires de France), pp. 175–76. Also quoted by Fiser, op. cit., p. 42.

leurs différences d'aspect une même espèce d'attention, et en quelque
sorte le même degré de tension, on accoutumera peu à peu la conscience à une disposition toute particulière et bien déterminée, celle
précisément qu'elle devra adopter pour s'apparaître à elle-même sans
voile.

We have already ample evidence in Chapter II of Proust's use of
this technique. Any theme, whether it be complex or very simple,
has associated with it a great variety of images drawn from the most
disparate sources.[1] Sometimes we find a single image in a particular
category, but more often we find a large number of them.

It is part of Proust's technique, once he has used an image, to
return to it again very soon or perhaps to use it several times in short
order and then either drop it completely or not employ it again for
some time. There are exceptions to this generalization, of course.
Certain images are invariably associated with given themes, e.g.
flowers with young girls, religious terminology with Charlus and
illness with love. Even so, within these categories one often notices
that a particular type of image may follow the pattern just set out,
i.e. similar images tend to cluster in particular parts of the book.[2]

One has only to examine the examples grouped together in
Chapter III to find overwhelming proof of this statement. Bird
imagery associated with Albertine and her friends all occurs in
Volume VI except for one figure in Volume X. Images drawn from
hunting, knightly pastimes, etc. are mostly found in Volumes VII and
VIII. Albertine is compared to a child numerous times in Volume
XI. The Princesse de Parme in a novel social situation is said to be
like a sea bather no less than five times in Volume VIII.

When Proust employs this technique quite consciously and
elaborates purposely on a metaphor or a simile, we have what we
may call extended images. The most famous of these figures is the
lengthy comparison of the members of the Faubourg St.-Germain
set at the theatre to marine deities or fish (VI, 47–49, 51, 63, 67, 69).
Other examples, however, are to be found in the comparison of the
restaurant at Rivebelle to a solar system (V, 58), the comparison of
the rotunda in the hotel at Balbec to the staging of one of Racine's
religious plays (IX, 223–24), the comparison of street sounds to

[1] In a different stylistic approach Yvette Louria in *La Convergence stylistique chez
Proust*, Genève (1957) deals with the same technique applied to Proust's multiple choice
of adjectives, adverbs, etc.
[2] Proust occasionally uses identical images in different parts of his book, e.g.
embarrassment is compared to that of a guest who appears at a formal party in a lounge
suit (VI, 23–24; VII, 238).

music (XI, 144–47) and the comparison of the encounter of Jupien and Charlus to the fertilization of a rare orchid by a bee (IX, 11, 14, 39–45). There are other extended images, as well, but these are the important ones.

This virtuoso technique in Proust's writing can be compared to nothing quite so readily as to the elaborate cadenzas in music which a solo performer brilliantly executes as he plays in public a great concerto. This aspect of Proust's style lends itself to burlesque when it is carried to extremes but it serves a function in showing us that analogies may be extended and that, depending on our vision of things, the whole universe may be completely different from what we think it is.

The great merit in Proust's images is their content of universal truth. They are the result of a unique vision of the world, but once we have grasped what our author is trying to say, his comparisons remain just as apt for us to-day as they were when he wrote them. A restaurant like a solar system—of course! And the unvarying circulation of waiters around tables and the cross-movements of patrons from group to group will continue to characterize restaurants as long as they exist.

At the theatre, too, the remote social set are like the eternal Greek gods and goddesses. This is true for any society once we have our eyes opened to the possibility.

All the other extended images mentioned above attain the universal plane. The music and liturgy of the Catholic Church, the presentation of plays and fertilization of flowers by vagrant insects are fundamental aspects of life as we know it. The latter phenomenon is biological but the other two date back to the very beginnings of our civilization and cannot be separated from it.

There is another facet to this use of a variety of images in Proust which is probably closer to what Bergson had in mind in the passage already quoted. This is the close juxtaposition of apparently conflicting images. Sometimes Proust uses two or three together and sometimes he piles up eight or more. This particular penchant of his is another of those distinguishing characteristics which lend themselves so easily to parody when they are exaggerated but which are wonderfully effective when they are used discriminately.

Sometimes Proust ties a number of similes to one object which he is describing. The leaves in the cup of tea at Combray make him think successively

> . . . d'une aile transparente de mouche, de l'envers blanc d'une
> étiquette, d'un pétale de rose, mais qui eussent été empilées, con-
> cassées ou tressées comme dans la confection d'un nid (I, 75).

Sometimes he coerces metaphor and simile without distinction
and applies them in the description of one feature. For example the
hair of a valet at the home of Mme de Saint-Euverte is described
thus:

> Une chevelure, par l'enroulement lisse et les becs aigus de ses
> boucles, ou dans la superposition du triple et fleurissant diadème de
> ses tresses, a l'air à la fois d'un paquet d'algues, d'une nichée de
> colombes, d'un bandeau de jacinthes et d'une torsade de serpents
> (II, 145).

All of these images are completely logical, but their variety gives
us a complex picture which seems to have more life than a single
image could convey.

Frequently, also, Proust starts out with one image only to move
tangentially to another suggested by or based on the first. He may
use different images to describe different aspects of one experience,
and the result here is to add, as it were, a third dimension to his
descriptions. Their progress is no longer rectilinear but spatial. An
excellent example is the following description of sunlight in the
grandmother's room at Balbec:

> Des rayons . . . mettaient sur la commode un reposoir diapré
> comme les fleurs du sentier, suspendaient à la paroi les ailes repliées,
> tremblantes et tièdes d'une clarté prête à reprendre son vol, chauffai-
> ent comme un bain un carré de tapis provincial devant la fenêtre de
> la courette que le soleil festonnait comme une vigne, ajoutaient au
> charme et à la complexité de la décoration mobilière en semblant
> exfolier la soie fleurie des fauteuils et détacher leur passementerie,
> cette chambre, que je traversais un moment avant de m'habiller pour
> la promenade, avait l'air d'un prisme où se décomposaient les couleurs
> de la lumière du dehors, d'une ruche où les sucs de la journée que
> j'allais goûter étaient dissociés, épars, enivrants et visibles, d'un
> jardin de l'espérance qui se dissolvait en une palpitation de rayons
> d'argent et de pétales de rose (IV, 129–30).

Another example worth quoting is the following description of
the manner in which Charlus shakes hands with a young man:

> Il le salua comme il eût salué un prince à Versailles, et pour
> profiter de l'occasion d'avoir en supplément un plaisir gratis—
> comme quand j'étais petit et que ma mère venait de faire une com-

mande chez Boissier ou chez Gouache, je prenais, sur l'offre d'une des dames du comptoir, un bonbon extrait d'un des vases de verre entre lesquels elle trônait—prenant la main du charmant jeune homme et la lui serrant longuement, à la prussienne, le [fixait] des yeux en souriant pendant le temps interminable que mettaient autrefois à nous faire poser les photographes quand la lumière était mauvaise (XIV, 159).

This wealth of images for every purpose is one of the basic features of Proust's style. Here is how André Gide describes its effect:

> L'écriture de Proust est (pour employer un mot que les Goncourt m'avaient fait prendre en horreur, mais qui, lorsque je songe à Proust, cesse de me déplaire) la plus artiste que je connaisse. Par elle il ne se sent jamais empêché. Si, pour informer l'indicible, le mot lui manque, il recourt à l'image; il dispose de tout un trésor d'analogies, d'équivalences, de comparaisons si précises et si exquises que parfois l'on en vient à douter lequel prête à l'autre le plus de vie, de lumière et d'amusement, et si le sentiment est secouru par l'image, ou si cette image volante n'attendait pas le sentiment pour s'y poser.[1]

The only quarrel one might have with this appraisal is over the statement *Si, pour informer l'indicible, le mot lui manque*; Proust was never at a loss for the right word, and he chose images in preference to straightforward description. Proust believed, as Bergson did, that you can get at the truth more easily through what appears to be an indirect means than you can by a frontal attack.

We have already mentioned some categories of reciprocal images which Proust uses. These could be extended almost indefinitely. Music is like natural sounds and natural sounds are reminiscent of music. Landscape effects make one think of the sea and the sea in turn looks like rugged land. In the artistic representations of the sea and the land in Elstir's paintings, the two are also transposed. Flowers and sunlight are like cloth in their texture, and cloth in turn reminds one of flowers or sunshine. Flowers are also like young girls and young girls can be identified with beautiful flowers. The moon is like an actress and the actress Rachel reminds us of the moon. Portraits remind the narrator of people, and individuals of his acquaintance look like portraits. Men often remind one of women and women sometimes look and act like men. Pure exalted family love is like passionate love and vice-versa. The effects of love

---

[1] 'Billets à Angèle', *Œuvres complètes*, XI, pp. 45–46, (originally in NRF, 1921.)

are like those of drugs, illness and death, and these pre-occupations themselves affect us with the intensity of love affairs.

In his images, Proust decidedly cultivates this penchant for paradox, until we are ready to admit with him that black is white and white black. The culminating point of this sort of controversy comes when he states, in connection with love, that: *De même qu'il y a des avares qui entassent par générosité, nous sommes des prodigues qui dépensons par avarice* (XI, 119). And we are quite ready to agree with him!

A further, much bigger category of such reciprocal images in Proust is the animation of the inanimate and its converse, or the use of personification along with the dehumanization of the human.

It is just extraordinary how extensive a use Proust makes of personification, which is fundamentally, of course, a form of metaphor. In the realm of nature, the sky, clouds, the wind, the sun, rays of the sun, the moon, trees, leaves, flowers, cliffs and the countryside are all personified. Buildings, rooms, windows and arches receive the same treatment, and even the garden gate at Combray is spoken of as though it were a person (I, 158). Trains and boats are personified by Proust along with less distinct entities such as cloth (IV, 28) and food (V, 169). The fire, lamps, clocks, and numerous household articles undergo the same process. Proust also personifies separate parts of the body which seem to have a life of their own together with the will, illness and death. Music and phrases in music are given human attributes.

From the opposite point of view, people are compared by him to flowers, plants, fruit, trees and numerous other botanical forms of life. They are also compared to insects, butterflies, polyps, fish and all sorts of zoological specimens. Individuals are said to be like birds or even birds' eggs, and they are identified with domestic animals such as the cat, dog and horse as well as wild animals and weird prehistoric creatures. In more far-fetched comparisons, Proust also compares humans to the countryside (II, 218; XI, 84), the beach (III, 194–95), food or cakes (IX, 269; X, 68), jewellery (V, 220; III, 206) and land, rivers, lakes, etc. (I, 23; V, 53; VII, 97, 231; IX, 312).

An extension of this same concept is the refusal by Proust to separate clearly people and their environment. Mme de Guermantes and Françoise are like linguistic or historic atlases of France, and many of the other characters in the novel are said to be like animate human representations of the regions from which they come.

Our friends are like a building in which we live (I, 261), and when we are in love, the loved one seems to be a part of our body (XII, 157). She lives in us and we live in her. For a beautiful woman like Odette, costume is an integral part of her personality. The narrator himself regards his own room as an extension of his body (IV, 84), and La Berma 'wears' the theatre in which she plays (III, 26).

By obliterating the rigid distinction between the animate and the inanimate, and by comparing all sorts of so-called higher and lower forms of life, Proust helps us to partake of his vision of life in which man is a member of a species that has much in common with all other orders of things both animate and inanimate. The geological and chemical nature of man's intellect, the electrical nature of memory, the photographic powers of the eye and the characteristics of the body which relate it to other biological forms as well as to the physical features of our environment, place us in the midst of natural phenomena which we sometimes suppose that we transcend.

We have already had occasion to refer to the symbolism of Proust's images. It is in similes and metaphors which exploit man's place in the physical universe especially—man's existence as a biological and material entity—that we discover these symbolic figures of speech. Young girls are flowers or birds. They are the rosy dawn[1] or the blossoming spring, and they are song birds or young animals. They are butterflies and soft clay, and they are little ocean waves on a clear calm morning. Older men and women, on the other hand, are dried up fruits or seeds. They are the dull evening or mournful autumn and winter. They are like old animals at the zoo or butterflies encased in a hard chrysalis. They are stone statues or crumbling monuments and they are the icy, wintry sea.

Proust's whole book is a cycle which begins with an experience of the involuntary memory and ends with him sitting down to write his book. Life itself is a grandiose cycle from birth to death, and the secret which Proust discovers in his book is his own personal relation to the time cycle.

In order to integrate these two vast cycles and to relate to them

[1] It is interesting to note how rose is always associated by Proust with the most pleasant experiences. The narrator's favourite hawthorns are rose, and cheese with strawberries crushed in it is a special treat. The tea leaves in the cup at Combray are rose, and young girls are like the rosy dawn or rosy fruit or even roses! Mme de Guermantes is rosy in complexion as well as dress (VI, 42), and Odette, when she impresses so forcefully the young Marcel at his uncle's, is *la dame en rose*. Memories of Rivebelle vein the dark stone of Combray with rose (VIII, 25).

all the subsidiary ideas which he wishes to express, Proust utilizes in a series of symbolic images the lesser cycles of day and night, spring, summer and winter with the botanical phenomena associated with them, insect, animal and bird life. The vast number of reciprocal images and the reversible reaction of personification and dehumanization can also all be regarded as mysterious but eternal cycles. 'A rose is a young girl is a rose'. Music is nature and nature is music. Art is life and life is art. One starts anywhere on the circle and one is carried back to where one started.

We have here also the explanation of why water imagery plays such an important part in Proust's work. The sea is the symbol for the eternal. It is scarcely connected with the cycle of life and death that goes on in it and around it and, despite its constant variety, it remains always the same. Life is like that too, for even though individuals come and go along with social, political and artistic changes, the fundamental nature of life, like the sea, remains unchanged.

The real significance of Proust's novel does not become apparent until the final volume of *Le Temps retrouvé*. To a certain extent, the same thing may be said for Proust's imagery and particularly for all symbolic imagery. Old people do not appear in the work in any great numbers until the final section, and it is only when the missing image-links are fitted into the cycles that their pattern becomes apparent. It is only in the last part of the work that we find many references to the crumbling statuary, the winter and snow of old age and its icy immobility.

Moreover, it is only in the last part of *Le Temps retrouvé*[1] that we find the very obvious key to what Proust means by water imagery.[2] Retroactively, this passage throws new light on all the images that have preceded.

The whole question of Proust's etymologies is one that urgently needs to be studied in some detail. It has already been suggested in this essay that proper names provide Proust with an intriguing form of private symbol.[3] Combray and Balbec are undoubtedly water symbols and the name Swann would appear to be another such image.

Evidence already cited is very strongly in support of an etymo-

[1] XV, 134–35.
[2] See p. 121 above. Cf. J. Vendryes, 'Marcel Proust et les noms propres', in *Choix d'études linguistiques et celtiques* (Paris, 1953), pp. 80–88.
[3] See p. 121 above.

logical interpretation of the name Guermantes which would relate the syllable *Guerm* to Indo-European *$gh^{w}erm$* which gives English and German *warm*, etc.[1] That Proust had in mind such a derivation is indicated by his repeated references to the orange or reddish colour of the word and his division of the name into the syllables *Guerm* and *antes* instead of *Guer* and *mantes* which would be more logical phonetically.[2]

Let us quote Proust himself to prove that he was used to thinking synaesthetically about names and works of fiction. In *Contre Sainte-Beuve*, in speaking of Gérard de Nerval's *Sylvie*, he says:

> La couleur de Sylvie, c'est une couleur pourpre, d'une rose pourpre en velours pourpre ou violacée, et nullement les tons aquarellés de leur France modérée. A tout moment ce rappel de rouge revient, tirs, foulards rouges, etc. Et ce nom lui-même pourpré de ses deux I—Sylvie, la vraie fille du Feu.[3]

When we consider such a subtle analysis, surely it is a little too obvious to propose that Proust's ideas on the colour of the Guermantes name were probably suggested to him by the analogy of *Guermantes* and *amaranthe*, the reddish-purple flower whose colour the name reflects.[4] The amaranth stands for immortality, and this is a connotation which Proust wants associated with the name *Guermantes* (VI, 15), but the pattern of imagery is much more profound than that.

Some of the proper names Proust invents are simple anagrams. Elstir (which probably comes from Whistler) may have some significance in itself, but no obvious suggestion presents itself. On the other hand, certain other names would seem to have been derived more facetiously. Vinteuil (Old French for *vingt yeux*) could conceivably have been suggested by Saint-Saëns who has certain features in common with the musician. Jupien may have the *jupe* (skirt) in his name because of his homosexuality.

[1] See p. 70 above.

[2] The late Professor A. Dauzat, unable to shed any light on the origin of the name Guermantes, suggested in a letter to this writer that the root is probably the same as that of the names *Guérin*, *Guétard*, etc. This suggestion would not appear to be correct, and for Proust, at any rate, the root is definitely *Guerm*.

In the *Correspondance Générale*, Plon, 1932, Tome III, pp. 301–303, Proust asks Martin-Chauffier about the etymology of the name Guermantes. Unfortunately, the latter's reply has never been published and I have been unable to find out where it might be.

He also apparently asked François de Pâris the same question. See E. de Clermont-Tonnerre, *Robert de Montesquiou et Marcel Proust*, Paris (1925), p. 234.

[3] Op. cit., p. 168.

[4] Cf. Stephen Ullmann, *Style in the French Novel*, p. 200.

R

One of the means by which images are suggested to Proust is that of association of ideas or words, and this common tendency in his normal method of forming images would seem to lend some support to the above hypothesis. It is doubtful if anyone will ever do for Proust what John Livingstone Lowes did for Coleridge, but a few examples will show how this process of association works as far as Proust is concerned.

We have already seen numerous instances of association in Chapters II and III. Many images connected with Françoise are drawn from food and cooking. Bloch and other Jews have Biblical or Oriental figures of speech used to describe them. Imagery drawn from war and battles is associated with the soldier Saint-Loup. To their inferiors, members of a superior class are like gods and goddesses or high-ranking nobles.

All of these might be called logical images, since they obviously connect individuals with their primary interest or with the feature which distinguishes them as members of a particular class. One might also say that the narrator (or Proust, the writer), in individual cases draws images from the source which interests him most under particular circumstances. It is Françoise who prepared the food he eats, and for that reason imagery connected with this phase of her character leaps to mind when he thinks of her. On the other hand, when he is particularly hungry, other things also remind him of food. Sunday morning after mass, the church tower is like a huge fresh loaf of bread (I, 93), and at Balbec, before dinner, the evening sky is the colour of salmon and mullet (V, 50). Conversely, the delicious fruits passed on to the narrator and his grandmother by Mme de Villeparisis remind him of the beautiful autumn season and the passage of the days which will soon bring an end to his sojourn at the sea-coast (IV, 122).

One does not have to look very far to see why Proust compares the church at Combray, surrounded by houses as it is, to a shepherdess protecting her sheep (I, 71). Also, when the narrator drives home from the park with his sick grandmother, the shadow of the coach on the wall, in retrospect at least, is *comme un char funèbre dans une terre cuite de Pompéi* (VII, 174). The whole long image of the theatre boxes with their marine deities probably is elaborated from the associations of the French term for box (*baignoire*) and the fact that they were draped in purple.[1]

[1] See VI, 45 and VIII, 41.

Mouton points out that very often Proust introduces a longer comparison with a metaphor which prepared for it and sets the tone.[1] Actually, it would be difficult to decide retrospectively whether the simile grew from the metaphor or whether the metaphor was introduced because of the simile. At any rate, the artistic result is most effective, since the reader has suggested to his mind a comparison which, when it is elaborated, seems completely reasonable even though it may be quite far-fetched.

The 'lines' of Mme de Guermantes's face in a picture allow Marcel to study her features like a treatise on geometry (VI, 96), and Albertine's enigmatic 'body' must correspond to some table of logarithms to have affected him so much (XII, 197). Albertine's note asking Marcel to come to her room, since (in her words) *'je m'endormirai vite après, car je suis comme une morte'* (XII, 197) prepares the way for the comparison which the narrator draws between her and a corpse or a funereal statue, just as Swann's announcement to the Duke and Duchess that he is soon to die, makes more significant the Duke's remarks playing on the same word: *elle arrivera au dîner morte . . . moi, je meurs de faim*, etc. (VIII, 260).

The metaphors that introduce all of the above comparisons can be regarded technically as pivot words. They have both a literal and a figurative meaning, and Proust uses one or the other as a sort of springboard taking him off along the tangent which has the opposite sense of that in which the word was first used. Albertine's use of the word 'death' in her note is metaphorical, and Proust here moves from the figurative to the literal. In the case of Swann, on the other hand, his reference to his own death is quite literal but the figures of speech which follow are purely metaphorical.

One can find in Proust's work many comparisons based on pivot words, and the technique is no less common for incidental images than for long elaborate ones. Examples are:

1. Ces *ombres* d'arbres, légères comme des *âmes* (XIV, 56).
2. Ses regards engageants [de Cottard à Charlus], accrus, par leur sourire, n'étaient plus contenus par le *verre* du lorgnon et le *débordaient* de tous côtes (X, 73).
3. Un homme grand et fort [*l'Editeur* de Paris] avec quelque chose de *tranchant*. Il avait l'air d'un *couteau à papier* en ébène (X, 55).[2]

---

[1] Op. cit., p. 104.
[2] Pierre-Quint describes these images as puns, op. cit., p. 294. This is particularly true of section 2 above. The italics in all the examples cited are mine.

A most interesting case is that of the word *aile* (literally, 'wing') which in French is also used for the wing or nostril of the nose and the wing of the stage. This leads Proust to say of the actress Rachel that *les* ailes *de son nez charmant étaient restées dans la perspective, entre la salle et* la scène, *tout comme le relief* des décors (VI, 216). When he speaks of Saint-Loup, he pivots in the other direction and remarks that in his case, it is a fine thing *que les* ailes *du nez soient délicates et d'un dessin parfait comme celles des petits* papillons *qui se posent sur les fleurs des prairies* (VIII, 38).

In two later examples of these same images, Proust omits the pivot word and we get comparisons whose origin would be more difficult to trace if we did not have the earlier examples. He says of Swann that *ses* narines, *que le parfum de le femme grisait*, palpitèrent comme un papillon *prêt à aller se poser sur la fleur entrevue* (IX, 140). Then in describing the effect on Swann of his last illness, he associates him with the image he used in connection with Rachel:

> Ce visage duquel la maladie avait si bien rongé les joues, comme une lune décroissante, que, sauf sous un certain angle . . . elles tournaient court *comme un décor* inconsistant auquel une illusion d'optique peut seule ajouter l'apparence de l'épaisseur (IX, 118).

Rachel and Swann are both Jewish, and this mental association is rendered the more plausible because of the earlier comparison of Rachel's face to the moon (see p. 31 above).

The permeation of a comparison by accurate and vivid metaphors is an aspect of Proust's style that can only be compared for virtuosity to the dense images of Keats. Mouton quotes the example of Marcel's Aunt Léonie whose energy and force, since they were *taries à la moindre fatigue, ne lui revenaient que goutte à goutte au sein de son repos, le réservoir était très long à remplir* (I, 159). Curtius examines the description of lilacs from the same point of view.[1]

> Quelques-uns effusaient encore en hauts lustres mauves les *bulles* délicates de leurs fleurs, mais dans bien des parties du feuillage où *déferlait*, il y avait seulement une semaine, leur *mousse* embaumée, se flétrissait, diminuée et noircie, une *écume* creuse (I, 185).

One could add many other instances to this list. Madame Cottard in society is *comme dans une fleur un insecte bourdonnant et volage, qui ensuite, au hasard de ses visites* répandra, *on l'espère du moins, la*

[1] Op. cit., p. 63.

nouvelle, le germe *dérobé d'envie et d'admiration.* She knows exactly how many *calices bourgeois* she can visit in an afternoon, *cette active ouvrière.* And she also knows *le pouvoir de dissémination* (III, 111). The extended images already mentioned make use of the same technique which is really a subsidiary stylistic feature strengthening and concentrating the image pattern.

The effect of introducing an image by a related metaphor is to make the image seem the more logical and inevitable. The concentration achieved by permeating the image with many related terms gives to it a density and a sort of overwhelming force that makes it utterly convincing except in the few cases we have already noted.

On occasion, Proust also employs another technique to add to the power of his images and to make the reader feel that he ought almost to have thought of some of them himself. He bases them on common proverbs which he varies slightly for his own purposes, or he introduces into an extended image a comparison based on a proverb, which has the effect of giving authority and solidarity to the other neighbouring comparisons.

An excellent example occurs in a description of Albertine's face. The impression left by that pale oval marked with little brown specks and two vaguely blue spots is like that of a bird's egg or an agate polished only in two places, *où, au milieu de la pierre brune, luisaient, comme les ailes transparentes d'un papillon d'azur, les yeux où la chair devient miroir et nous donne l'illusion de nous laisser, plus qu'en les autres parties du corps, approcher de l'âme* (V, 220).

The prestige of the common old proverb that *les yeux sont le miroir de l'âme,* coming as it does at the end of a series of analogies, seems to stamp them with its approval and to convince the reader, who would in any case admit the veracity of Proust's comparisons, that they are almost self-evident. This is a very clever trick.

Proverbs (which are generally what we may call faded metaphors) actually appear most often in Proust in conversational images. This is artistically fitting, since ordinary speakers tend to turn for their images to that vast repertory of fixed and almost colourless folk expressions. *C'était elle qui tenait la corde, maintenant elle n'est plus bonne à donner à manger aux chiens* (IX, 261); *fine comme l'ambre, maligne comme un singe* (VIII, 83); *jaloux comme un tigre* (XII, 121), and dozens of similar expressions which Proust introduces into conversational images are used and understood by all French speakers without any reference to the literal meaning or any understanding of how the figure arose.

Almost all of Proust's thousands of images are patently logical, despite any underlying pattern or *raison d'être* they may have. Their purpose and their function is perfectly obvious, and once we have classified and analyzed them, there remains no vague aureole of uncertainty, no fringe of ambiguous content which eludes our grasp and suggests far more spiritually and emotionally than the mere words.

It is difficult to distinguish succinctly the difference between a logical image and what we may call a poetic image. The former can easily be analyzed from the point of view of origin and purpose. Typically, it is concrete, specific and illustrative, and it is clearly intended to bridge the gap between the writer's thought and the reader's comprehension.

A poetic image, on the other hand, makes no concessions to its readers. Very often, intermediate links are left out and the reader is challenged, not only to supply them but to penetrate to the author's thought. This is never quite possible, because a poetic image has a content of personal emotion or association which allows each reader to interpret it in his own way. A poetic image cannot be tied down and its implications are ever new, ever fresh and challenging.

Some twenty or thirty of Proust's images can be classified as poetic. They are so almost in spite of their creator, because it was his constant aim to express clearly and in a fully logical way the most abstruse of human conceptions. These poetic images, despite their difficulty, must not be considered as logical images that failed, since some of them are among the very greatest Proust ever thought of. They are rather flights of fancy such as he did not ordinarily permit himself.

It is sometimes inferred that Proust's style is a virtuoso style showing no restraint, but as far as images are concerned, the opposite is nearer to the truth. The figures he employs are seldom spontaneous, effervescent creations; they are, rather, carefully considered and logically constructed comparisons. The few ebullient metaphors which do not pass through the alambic are neither inferior nor superior in kind; it is just that the transmuting power of Proust's logic has not worked its alchemy on them.

Proust's poetic images are neither learnèd nor fantastic. They employ no obscure references and they are wonderfully effective too. Their implications, however, reach far beyond the surface meaning and, in many cases, would permit of almost indefinite elaboration. Two wonderful examples already examined in some detail are the comparison of Albertine to a *Victoire* and a *pesante esclave* and the association of great works of literature and Manet's '*Déjeuner sur l'herbe*.'[1]

Consider, in addition, Proust's description of

> . . . un grand oiseau solitaire et hâtif [qui] . . . fouettant l'air du battement régulier de ses ailes, passait à toute vitesse au-dessus de la plage tachée çà et là de reflets pareils à des petits morceaux de papier rouge déchirés . . . comme un émissaire qui va porter bien loin un message urgent et capital (IX, 293).

The appearance of this bird in a context in which Albertine appears is significant, because of the bird and water imagery associated with her. The moment is even more fraught with implications because it is just the beginning of the fateful and prolonged liaison between the narrator and Albertine. The bird flying directly away surely symbolizes her final flight from him, and the reflections like torn red paper may be his grief or her death or the letters from her, actually received by him after her death.

Another wonderfully suggestive poetic image is the following which describes how Legrandin and the narrator are drawn together by their common origins, despite the incompatibility of their characters:

> Certains souvenirs sont comme des amis communs, ils savent faire des réconciliations; jeté au milieu des champs semés de boutons d'or où s'entassaient les ruines féodales, le petit pont de bois nous unissait, Legrandin et moi, comme les deux bords de la Vivonne (VI, 188).

It is significant that the link uniting Marcel and Legrandin should be a bridge because of the water imagery associated with Combray. The feudal towers and the golden yellow buttercups recall various references to the Guermantes family and Saint-Loup in particular and they remind us of the fact that Legrandin is very jealous of the Guermantes clan with whom the narrator is so friendly. The wood of the bridge echoes the *bois jaunissants* which the narrator sees in Mme de Guermantes's name, and we sense throughout this image

[1] See pp. 68 and 184 above.

many other associations which Marcel and Legrandin have with Combray apart from those merely geographical.

For sheer beauty of poetic imagery—what Musset calls the power to

> Chasser tout souvenir et fixer la pensée;
> Sur un bel axe d'or la tenir balancée,
> Incertaine, inquiète, immobile pourtant,[1]

this description of twelve o'clock striking in the church tower at Combray can hardly be equalled:

> L'heure altière de midi, descendue de la tour de Saint-Hilaire qu'elle armoriait des douze fleurons momentanés de sa couronne sonore (I, 100).

Proust's language in images often approaches the language of poetry, and the cadences of its music together with the rhythmical counter-balance of phrases which rise and fall in a manner completely satisfying to the ear also help to make the images utilized appear inevitable.

In the following example, the phrases can almost be scanned and the use of alliteration and vowel assonances is almost excessive:

> Dans les joues de la duchesse de Guermantes . . . composites maintenant comme un nougat, je distinguais une trace de vert-de-gris, un petit morceau rose de coquillage concassé, une grosseur difficile à définir, plus petite qu'une boule de gui et moins transparente qu'une perle de verre (XV, 96).

Readers undoubtedly accept these images and, at first thought, one might consider that we have here a series of logical comparisons. A moment's reflection, however, will prove that these are actually poetic images. Notice, first of all, the colour of the little growth on Mme de Guermantes' cheek. It is said to be greenish (like verdigris), then rose, and finally (although colour is not actually the comparison sought) it is related to mistletoe berries and imitation pearls, both of which are whitish. This is certainly not logical.

The comparison of the little growth to a bit of rose shell recalls both the earlier healthy rose color of Mme de Guermantes's complexion, and the water imagery associated with her. The rose colour is reminiscent of her lovely red costumes and her rubies. These

---

[1] 'Impromptu' (Poésies Nouvelles).

jewels, and the jewel-like quality of her eyes are also suggested by the pearl comparison, and the mistletoe recalls the ancient history of the family and the Druidic character of Mme de Guermantes herself. What verdigris suggests is not readily apparent, and we are forced to conclude that even though these images are poetic and aesthetically satisfying, they are actually not logical or clear.

The concluding portion of this Chapter has dealt, of necessity, with certain exceptional features of Proust's techniques in the use of images. It would be impracticable to try to analyze all the poetic images in *A la recherche du temps perdu* even though their number is restricted. Enough indications of Proust's procedure have already been given, however, that the reader ought to be able easily to analyze individual images by drawing on the source material contained in Chapters II and III.

We have remarked before that categories of images in Proust are infinitely varied. The same statement applies to techniques. It would be quite wrong to seek an opening metaphor for every one of Proust's images or to look for a hidden significance. Less than a quarter of the images on which this study is based could be said to have any 'preparation' in their context and fewer than one in ten images could be said to have any symbolic function. Once the reader's attention has been drawn to this and other tendencies, however, he can examine Proust's text in a way not previously possible. Ours is a course of orientation lectures to show what the oculist is doing in changing one's method of seeing. The treatment itself may be painful, but the propaganda that goes with it should be convincing proof of its necessity!

CONCLUSION

We have now completed the cycle which constitutes our study of Proust's imagery and we arrive back at a general consideration of underlying patterns, but with a new vision of just what that means. We have gained some insight into what Proust meant when he said that *la métaphore seule peut donner une sorte d'éternité au style*.[1] Imagery is an integral part of Proust's style. This is patently evident from the very frequency with which images are used. Moreover, from a consideration of images alone, we have been able to examine all the important themes in *A la recherche du temps perdu* and to draw conclusions which are in harmony with those of more general critical works, even though the emphasis may differ slightly.

Proust chooses his images consciously, whether they are brief and incidental or long and fundamental. He prides himself on the fact that they are strong, appropriate and an essential part of the text (unlike those of Flaubert or Gautier). They are indeed polished, integrated and, as it were, welded to their context by such a variety of techniques that they are inseparable from it. It is wrong to suggest as Feuillerat does,[2] that the use of images characterizes a certain early period in Proust's style, and even though similes or simple analogies slightly outnumber pure metaphors in his work, it would be quite impossible to extract any of them without mutilating the text.

Statistics reveal that the images in *A la recherche du temps perdu* are typically visual, logical and concrete, despite the fact that Pommier has declared that olfactory and gustatory images predominate[3] and Jacques Bret that Proust's images are fanciful and illogical.[4]

Proust's medium is the written word and words themselves appear to him as visual images (in the psychological sense). He absolutely refuses to compromise with the elusive or the intangible and he generally translates them into similes and metaphors which are basically visual. Though his other senses are also keenly developed, Proust frequently reacts visually to auditory, olfactory or gustatory sensations and his images, by preference, are visual and concrete.

[1] 'A propos du 'Style' de Flaubert,' *Chroniques*, pp. 193–94.
[2] Op. cit., p. 135.
[3] Jean Pommier, op. cit., p. 57, and André Maurois, op. cit., p. 187.
[4] Op. cit., p. 58.

By carefully counting images and analyzing them from different points of view, we have been able to produce unassailable evidence on which to base our generalizations about which images Proust favours or which predominate in his work. We discovered, for instance, that the most important single category from which Proust derives images is not the world of the arts, as Mouton suggests,[1] but nature, and, within nature, the sea and water. For Proust, the sea stands for the eternal, and he relates his own experience and life to the world conscience by means of water imagery. Etymologically, Combray means the junction of a river and its tributary, while Balbec also stands for a kind of stream. Proust gives us keys to these and other private symbols he uses, and once we have apprehended them much is added to the piquancy of his writing.

Proust uses images symbolically, and, apart from the private symbols he employs, he frequently draws on the numerous shorter cycles which are analogous to the longer cycle of human life, to form readily apprehended public symbols. Young girls are flowers, playful kittens, the rosy dawn or spring. Older women are dried-up fruits or hard seeds, tired old animals, the evening or cold, bleak winter. Images drawn from these lesser cycles are like the polyphonic orchestration of the vaster cycle of the whole novel and they contribute to the unity of 'the pattern below the level of plot and character'.[2]

Apart from underlining the importance of images drawn from nature (and especially water), our statistical analysis revealed one or two other startling things. It revealed, for instance, the very important part imagery drawn from religious sources plays in novel and it high-lighted the relative importance of images from closely allied categories e.g., music vs. painting or the theatre and biology vs. the other sciences.

By his images, Proust interrelates all forms of life and many apparently disparate phenomena. He animates the inanimate and dehumanizes the human. He uses transpositions (e.g., the sea is described in terms of the land, and the land in terms of the sea), correspondences (a stimulus to one sense calls forth a response in another) and reciprocal images (e.g., art is compared to life and life to art).

[1] Op. cit., p. 77.
[2] T. S. Eliot, quoted by Wellek and Warren, op. cit., p. 216. This quotation was referred to in the Introduction, p. vi.

By associating a large number of different images with one phenomenon, Proust manages to make us see it in a variety of ways so that it appears living and dynamic, and not static. Apparently contradictory images are chosen quite deliberately so that we may see the different facets of what we call the truth.

At the same time, a single source of imagery may be used in connection with a great number of different phenomena. This has the effect of showing us that things which we might consider completely unrelated actually have something in common.

The association of images with themes and the utilization in a variety of ways of images drawn from the same sources adds immeasurably to the unity of Proust's work. In the vast fabric of *A la recherche du temps perdu* the woof might be said to correspond to the sources of images which remain the same and run throughout a great number of themes. The warp, on the other hand, is like the themes themselves, and it comes in contact with images from many different categories.

It is largely through images that Proust reaches the universal plane. After all, his story is an individual story set among circumstances which are rather unusual. But, by the figures of speech which the narrator associates with *his* love, the girls *he* loves, the society *he* frequents, etc., etc., Proust brings out the eternal truths in these situations.

Proust's method of perception is metaphorical. His whole work is based on images, and, for him,

> ... plus que pour n'importe quel autre auteur, c'est d'abord dans le style qu'il faut rechercher non pas seulement la beauté de l'œuvre, mais son sens profond, sa véritable raison d'être.[1]

The core of Proust's style is his use of images, and without a full understanding of them, one cannot appreciate either the unity or the profound meaning of his work.

[1] Bret, op. cit., p. 69.

APPENDICES

| | Actual Figures | | | | Percentages | | |
Volume Number	Analytical (1)	Descriptive (2)	Conversational (3)	Totals	Analytical (1)	Descriptive (2)	Conversational (3)
I	150	262	17	429	35	61	4
II	163	124	3	290	56	43	1
III	202	49	10	261	77	19	4
IV	167	99	0	266	63	37	0
V	197	116	2	315	63	37	0
VI	213	96	7	316	68	30	2
VII	187	59	6	252	74	23	3
VIII	209	55	11	275	76	20	4
IX	318	81	8	407	78	19	3
X	240	62	9	311	77	20	3
XI	289	61	6	356	81	17	2
XII	219	57	18	294	74	19	7
XIII	260	52	3	315	83	17	0
XIV	132	51	1	184	72	28	0
XV	228	77	2	307	74	26	0
Totals	3174	1301	103	4578	69	28	3

Appendix 2 overleaf

APPENDIX 3
DISTRIBUTION OF IMAGES ACCORDING TO TYPE

| | Actual Figures | | · | Percentages | |
Volume Number	Simile (1)	Metaphor (2)	Totals	Simile (1)	Metaphor (2)
I	308	121	429	72	28
II	179	111	290	62	38
III	162	99	261	70	30
IV	169	97	266	63	37
V	159	156	315	50	50
VI	182	134	316	58	42
VII	152	100	252	60	40
VIII	134	141	275	50	50
IX	211	196	407	52	48
X	162	149	311	52	48
XI	139	217	356	39	61
XII	127	167	294	43	57
XIII	156	159	315	50	50
XIV	106	78	184	58	42
XV	153	154	307	50	50
Totals	2499	2079	4578	54	46

APPENDIX 2

Distribution of Images according to Concreteness or Abstractness

Volume Number	Actual Figures				Totals	Percentages			
	Concrete (1)	Abstract-Concrete (2)	Abstract (3)	Concrete-Abstract (4)		Concrete (1)	Abstract-Concrete (2)	Abstract (3)	Concrete-Abstract (4)
I	229	186	5	9	429	54	43	1	2
II	163	124	1	2	290	56	43	0	1
III	112	146	1	2	261	43	56	0	1
IV	150	113	1	2	266	56	43	0	1
V	241	71	1	2	315	76	23	0	1
VI	248	65	3	0	316	78	21	1	0
VII	212	36	4	0	252	84	14	2	0
VIII	207	64	4	0	275	75	23	2	0
IX	363	44	0	0	407	89	11	0	0
X	251	58	2	0	311	81	18	1	0
XI	263	92	1	0	356	74	26	0	0
XII	239	53	0	2	294	81	18	0	1
XIII	270	43	1	1	315	86	14	0	0
XIV	149	34	0	1	184	81	18	0	1
XV	211	96	0	0	307	69	31	0	0
Totals	3308	1225	24	21	4578	72	26	1	1

APPENDIX 4

Distribution of Images in the Grasset Proofs and the later Additions to those Proofs

Volume Number	Number of pages of original edition (1)	Number of Similes (2)	Number of Metaphors (3)	Total (4)	Number of pages added to proofs (5)	Number of Similes (6)	Number of Metaphors (7)	Total (8)
III	147	81	45	126	114	81	54	135
IV	186	102	58	160	80	67	39	106
V	253	123	130	253	62	36	26	62
VI	244	126	87	213	72	56	47	103
VII	65	32	15	47	71	40	23	63
Totals	895	464	335	799	399	280	189	469

APPENDIX 5
Distribution of Images according to Quality

Volume No.	Actual Figures — No. of pages	Actual Figures — Auditory	Actual Figures — Visual	Actual Figures — Kinaesthetic	Actual Figures — Synaesthetic	Actual Figures — Mental	Actual Figures — Gustatory	Actual Figures — Olfactory	Total No. of Images	Percentages — Auditory	Percentages — Visual	Percentages — Kinaesthetic	Percentages — Synaesthetic	Percentages — Mental	Percentages — Gustatory	Percentages — Olfactory
I	282 } 550	25	306	28	30	33	2	5	429 } 719	6	71	7	7	8	0	1
II	268	9	178	35	36	30	1	1	290	5	61	12	12	10	0	0
III	211 } 634	15	170	15	16	44	1	0	261 } 842	6	65	6	6	17	0	0
IV	200	8	202	21	13	20	2	0	266	3	76	8	5	8	0	0
V	223	16	232	22	10	32	1	2	315	5	74	7	3	11	0	0
VI	215 } 715	23	233	20	12	25	0	3	316 } 843	7	74	7	3	9	0	0
VII	246	17	157	18	13	46	1	0	252	7	63	7	6	17	0	0
VIII	254	16	158	29	6	61	4	1	275	6	57	11	2	23	1	0
IX	330 } 661	20	244	29	16	96	0	2	407 } 718	5	60	7	4	24	0	0
X	331	22	188	30	4	66	0	1	311	7	60	10	1	22	0	0
XI	245 } 499	33	170	41	15	95	1	1	356 } 650	9	49	11	4	27	0	0
XII	254	19	138	28	29	80	0	0	294	7	47	9	10	27	0	0
XIII	324 } 324	7	155	45	15	92	1	0	315 } 315	2	39	14	5	30	0	0
XIV	200 } 423	11	94	12	8	59	0	0	184 } 491	6	51	6	5	32	0	0
XV	223	9	202	19	8	68	1	0	307	3	66	6	3	22	0	0
Totals	3806	250	2827	392	231	847	15	16	4578	5	62	9	5	19	0	0

APPENDIX 5 (continued)

Actual Figures

Section	No. of pages	(group)	Auditory	Visual	Kinaesthetic	Synaesthetic	Mental	Gustatory	Olfactory	Total No. of Images	(group)
S Pt. 1	240		22	292	27	25	27	2	5	400	
Pt. 2	253	550	10	116	29	33	23	1	1	213	719
Pt. 3	57		2	76	7	8	13	0	0	106	
JF	634	634	39	604	58	39	96	4	2	842	842
G	415	715	34	345	32	21	60	0	3	495	843
Ch. 2	300		22	203	35	10	72	5	1	348	
SG Pt. 1	40		1	41	1	1	28	0	0	72	
Pt. 2	148	661	12	114	10	2	42	0	2	182	718
(Less intermittances du Coeur)	473		29	277	48	17	92	0	1	464	
P Ch. 1	229		33	158	41	15	88	1	1	337	
Ch. 2	162	499	11	85	9	16	63	0	0	184	650
Ch. 3	108		8	65	19	13	24	0	0	129	
AD Ch.1	166	324	5	88	37	5	48	1	0	184	315
Ch. 2	158		2	67	8	10	44	0	0	131	
TR Ch. 1	32		2	9	2	2	6	0	0	21	
Ch. 2	153	423	8	69	8	3	49	0	0	137	491
Ch. 3	238		10	218	21	11	72	1	0	333	
Totals	**3806**		**250**	**2827**	**392**	**231**	**847**	**15**	**16**	**4578**	

Percentages

	Auditory	Visual	Kinaesthetic	Synaesthetic	Mental	Gustatory	Olfactory
S	5	67	9	9	9	0	1
JF	5	72	7	5	11	0	0
G	7	65	8	4	16	0	0
SG	6	60	8	3	23	0	0
P	8	47	11	7	27	0	0
AD	2	50	14	5	29	0	0
TR	4	60	7	3	26	0	0

S

APPENDIX 6

DISTRIBUTION OF IMAGES ACCORDING TO SOURCE[1]

Source of Images	No. of Examples	Totals
NATURE		
Flowers and Gardens	100	
Plants, Bushes, Trees	45	
Fruits, Seeds	46	
Seasons, Weather	180	
Landscape, Perspective	21	
Birds	101	
Animals	74	
Rural Life	51	
Sea, Water	326	944
COMMON OBJECTS		
Metals, Jewels and Enamel	65	
Mirrors	25	
Household Articles	135	
Divisions, Pieces, Fragments	22	
Chains, Links, Networks	23	
Thermometers, Barometers, Clocks	17	
Materials and Trades	50	337
SCIENCE		
Biology	160	
Physics	59	
Mathematics	32	
Astronomy	45	
Geology, Archeology	16	
Chemistry, Alchemy	35	
Inventions	56	403
LITERATURE		
General	279	
Folk Lore, Arabian Nights	105	
Knighthood, Hunting	30	
Classics, Mythology	176	
Religion and the Bible	305	
Geography, Travelling	132	1,027

[1] Estimated totals do not include private images, e.g., Balbec, Combray, etc. The only category that would be increased materially if this were done is that of Sea, Water under Nature.

THE ARTS
    Painting   203
    Sculpture   87
    Architecture and Ruins   30
    Music   171
    Theatre   194
    Ballet   10   695

SOCIAL AND DOMESTIC INSTITUTIONS
    Childhood   58
    Games   70
    School   30
    Social Customs   55
    Hierarchy   53
    Military   79
    Commerce   13
    Law   58
    Love   69
    Food   77   562

INTROSPECTIVE PROCESSES
    Bodily Sensations   58
    Illness, Medicine   298
    Drunkenness   19
    Death   63   438

Personification   69
Conversational Images (not analyzed)   103   172

GRAND TOTAL   4,578

APPENDIX 7

DISTRIBUTION OF SEA AND WATER IMAGES ACCORDING TO VOLUME

Volume Number					*Number of Examples*
I	...	...	...	...	30
II	...	...	...	...	23
III	...	...	...	...	22
IV	...	...	...	...	18
V	...	...	...	...	36
VI	...	...	...	...	18
VII	...	...	...	...	25
VIII	...	...	...	...	15
IX	...	...	...	...	20
X	...	...	...	...	20
XI	...	...	...	...	26
XII	...	...	...	...	12
XIII	...	...	...	...	24
XIV	...	...	...	...	16
XV	...	...	...	...	21
TOTAL	...	...	...	...	326

BIBLIOGRAPHY

I. Works Cited:

A. Proust's Works:
Marcel Proust, *A la recherche du temps perdu*, Paris, Gallimard, Edition de la Nouvelle Revue Française, 15 volumes.
—— *Chroniques*, Paris, Gallimard, NRF, 36e édition.
—— *Correspondance générale*, Paris, Plon, (1930–1936), 6 volumes.
—— *Les Plaisirs et les jours*, Paris, Gallimard, NRF, 73e édition.
—— *Pastiches et mélanges*, Paris, Gallimard, NRF, 44e édition.
—— *Contre Sainte-Beuve*, Suivi de nouveaux mélanges, préface de Bernard de Fallois, Paris, Gallimard, 1954.

B. Works about Proust:
Beckett (Samuel), *Proust*, London, Chatto and Windus, 1931.
Benoist-Méchin (Jacques), *La Musique et l'immortalité dans l'œuvre de Proust*, Paris, 1926.
Bret (Jacques), *Marcel Proust*, Etude critique, Genève, Collection Action et Pensée aux éditions du Mont-Blanc, 1946.
Briand (Charles), *Le Secret de Marcel Proust*, Paris, Editions Henri Lefèbvre, 1950.
Chernowitz (M. E.), *Proust and Painting*, New York, 1945.
Clark (Charles N.), 'Love and Time: The Erotic Imagery of Marcel Proust', *Yale French Studies*, no. 11 (1953), pp. 80–90.
Clermont-Tonnerre (E., Duchesse de), *Robert de Montesquiou et Marcel Proust*, Paris, E. Flammarion, 1925.
Crémieux (Benjamin), *Du Côté de Marcel Proust*, Paris, Lemarget, 1929.
Curtius (Ernst Robert), *Marcel Proust* (traduit de l'allemand par Armand Pierhal), Paris, Editions de la Revue nouvelle, 1928.
Dandieu (Arnaud), *'La Signification de la métaphore'* (Article extrait d'un ouvrage d'Arnaud Dandieu sur Marcel Proust), Paris, *Bulletin Marcel Proust*, Le Rouge et le noir, 1930.
Feuillerat (A. G.), *Comment Marcel Proust a composé son roman*, Yale Romanic Studies, VII, New Haven, Yale University Press, 1934.
Fiser (Emeric), *La Théorie du symbole littéraire et Marcel Proust*, Paris, Librairie José Corti, 1941.
Graham (V. E.), 'Proust's Alchemy', *MLR*, LX (1965), pp. 197–206.
—— 'Water Imagery and Symbolism in Proust,' *RR*, L (1959), pp. 118–28.
Hier (Florence), *La Musique dans l'œuvre de Marcel Proust*, New York, Columbia University Press, 1933.
Hindus (Milton), *The Proustian Vision*, New York, Columbia University Press, 1954.
Hommage à Marcel Proust (Les Cahiers Marcel Proust 1).
Levin (Harry), *The Gates of Horn*, Oxford University Press, 1963.
Linn (J. G.), 'Proust's Theatre Metaphors', *RR*, XLIX (1958), pp. 179–90.

Louria (Yvette), *La Convergence Stylistique chez Proust*, Genève, E. Droz, 1957.

March (Harold), *The Two Worlds of Marcel Proust*, Philadelphia, University of Pennsylvania Press, 1948.

Matoré (Georges), 'Les Images gustatives dans *Du Coté de chez Swann*', *Annales Universitatis Saraviensis VI* (1957), pp. 685–92.

Maurois (André), *A la recherche de Marcel Proust*, Paris, 1949.

Monnin-Hornung (Juliette), *Proust et la peinture*, Genève, 1951.

Moss (Howard), *The Magic Lantern of Marcel Proust*, New York, Macmillan Co., 1962.

Mouton (Jean), *Le Style de Marcel Proust*, Paris, Editions Corrêa, 1948.

Picon (Gaétan), *Lecture de Proust*, Mercure de France, 1963.

Pierre-Quint (Léon), *Marcel Proust, sa vie, son œuvre*, Paris, Editions du Sagittaire, 3e édition, 1935.

Piroué (Georges), *Proust et la musique du devenir*, Paris, Denoel, 1960.

Pommier (Jean), *La Mystique de Marcel Proust*, Paris, Droz, 1939.

Poulet (Georges), *Etudes sur le temps humain*, Edinburgh, 1949.

—— *L'Espace proustien*, Paris, 1963.

Shattuck (Roger), *Proust's Binoculars. A Study of Memory, Time and Recognition in A la recherche du temps perdu*, New York, Random House, 1963.

Seznec (Jean), *Marcel Proust et les Dieux* (The Zaharoff Lecture for 1962), Oxford, Clarendon Press, 1962.

Stockwell (H. C. R.), 'L'Image dans l'œuvre de Marcel Proust', article in *Modern Languages*, vol. XXVI, 1944–45, pp. 10–15.

Tiedtke (Irma), *Symbole und Bilder im werks Marcel Prousts*, Hamburg, Paul Evert Verlag, 1936.

Ullmann (Stephen), *Style in the French Novel*, Cambridge University Press, 1957.

—— *The Image in the Modern French Novel*, Cambridge University Press, 1960.

Vance (Vera L.), 'Proust's Guermantes as Birds', *French Review*, XXXV (1961–62), pp. 3–10.

Vendryes (Joseph), 'Marcel Proust et les noms propres', in *Choix d'études linguistiques et celtiques* (Paris, 1953), pp. 80–88.

Virtanen (Reino), 'Proust's Metaphors from the Natural and the Exact Sciences', *PMLA*, LXIX (1954), pp. 1038–59.

C. General Works:

Bachelard (Gaston), *L'Eau et les rêves*, Paris, José Corti, 1942.

Bayley (Harold), *The Lost Language of Symbolism*, 2 vols., London, Williams and Norgate, reprinted edition 1951.

Foulquié (Paul) et Deledalle (Gérard), *La Psychologie Contemporaine*, Paris, Presses universitaires de France.

Gide (André), *Œuvres complètes*, NRF.

Jung (C. J.), *Psychology of the Unconscious* (transl. B. M. Hinkle), New York, Dodd, Mead and Co., 1947.

Langer (Susanne K.), *Philosophy in a New Key* (A study in the Symbolism of Reason, Rite and Art), New York, The New American Library, 1948.

Wellek (René) and Warren (Austin), *Theory of Literature*, New York, Harcourt, Brace and Company, 1949.

II. Works not cited but Containing Material found useful in this Study:

Brown (Stephen J.), *The World of Imagery*, London, Kegan, Paul, Trench, Trubner and Co., 1927.

Day Lewis (C.), *The Poetic Image* (The Clark Lectures given at Cambridge in 1946), London, Cape, 1947.

Hornstein (Lillian H.), 'Analysis of Imagery: a Critique of Literary Method', *PMLA*, LVII (1942), pp. 638–53.

Konrad (Hedwig), *Etude sur la Métaphore*, Paris, Maurice Lavergne, 1939.

Murry (J. Middleton), *The Problem of Style*, Oxford, Oxford University Press, 7th edition, 1949.

Peillaube (E.), *Les Images*, Paris, 1910.

Reiser (M.), 'Analysis of the Poetic Simile', *Journal of Philosophy*, XXXVII, No. 8, April 11, 1940.

Ullmann (Stephen), *Language and Style*, Oxford, Blackwell, 1964. Ch. IX: 'The Nature of Imagery.'

INDEX

This index does not pretend to include references to *all* images in *A la recherche du temps perdu*. Only those considered in the text have been listed here, grouped as far as possible under thematic headings. Proper names which recur with great frequency have been omitted except for references to the section where they are discussed specifically.